Travels in Blood and Honey

For Rob, the hero of my story

Travels in Blood and Honey

Becoming a Beekeeper in Kosovo

Elizabeth Gowing

Elizabeth Gowing (signature)

Signal Books
Oxford

First published in 2011 by
Signal Books Limited
36 Minster Road
Oxford
OX4 1LY
www.signalbooks.co.uk

A catalogue record for this book is available from the British Library

ISBN 978-1-904955-90-0 Paper

Design & Production: Devdan Sen
Cover Design: Paddy McEntaggart & Su Jones
Cover Images: Paddy McEntaggart & Su Jones
Photographs: © Elizabeth Gowing; Robert Wilton (p.64, p.81); Paddy
McEntaggart (p.70); (Alexandra Channer (p.243).
Printed by Short Run Press Ltd, Exeter

Contents

...Contents

Thanks

It takes 700 bees a lifetime to make a jar of honey, and it has needed the help of almost as many people to produce this book.

First thanks must go to my wonderful family – Gowing, Wilton, Ward, Greenslade and Lucas. You launched and supported me on this and so many other journeys.

And then sincere thanks to all the people who helped me in my adventures in Kosovo, opening their homes or their hives to me, helping, teaching and befriending me. Chief among them must be Adem and Xhezide Ibrahimi, and Gazi Bërlajolli. *Faleminderit për gjithçka.*

For help in the process of turning those experiences into a book, first my thanks must go to James Ferguson. But thank you, too, to the members of the Magnetic North writers group in Greenwich and the members of the writers group who meet at Dit e Nat in Pristina; for their detailed constructive criticism – and for the spontaneous applause when I read the chapter on Kosovo's independence. Enormous thanks, too, to all those others who commented on the manuscript and saved me from myself, including many of those mentioned above or in the text but also David Banks, Rosie Whitehouse, Shiraz Chakera, Sybille Raphael, Tim Albert, Tim Judah and Tracey Byrne.

Thanks, too, to all those who helped me with the recipes – as well as those mentioned in the text or above, thanks to tasters from Network Cornwall (including Althea, Candida, Debbie, Jacquelin, Jenny, Jo, Lyn, Rachel, Ruth, Sharyn, Sue and Suzy) and beyond (Anna, Cassia, Kerri and Martha).

Finally, thanks to Su Jones and Paddy McEntaggart for, amongst other things, making this book look so beautiful.

1.
Starting with the birds, not the bees

New Albanian vocabulary: *më fal* (sorry), *sigurim* (insurance)

Kosovo's black birds start massing, whirling – and gleefully shitting – just as the sun is going down. Their instincts are attuned to the same triggers which send the *hoxha*s of Pristina's mosques to their loudspeakers to call the faithful to prayer. But I have watched carefully, and the birds rise into the skies before the call to prayer begins – they are not obeying it. I don't think these birds are Muslims.

At about the time when people are coming home from work, or sitting down to dinner (at *exactly* the time when they are sitting down to dinner during the Muslim month of Ramadan, with its requirement for fasting during the hours of daylight), the sky splits open with the moan from the first mosque. A second wail starts up, chanting echoes that aren't quite in agreement, although the words are the same. If you are in the right place in Pristina you will be able to hear a third and maybe a fourth. And the digestive juices of the population sing in harmony.

It is at this point, while the sense of taste and of sound is being sated, that the birds rise in a ragged black mass – thousands strong – against the darkening sky. It's impossible not to be impressed, not to think of Hitchcock – or maybe the computer generated scarabs in *The Mummy*, depending on your age.

And it is to these birds that this land really belongs: the word 'Kosovo' comes from the Serbian for The Field of Blackbirds. Or perhaps it is The Field of Black Birds. No-one seems very sure about exactly which birds wheel around or through a possible gap in the English words translating the name. Certainly, during my time in Kosovo I never saw a yellow-beaked, Beatles-style blackbird singing. But at dusk each day in autumn and winter I have seen the black (-space-) birds – hooded crows, or maybe rooks, or members of the jay family (my ornithological friends disagree with one another) in their

sinister, glorious, frightening, deafening mobbing across the city.

And it was the 1389 battle which took its name from these birds – the Battle of the Field of Blackbirds – which defined Kosovo, not only etymologically, but politically and culturally for the next 600 years and more.

Appropriately, the story of this battle was my introduction to Kosovo's history. I had been in the country for less than an hour – a bewildering hour of worry and mispronunciation and worry about mis-pronunciation. Rob and I had spent most of the hour standing at the baggage carousel of Pristina airport hoping that some of our posses-sions would soon circle into view, and when they did, hoping that the word we were repeating as we pushed past the men blocking our way sounded something like the apology we were attempting in their strange language.

Then we were out of the airport, greeted by a car from the British Office (in practice the British Embassy, but because Kosovo didn't have the status of a country, it couldn't have an embassy) to drive us to our hotel. I had learned quite a bit about our hotel in the last twenty days – the period that we had had after Rob had been told that he had been accepted by both the British government and the Prime Minister of Kosovo to be funded by the former as adviser to the latter. Twenty days weren't quite enough to pack up a house, say proper goodbyes to people who mattered, and learn about the language, culture and politics of your new home. So I had spent those days packing the house and saying my goodbyes, and only wondering where to start on learning about Kosovo. They had been days of excitement as well as a little healthy fear.

Rob and I had met at university and moved to North London together, enjoying ten years of public sector careers. For me that meant mainly teaching, with some poetry. One Saturday morning Rob had gone out to get his newspaper and had come back to read it over his mug of hot chocolate by the window, looking out over our patch of gently maturing garden. In a moment of quiet epiphany he put down the foreign news story he was reading. 'Do you realise that on current form there is nothing to stop me doing this, right here, every Saturday morning for the next forty years?' We had both shivered a little, and in the conversations that followed we agreed that it was time for some-thing more like adventure. Most of our friends seemed to have embarked on domestic adventures involving the birth of children. We had decided not to go down that route. When the call had come through inviting Rob to move to Kosovo, I felt the prickling of adrenaline.

While Rob had years of working on the Balkans behind him, I had had less than three weeks to educate myself. His books, with the unpronounceable titles, had been stacked on the shelves in our bedroom, and sometimes I had idly tried to sound out the words along the spines. But they were his, his hobby; I hadn't properly understood until now that they were also real life for millions of people on the other side of Europe, or that they might become real life for me, too.

So as we took off from Gatwick, for what amounted to an extended blind date with this place, my knowledge of my new home had been largely based on two things. First was the Wikipedia article on Kosovo. Significantly, it is a 'locked' article because of the rival amendments being so angrily and regularly proposed by different ethnic groups. That was probably one of the most important things I did learn about Kosovo during those days, and it made me realise, too, how my entry into this debate would be perceived as partisan, by both sides. The second source of information I had was the website of the Hotel Baci. As a result, before arriving here I had picked up only a healthy respect for the ethnic differences within my new home, and a healthy disrespect for its taste in interior décor.

My only other guide to the place was an Albanian-English dictionary. As we drove in the British Office car through the dusty, baffling streets of Pristina's suburbs, I looked up as many words as I could. The images flickering past my window – half-finished houses, dark-haired, dark-eyed young women in tight jeans, overloaded cars, people greeting one another enthusiastically as they passed in the streets – were untranslatable. Who were these people? Which were Serbs and which Albanians? What were they thinking? Translating the words on billboards and small business frontages was at least a start at understanding a place. I learned the words for insurance and depilatory cream, and one of the first words I looked up on that drive was displayed on the sign that announced 'Fushë Kosovë'. There was something written in Serbian underneath it, but it had been spraypainted out. Anyway, I didn't yet have a Serbian dictionary.

'Kosovë' I thought I recognised. If I could just find out the meaning of 'fushë' I hoped I might be able to translate my first Albanian phrase. I looked it up; it means 'field' or 'plain'. I had found myself the Plain of Kosovo, and if I'd had that Serbian dictionary with me then I would have had a clue earlier on as to what I might find flying above it.

The Plain of Kosovo stretched out around us – flat, rich but mainly uncultivated land extending to the lines of mountains in the distance with snow still on them. The British army officer driving us told us that this was the site of the Battle of Kosovo. Since he had just told us about the military showdown that had taken place at the airport between NATO and the Russians in 1999, I wasn't immediately sure what century this other battle might have happened in. The confusion was appropriate as it turned out, because you could argue that this was a battle fought in 1389 for 600 years. It is the Dunkirk of the Serbian people – the military defeat proudly displayed centuries later: not like a scar, but like a scab.

We were driving past mosques and small modern Orthodox churches scribbled round with barbed wire. Rob had told me about the epic poem about the Battle of Kosovo, where the Turkish Sultan tells the Serbian prince Lazar about this land, 'We cannot both together rule here.' The army officer filled in some military details to my literary framework. The Battle of Kosovo was between Ottoman Turks and fighters now usually referred to as Serbs. They were soldiers led by a Serb prince, but it seems likely that the 'Serb' army in fact included men who were Albanian, and from many other ethnic groups across the Balkans. It is seen as the point at which the Serbs – and the Serbian church – lost Kosovo to the Turks, and to Islam. The battle actually ended in a draw – both the Serbian and the Turkish commanders were killed, and the Ottomans retreated to regroup under their dead sultan's son before they came back a generation later to stamp their rule on this country.

What really happened, however, is less important than the poem – the way that the epic, heroic story has been told and used since. This scruffy suburb, named after the battleground, where we were driving was the setting that Milošević chose in 1987, and then on the 600th anniversary of the battle, in 1989, for picking at his nation's scab –

reiterating the claims of Kosovo as a Serb homeland, which led to nationalist policies brutally enforced against Kosovo's Albanians.

The subsequent ten years, with their atrocities and injustices of the Serbian administration against the Albanian majority across Kosovo finally led to the 1999 NATO bombing and the UN administration of Kosovo. They led to the establishment of what was called the Provisional Institutions of Self-Government, and the appointing of its Prime Minister keen for British connection and advice. They led to Rob's appointment as the PM's adviser, and to him and his baggage being driven from the airport at the end of May 2006, wordlessly looking things up in a brand new dictionary, starting a new life on the Field of Blackbirds.

2.
A lone bee

New Albanian vocabulary: *mirëmëngjes* (good morning; this was part of Rob's legacy to me from the language lessons he had had in London before our departure. I asked him to pass on a word a day as my start-ing point in Albanian, which he conscientiously tutored me in as we got up together every morning), *shpi* (house), *ju lutem* (please), *lirë* (cheap)

The Baci Hotel was even more mustard-coloured than its website had led me to imagine. Later, I might have charitably called this a honey tone, but in the dusk our official car pulled up outside what seemed to me to be a building definitely the colour of mustard. I recognised the place from a grainy jpeg image. We were shown up to a mustard-coloured room where the bed had a mustard-coloured nylon eider-down. The sitting area had a mustard-coloured sofa and matching curtains.

The man from Reception set down our luggage and left us. We sat down on the bed and looked at one another. And grinned. It was really happening. This felt like an adventure, whatever the colour scheme.

We were to stay in the mustard hotel for a week while I looked for a home in subtler shades. I had wondered what I would do with myself without a paid job while Rob was at work. This was the first time we had ever been in this situation – I had always worked, and often earned more than him. When he left me my first pile of euros on the bedroom chest of drawers, I was furious.

But I realised my first project had to be house-hunting. It was a project made more complex because I had to try to do it in Albanian. As Rob walked out of our hotel room in the morning I would say goodbye with all kinds of regret. I was losing a friend and ally, but I was also losing the only person I could speak English with.

Until Rob came back from work my day was spent in a strange parlour game of mime and word association. On my first morning alone

I went to buy myself a mobile phone (the roaming facility on my British mobile had worked fine all over New Zealand, India, Russia... In Kosovo it would only work in Serbian villages where companies from Serbia had put up phone masts).

I walked carefully through the throbbing, thrilling streets. Pristina sits in a bowl, surrounded by hills, and to the south west, that Plain of Kosovo. It has a creaking power station burning the so-called 'dirty coal', lignite. As a result, the air quality is terrible – but, as I would discover that evening, the dust-fragmented light of its sunsets is spectacular.

Concrete towered above me, in quick-fix buildings that were half-finished, unrendered, spiky with reinforcing rods. The pavements were almost unwalkable – muddy piles of plastic bottles and other drifts of litter would suddenly mire my shoes, and I was forced into detours by huge holes in the paving, or sewers revealing themselves metres beneath me, where manhole covers had been prised up to be sold as scrap metal. Cars parked anywhere, forcing pedestrians into the streets. And the traffic weaved around it all, cheerfully anarchic. Everywhere there were beautiful, angular young girls in short skirts and low tops, walking in pairs to work or towards the university. They stepped out into the crazy traffic without looking left or right. It seemed they didn't need to – they were invincible. I had to keep my eyes down, treading carefully in

my sensible shoes over the mud with its little square wormholes where the invincible young women had jabbed their confident stiletto heels.

Finally I found a kiosk selling phones. As I walked towards it I looked up in my dictionary the word for 'cheap'. I practised the sentence under my breath and went in to the phone shop. Painstakingly, I strung the words together. 'Excuse me, what is most cheap?' I asked carefully. The shop-owner frowned at me. I repeated myself. 'Most cheap?'

'We have no "cheap",' he replied, echoing the Albanian word I had used. It was a surprising sales pitch in this rather dirty little space with secondhand phones stacked on shelves and the assistant salesman picking his teeth, sitting on a plastic stool covered with a piece of cardboard for padding.

I waved the dictionary at him, wondering whether my pronunciation had been at fault, with all the Albanian 'q's that are 'ch's and the 'j's that are 'y's. I pointed at the word I had been using, and as I did so, I noticed the English translation a line above it. With the book jogging under my nose as I walked along the pavement, I had skipped a line. I had not been asking for 'cheap' but for 'cheat' phones.

I had many similar experiences with the shopkeepers, estate agents, landlords, electricians and everyone else I met in those early days. But all these transactions reinforced that I was really here to stay. Within a week we had a house, and intermittent electricity. With no way back, I realised that I was embarking on more of an arranged marriage than a mere blind date with Kosovo.

So I had better make it work. And I had better make me work. With my experience in education, I was sure that I would be able to find some useful role here. After all, Kosovo has plenty of children – with 25 per cent of the population under 18 it is the youngest country in Europe. I sent out increasingly hyperbolic CVs to new contacts at the Ministry of Education, to local schools – both English-speaking private schools and Albanian-language state schools. I offered training within the education programmes of NGOs, UN agencies, the professional development section of the Kosovo Police Academy. I offered myself as a consultant and as a volunteer. I met for coffee with anyone who was willing to spare me the time. I would sit carefully deploying chunks of my resumé while *makiatos* steamed on the table, thinking about J Alfred Prufrock and what it meant to have measured out my life with coffee spoons. In between meetings I fretted about the book I had been halfway through writing when the call to Kosovo had come. I had checked that we could have things delivered from Amazon, but I couldn't build up any enthusiasm for books for research on the library towns and patrons of England when I felt I had just embarked on a multimedia study programme on Kosovo.

And each day when I had worked through my list of contacts to try, and work to chase, I treated myself to sending messages back home, toiling down to the nicotine-rich internet café on Bil Klinton Bulevard.

Most of the road names were simply bewildering to me in those first days, usually being the names of notable Albanians who are less notable outside their native lands. But there were some exceptions to this – for example, Pristina's main thoroughfare, Mother Theresa Street (she was ethnically an Albanian born in what is now Macedonia), and this main road from the airport that intersects it. Rob pointed out that the location of our house was best described as being at the junction of Mother Theresa and Bill Clinton – a mind-boggling concept.

There is, or was, also a Toni Bler Road, we were proud to be told. Unfortunately, when we subsequently went to find it, we discovered that it had been a minor road in the block of houses now commandeered by the American Office. The paranoid could read something into that.

Bil Klinton Bulevard had been Lenin Street under Communist rule – the name change was just one of the tit-for-tat changes that had been made following the NATO campaign, by a people eager to use every opportunity to remove Serbian fighting heroes from their lives. The road named for the Yugoslav army was similarly changed to KLA Street, after the Kosovo Liberation Army guerrillas who fought the Serbs, and Belgrade Street was renamed Tirana Street to signal a shift in cultural identity from Serbia to Albania. The road names are party political as well as patriotic – incoming mayors find this an economical way to share their values, honour their patrons, repay debts. Since at one point the road names in towns were changing on a nearly annual basis, many people – both native and foreign – gave up on using the road signs, and used landmarks or invented names in conversation; my difficulties in navigating lasted well beyond those first days.

Our new address was in Musine Kokollari Street (ominously named after the Albanian woman who was a teacher and writer but who I was told committed suicide as a result of the poor reception of her work). I had change of address cards printed, and sent to friends and family in the UK. The cards went out signed 'Bee'. At that point, the only bee in my life was this one, myself, carrying the family nickname I'd had since childhood, as a result of a babbling younger sister who could only handle the last syllable of my name.

Bees don't last long if they are isolated from their colony. They can't collect, store and protect their food stocks alone. By necessity, not just by choice, they are social creatures. If I was to survive, let alone thrive, I needed to work fast to find some points of contact in this concrete garden I had just flown into.

3.
'Homogenised, industrialised': shopping for honey in Kosovo

New Albanian vocabulary: *përbërësit* (ingredients), *pazar* (market: of course not an Albanian word originally, but an etymological item of barter and exchange, being linked like our own version, *bazaar*, to the Turkish and Persian traders who have left their traces in markets across the world)

I'd found us a house – a disconcertingly large place with a downstairs reception room we nicknamed 'the ballroom' and never sat in on our own, because we felt we couldn't quite live up to it. We were in the centre of town but we had a garden with rosebushes and apple trees. It was a place that felt like it could become a home, and my first instinct was to fill its cupboards. I was hungry for home cooking; the simple processes of creating and sharing meals in our own space. I needed groceries.

The first place we tried was one of the large out-of-town supermarkets. The names of these large chains could as well be brand names for industrial solvent or powerful prescription drugs – Maxi, Interex, Intereminex, Albi, Ardi, Era, Ben Af. The latter, as Rob pointed out, could also have been the nickname for the lover of *J Lo*.

Our first visit to one of these stores, piled high with imports, was reassuring, if not exciting. You could buy Nutella in Kosovo, you could buy balsamic vinegar, and wholemeal pasta, Milka chocolate, even Worcestershire sauce, and French wine. Really, there wasn't much you couldn't buy (cheddar cheese was our one constant slice of homesickness, although we did find something called cheddar, produced in what must be Somerset's Turkish dominion).

However, we had been trained like good wholemeal-pasta-eaters that we should be mindful of the food miles of the products we bought. And whilst I wasn't willing to exchange the local equivalent,

'Eurokrem' (another solvent?) for my Nutella, and was doubtful of finding an alternative to Lea and Perrins, I wanted to try as much as possible to buy local.

So I set off to explore the covered market in the old quarter of Pristina. The Cairo souk it ain't, but it was still a lot more of an adventure than Sainsbury's had ever been. Small radios bleated local pop music, distorted by being cranked up to full volume on fragile speakers. Handsome young men with eyes that flickered back and forwards stood next to towering walls of bootleg Marlboro Lights. Old men sat on wheelbarrows waiting for someone to pay them to transport sacks of vegetables. Stallholders greeted everyone with a smile, called out enticing prices and provenances of their stock. I love markets for the way that, like dancing, they offer a form of ritualised licensed flirting. The stalls were piled high with heaps of spinach, bosomy mounds of nectarines, sleek-buttocked peppers, kept looking fresh all day by the traders who use old plastic mineral water bottles with holes punched in them as sprinklers.

It was crowded, not just with bodies, but with bags. The dance-floor of this market was the kind where everyone comfortably bumped up against one another's plump protrusions which could be belly, breast or bag of onions. You could only buy by the kilo or more, and the bowed figures with netted sacks of cucumbers and bleeding paper bags of cherries seemed little spots of indulgence in this concrete city of subsistence living I'd experienced up till now.

Kosovo's history and geography was laid out here, in its food. The market was all-Albanian, and this area, I had been told, had always been an Albanian part of Pristina. Even during the bombing campaign and the days of the most intense Serb paramilitary violence when so many Albanians had left Pristina, in this part of town Albanians had stayed hiding in their homes. But the names for vegetables here were Turkish, Serbian, imported along with all the delicious ingredients the Ottomans had brought to Kosovo – spinach, beans, tomatoes named with the Turkish name for aubergines, and aubergines given an additional colour description to form their name 'patëllxhan i zi' – 'black tomatoes'. Cucumbers were sometimes labeled with their Albanian name, 'tranguj', sometimes with the word, 'kastravec' adapted from Serbian. You could tell this was a country in transition.

I haggled inexpertly, worrying about the words for numbers and the conversion rate. Usually at the end of a transaction, the stallholder threw in an extra peach or potato anyway.

Following my nose, I found myself in the cheese section. It was quieter, an annex to the main market which looked like a garage. It smelt like sick.

As far as I could see, everyone there was selling the same kind of cheese. It is a white, fresh cheese moulded into small irregular, loaf-like lumps. It's kept in brine or in whey, and stored in barrels. They came in different sizes, in blond wood with darker bands with the bark still on, holding the staves in place. They were different from English barrels, starting from a wide base with gradually tapered sides. It wasn't fine craftsmanship, but it was elegant, neat and ergonomic in the way that handmade things are when they have a design that has been followed and refined for generations. The barrels were stacked high and I stared at them. The cheesemakers stared too, at this foreigner transfixed by such ordinary things. I got out my camera.

That clinched it. 'Do you want to buy?' asked the guy standing nearest to the stack of barrels, with an edge of hostility in his voice.

'Yes!' I realised that I did.

'How many kilograms?' he asked.

No, not cheese. I wanted to buy the barrel.

They tried to explain to me that I didn't have to buy the whole barrel, I could decide how much cheese I wanted. I tried to explain to them that their cheese made me feel like retching, but the barrel was beautiful. I had a plan to use it as a small table in our new sitting room.

Eventually we understood one another. They had never sold a barrel before, and they didn't have any bags big enough for it. I was taken to a stall selling dustbin bags where the cheese-seller explained what I needed it for.

'She wants to buy the barrel!'

'She wants to buy the barrel? Are you sure she doesn't just want some cheese? Are you sure you don't just want some cheese?' A small crowd gathered.

An old guy sitting on a wheelbarrow outside was summoned to carry my barrel for me. He held his nose humorously as we trailed back through the market, me processing in front with a little triumphant

smile on my face, and the wheelbarrow carrying its barrel like a madonna. People parted to let us (or maybe that pungent smell) pass.

I explained to the wheelbarrow guy that I wasn't ready to go home yet. I had come to the market not just in search of salad, certainly not in search of cheese-barrels, but really for some comfort food.

For some years now, Rob and I had had a Sunday afternoon ritual to take the edge off end-of-weekend blues. In the face of lesson planning and marking and all the other things that seep out of the classroom into the home, we had established a rule of no work after Sunday tea. As a consequence, Sunday tea had grown into an indulgent, celebratory, buttery time of togetherness round the toaster. All the baking I did was for this meal. We would close my lever arch file, the laptop lid, spread a tablecloth, and with warm scones, a cake, even homemade bread, we would stave off Monday morning.

That sacred part of the weekend felt just as important now, even though I wasn't working. Rob's new job was seeping in even more than my teaching had. As the Prime Minister's advisor he seemed to be as busy as the Prime Minister. Like the Prime Minister, he was required not only during office hours, but for all the official activity out-of-hours. Dinners with visiting VIPs, opening of fire stations, as well as text messages alerts whenever something happened that was significant for the government (ministers caught in compromising situations, car bombs, traffic accidents involving personnel working in Kosovo with the UN, EU etc – the so-called 'internationals'). It was fascinating stuff – for him, and for me as a spectator. I loved watching Rob becoming absorbed by this new system he was helping to create. But I was also determined not to let it overrun Sunday tea.

To be truly comforted by Sunday tea, you have to have two things. The first is a pot of Marmite – I had snuggled one inside the sleeves of a jumper in my suitcase for our journey to Kosovo. The second is honey.

The old man grinned toothlessly at me when I asked about honey – he was happy to wheel my barrel round as long as I wanted. He was becoming something of a comic hero to the audience we were attracting as we made our way through the market. He took me outside the covered section to the street where the country cousins sit on their haunches behind the dusty rugs where their goods are displayed. As well as meaner piles of fruit or vegetables from their gardens they bring Coke

bottles filled with the morning's milk, and purple plastic pails with slabs of more fresh white cheese smelling like babies.

They also bring their honey.

The honey sold here is all colours, and in jars of all sizes. As with the milk, the honey salvaged from this promising land is packaged in recycled containers – you can see the labels on the lids of jars showing the jams and pickles that the glass used to hold.

Smallholders recycling their packaging like this is exactly what I should be supporting. It was the reason that I came to this market and avoided all those neologistic supermarket chains. But once I got up close, in the whiff of the cheese, wondering how much of the taste of the pickle jar had transferred itself to the honey, and why exactly the colouring is different in each jar, it all looked far more like a *secretion* than I had anticipated. I couldn't quite bring myself to buy any of it. I apologised to the man who had brought me here, shaking my head, and then correcting myself. Round here, I had learned, that means 'yes'. Nodding instead, I asked him to take me to the bus stop, where he left me at the end of an unimpressed queue of people who realised they would be sharing a small hot space with me and my new purchase.

I spent the rest of the afternoon in the garden with a hosepipe and a bottle of bleach. I judged my success by the number of flies crowding round the barrel after each successive scrub and rinse. By the end of the day there was only one; I could live with him, and I left my new piece of furniture to dry out. I had achieved something, but it was with a sense of disappointment in myself, that I added 'honey' to the list of things to buy at InterAlbiMax on our next trip.

When we next went shopping in the supermarket I walked down the aisles of migraine lighting, and looked for the honey section. My options were ranged before me, all in identical jars with tidy labels. My little bourgeois honey-loving heart sang, and I chose a neat jar.

When we got home I tried it in a sandwich. It was a simple syrupy drool with none of the floral complexity of good honey. I wondered whether I had chosen the wrong brand. I examined the label more closely, looking to see where it was produced, from what flowers. I worked slowly because of the Albanian, but I did see something that I thought translated as 'ingredients'. This surprised me because I had imagined that the only ingredient would be 'honey'. Not so – this stuff

was made of 'glucose' and 'honey flavouring'. No wonder it tasted so foul.

The label on the front had the company's slogan – the one I had fallen for when I scanned the shelves at the supermarket. 'Homogenised. Industrialised', it proclaimed. Well, exactly.

If you don't have a smallholding, like the men with the weather-beaten faces outside the market, then 'homogenised, industrialised' produce is the easiest food to find. Increasingly, I was feeling that what-ever my education, my comparative material wealth, round here I was one of the dispossessed.

The next day I went back to the bandy-legged man in the market and bought myself a jar of the stuff that looked like earwax. It was deli-cious; Rob and I ate it on toast for tea on Sunday, balancing our plates on the bottom of the well-bleached upturned cheese barrel, in our house that was becoming a home.

4.
A first experience of honey served with Albanian hospitality – and *fli*

New Albanian vocabulary: *kar* (willy), *mjaltë* (honey: I was later to discover that this Albanian word is special – grammatically as well as gastronomically. It is one of a tiny group that behave strangely in their gender, suggesting they were part of an earlier neuter case that no longer exists. The other nouns in this group – *dough, wool, water, wax* – have ancient, fundamental significance and you can tell they have survived from early times despite their strangeness, being repeated from mothers to children in Albanian kitchens for thousands of years)

We had found ourselves a house, and we had stocked its cupboards so it felt like a home. But the Albanian expression told us that this could never truly be *our* home because 'a house belongs to God and the guest.' Inviting in the former would be changing the habit of a lifetime, but we were keen to fill our rooms with the latter; Rob and I sat down together to make a list of people we could have round for a housewarming brunch.

It was a long list for only a month in a new country; there were the British Office staff – that army officer with the confusing history lessons, the people who managed Rob's contract, whose address I was able to use for my Amazon deliveries. There were the Kosovan colleagues from the Prime Minister's Office; British army officers working with the NATO mission; a few other international advisers to the government, or with the United Nations Mission in Kosovo (UNMIK), which supported – or in some cases still ran – the government. The EU also had an office and huge staff in Kosovo, supporting its journey to meet EU standards that were one of the conditions for independence. I was learning about the way that these international missions brought others in their wake – the international charities, and local NGOs, big butch aid organisations who were as competitive and thrusting about their

budgets and their development initiatives as their corporate equivalents.

All of the names on the list were people we knew through Rob. I felt rather sad that I had no-one to bring to the party. Stubbornly, I insisted on including the guy who ran the internet café, and the electrician I had organised to come and sort out our fusebox and who had ended up also fixing the wiring for me on the waffle maker we would be using for brunch. Neither of them turned up on the day.

But Rob's colleagues did. They filled the ballroom, and spilled out of the French windows and stood on the terrace among the potplants and palms I had dotted hopefully around with an idea of offering attractive places for people to bring their company and conversation. Among the tanned British men cheerfully eating waffles and talking about Kosovan politics, with a cynicism undermined by enormous appetites, stood an elegant Kosovan woman of my age with a friendly smile.

She was introduced as Shpresa. Her name means 'hope' – one of many everyday Albanian nouns parents here give to their children as a kind of blessing. The school register must look like a compendium of all the things in life that one generation would want to bequeath to another – Praise, Butterfly, Improvement, Alphabet, River, Patience, Breeze, Dove, Swan, Love, Rainbow (Lavdim, Flutura, Përparim, Abetare, Lumi, Durim, Pohuiza, Kumria, Mjellma, Dashuria, Ylber).

Shpresa became my first friend in Kosovo. The day after our house-warming party she called me and invited me to lunch. It was typical of her, I would discover, and she told me later that it was an Albanian village tradition, to honour someone you've just met – something that had lingered in her approach to socialising despite her many years out of the village, out of the country. We sat in a busy café near her UN office and chatted about the people who drove her crazy at work, about her six-year-old son from her first marriage, about men. She told me about the years she had spent working in Germany in the 'nineties, after she had been excluded from the University of Prishtina, along with all the other Albanian students, and I asked her all the questions I had been saving up about Kosovo.

As we watched the waiters rushing salads and *makiatos* to the tables around us, she said, 'I used to work as a waitress in Germany. I swore that one day I would be the one coming out from my nicely-paid office job to sit for an hour in sunshine, and not the one sweating to serve the cus-

tomers in time.' But her job in Kosovo had its stresses too – she worked in the civil registry where people came for identity cards and UN travel documents (not passports – as Kosovars were constantly being reminded, they didn't really have a country).

She was always ready to criticise her country, bemused and sometimes angered by my compliments about the place, the things I singled out to comment on positively. One of my Kosovan friends told me later that he believes the sign that someone is truly Kosovan is when they tell you how much they'd prefer to live somewhere else.

I think Shpresa noticed before I did that I was ready to fall in love with this place. She seemed happy to act as matchmaker for me, suggesting walks before work out in the large park just outside Pristina, where she and I gossiped along the dappled trails and politely nodded good morning to the wheezing sixty-year olds in their velour tracksuits, taking an early morning walk for their health. She took me swimming in the outdoor pool set in rolling fields behind the ethnically Serb town of Gračanica, just outside Pristina, speaking politely fluent Serbian to the attendants. I asked carefully about her Serbian.

'Yes, of course I know how to speak Serbian. I played with local Serb kids as a child.' She treated racism with disdain, as yet another sign of Kosovo's backwardness.

She offered trips to the theatre with Rob and me, and I sat attentively through my least favourite Shakespeare play translated a century ago into incomprehensible Albanian. It was with Shpresa and her boyfriend that I first went to the nearest water to Pristina, a lake forty minutes outside the capital, where we sat eating fresh fish while the boyfriend told us about how the guerrilla Kosovo Liberation Army, the KLA, was funded. It was with her that Rob and I ventured to a sanatorium-style thermal spa with garish streaks of rust and minerals across its paintwork, but water that left my skin like a baby's.

I babysat her son, bought her books to fuel our pop psychology discussions (*I'm OK, you're OK* from Amazon), she introduced me to her friends, and taught me words of Albanian, including the swear words. She seemed as pleased to have a British friend as I was to have a Kosovan one.

One day she called me up. 'Are you and Rob free this evening? Would you like to come to supper at my family's home?'

It was from Shpresa that I had first learned the uselessness of a diary in Kosovo; all arrangements were made at a moment's notice. Her village was about an hour by car from our house. I wasn't insured on our Kosovan car, and I wondered whether Rob would be free from work in time. But this was the first time we had been invited into any Kosovan home.

I phoned Rob at work. 'Will we be able to go? Please?'

It was a hot summer's evening with a dusty haze softening the light across the rolling hills. As we drove out of the city we were entering a different world. Shpresa was born in a village, and there is no-one more keenly aware of the difference in mentality between the capital we were leaving behind and the rural community we were driving towards. This was the journey of Shpresa's life in reverse.

It was on this journey that I caught sight of my first beehive. Ranged in a field I saw a line of wooden boxes, as evenly placed as crosses in a military graveyard. The wooden boxes were about the same size as the slatted wooden weather stations you sometimes see by the road in the UK. Some were painted too. Shpresa explained what they were as we drove on past homes from which we caught whiffs of woodsmoke, as dinner was being prepared, and I wondered about Shpresa's mother getting supper ready for us in the house that Shpresa told us was yet some miles away.

We passed egg-shaped haystacks and sunburned men resting at the end of a day spent building them. Women with headscarves and lined faces stood with a hand on a hip and a glance at our car while they supervised skipping grandchildren in their front yards. Fields of maize shimmered. We saw the concrete representation of Kosovo's tight-knit families – repeated clutches of 'brother houses', each group of three or four identical houses set at a respectful distance from one another in a single field, where a family of brothers had used the same architect, like DNA, with only occasional differences in paint choices or an eccentric balcony showing the effect of nurture over nature.

We caught snatches of music distorted through loudspeakers from the week-long weddings which dominate the Kosovan summer. At the edge of villages, as we passed small clogged streams, we got sudden reminders of sewage. Far from Pristina's bars and politics, the 'internationals' and the big white UN cars that roamed the capital, this felt like

a place where the stuff of living was really going on.

I pointed out all these things to Shpresa in delight. As the journey went on and the road surface deteriorated she responded to me less and less enthusiastically.

'You need to understand the villager mentality, Elizabeth,' she said. The word 'villager' has two meanings in Albanian. It means someone who lives in a village, but also a peasant; it's a term of abuse by city folk. I wasn't sure exactly how Shpresa was using it now. But it was also clear that this 'mentality', where the world shrinks to the size of your own plot of land, wasn't something she wanted me to think she shared, and she didn't want me to be seduced by it.

Off the main road, and bumping along unmade tracks, Shpresa told Rob to stop when we came to a high wall with a high gate set in it. It opened and her mother and father came out to welcome us. Her parents looked old – older than they should have done for what Shpresa had told me of their age. Her father shuffled towards us and her mother stood stooped and smiling to greet us.

It was at Shpresa's home that I learned about Albanian greetings. When we arrived, Rob and I were introduced to her mother and father. The greetings procedure began, and for the first time, thanks to Shpresa, I had a translation of this key set-piece of Albanian social contact. I was to learn that these extended ritual greetings are almost identical, with the same insistence and concern, whether with a close friend or a sales assistant. The translation runs as follows:

'How are you? Are you well? Are you tired? Did you manage to get here? Your health? Are you feeling OK? Everything OK? How's your family? Father, mother, your husband?' The answers, of course, are set-pieces too. How am I? Well. Am I well? Yes. Am I tired? Just a bit. Did I manage to get here? Here I am. But it is a kind of competition because at the same time that these questions are being asked of me, I should be trying to ask them of my interlocutor. There are also some required responses to some of the answers and 'Thanks be to God' at appropriate moments. What's more, after this extended triangulation of my alleged state of health and well-being, attention was turned to Rob. How are you? Are you well? Are you tired?

Well, I thought we'd covered that – they'd asked me how my husband was a few minutes ago, even though they could see he was

standing right beside me in a state of peak physical fitness. Maybe I hadn't been convincing enough in my replies. The interrogation continued to him. He was answering as required – yes, he was well, no, he was only a bit tired, yes he managed to get here – here he is. And then they asked 'how's your wife?'

How many times do we have to tell you? Quite, quite well. But, in all honesty, now just a little bit tired.

It is a genuinely charming ritual. Where in the UK we might restrict ourselves to 'how are you?', perhaps throwing in the Protestant *How's work?* if we really want to reach into someone's soul, I got a sense that Kosovars were getting to the heart of things. A thousand miles from England, to be asked how my family was – Father? Mother? Everyone? I sometimes did get a lump in my throat and wanted to thank people for asking.

Once we had got through these preliminaries, Shpresa announced that her mother had prepared a special dish for us. This visit was to be our initiation into another important Kosovo Albanian institution: *fli* – with Kosovan honey. The enormous round tray of something like closely stacked pancakes was placed on the table and we sat down with the family – Shpresa and her parents as well as her brother who lives with his wife and two children in the family home. We all peeled off strips of *fli* with our fingers and ate it with helpings of yoghurt, home-cured cucumbers, home-grown tomatoes, a wedge of white cheese – and a dollop of honey.

I later understood that *fli* is the most lavish form of hospitality a Kosovan family can offer you; with it I had found my first comfortable role in Kosovo, in the sacred position of the guest.

My first taste of *fli*

Ingredients
• A triangular stand to go over a fire and support the *tepsi* (a round, deep baking tray; in this case about 50cm diameter)
• The *saç* – a metal dome which covers the *tepsi* and is itself covered with hot coals or ash (it's easiest to visualise this item if you know that the word *saç* is also used in Albanian for a satellite dish)
• A long metal hook for lifting the *saç* on and off the *tepsi*

• The flour, butter, yoghurt and salt water for making *fli*
• The family cow to produce the white cheese (something between Wensleydale, curd cheese and cottage cheese, a moist paste smelling like sour milk) for serving with the *fli*
• Honey to drizzle over it all

Grease the *tepsi*.

Heat the *tepsi* over the fire.

Sift 8 cups plain flour with 2 heaped tablespoons of salt.

Add water to the flour and salt until you have a thin batter – slightly thinner than for pancakes, but still able to coat the back of a spoon.

Drizzle strips of the batter into the *tepsi* in the form of sunrays from the middle. There is a theory that making *fli* with this distinctive design was a way of honouring the sun, which was sacred to the Illyrians – the ancient inhabitants of the Balkans.

Put the *saç* on top. Leave until the strips are golden with spots of brown.

Melt 400g butter and combine with 300ml of thick yoghurt.

Brush the golden strips with the butter/yoghurt mixture.

Drizzle new strips of batter into the spaces left between the 'sunrays' the first time.

Bake under the *saç* again.

Brush the more recent strips with butter/yoghurt, and continue alternating the batter with the butter/ yoghurt until all the batter is used up.

The resulting *fli* takes some hours to make, owing to the repeated layering and baking of the batter. I have since been told of a tradition that you shouldn't make *fli* alone. No-one has been able to confirm for me whether this is superstitious or practical advice, but it is certainly true that having two people at work (one slathering with butter or drizzling batter while one heats the *saç*-es) will speed up the process. Of course it is possible to make the dish in an oven too (200 degrees). The *fli* ends up two to three inches high, and enormously wide. It's an outsized food, making a statement about the outsized hospitality it represents. The laborious process and the huge, dense product at the end of it are the hallmark of Kosovan hospitality. I was later to eat *fli* in other homes, in a school where the staff had prepared it for me as a special

guest, in the traditional surrounds of a restored old stone *kulla* – and every time the feel of the solid slab in my stomach echoed the solid slap of the enthusiastic handshake of welcome I'd received from our host. *Fli* is a food and also a phenomenon.

5.
The definite article: *llokuma* with honey

New Albanian vocabulary: *ju bëftë mirë* (literally 'may it do you good': bon appétit. The usage of this phrase definitely doesn't translate from the equivalent in the UK – it has less of the sense of a fanfare before you stuff your face, more of the feeling of saying grace before you take nourishment. It really is a prayer that this food may serve you well, and as such it is said to almost anyone you see eating. You say *ju bëftë mirë* in the same way you might say 'bless you' in English when someone sneezes near you, even if you don't know them well – if at all), *krushq* (wedding procession), *zana* (fairy)

How can you know someone if you can't speak to them in ways they understand? I remember a newspaper I once bought in Chinatown. At the back was a strip cartoon of two animals with speech bubbles coming out of their mouths, filled with Chinese characters. In the middle picture, the cat was grinning, and in the third frame both he and the mouse were doubled over in hysterics. I had stuck it by my mirror and scanned it regularly, looking for a clue to the joke. I never got anywhere.

I thought about that cartoon a lot in my first weeks in Kosovo, as conversation flowed around, about and over me. If I couldn't find a way to communicate with this place soon, I would never feel at home here. I had started trying to learn Albanian on my own from a text book and with my best friend, the dictionary, with whose help I was still translating every poster and food packet I had time to look at. But I had been warned about Chapter Six.

'I had great plans like you, when I arrived. But honestly – have you seen what you have to learn? It's impossible once you get past chapter five.' We were at a barbecue with some other well-intentioned native English-speakers. And later that week, lying sunbathing in the garden sweating over my studies, I realised that they were right. Even when I'd

looked at the back of the book for the answers to some of the exercises, I couldn't understand why they were as they were. And I had no-one I could ask.

Rob's contract with the government had included a certain number of hours of language training for both of us. He had twenty hours in London before we moved – lessons with a Kosovo Albanian artist from whom Rob came home buzzing with adjectives and – his speciality and my bugbear with any new language – carefully conjugated verbs. When we arrived in Pristina he was immediately put in contact with a teacher to continue his studies but I had more trouble in setting up lessons. So when Rob and I were out together, I would ask him what I should say, would defer to him to order in restaurants or negotiate with shopkeepers. Meanwhile, all I could really do was smile through gritted teeth and try to look pretty. Shpresa suggested that it was excellent training for understanding the position of women in Kosovo.

I was wary of bothering Shpresa herself for anything more structured than the incidental vocabulary she offered when we were out together, but I increasingly felt the need for a teacher. Finally I begged Rob for the chance to come along for the first five minutes of his next lesson to get some help. I felt like the direct descendant of all those bright young Victorian women with furrowed brows who borrowed their brothers' schoolbooks to learn Latin.

Thankfully, Gazi the language teacher didn't really have Victorian values. He had a certain nineteenth-century intellectual pride though. It was only later that I discovered that he had lived in the UK while studying for his masters degree and had paid his way by working at Harrods. Asking this great mind and great linguist to help me with the tedious problems of the different forms of 'it' in 'I gave it to him' and 'I gave it to them' I felt rather like you might on walking into the grand decorated Food Hall and asking to buy a sandwich.

I greeted him in Albanian. He replied in a long sentence that I didn't let on that I didn't understand. I started again in English – would he be able to help me? He said he was rather busy at the moment.

I persisted – could he help me then for a few minutes this evening with some questions I had from the book I was using to teach myself? He glanced at Rob, and began an impatient series of questions about

what exactly I was misunderstanding.

'It's in Chapter Six.' I waited for the impact of this to sink in.

'You tried to cover Chapter *Six*?' He unbent. By the time I'd finished my drink, he had agreed to set up lessons three times a week with me.

We met in the café next to our house. I continued lessons with Gazi every week while we lived in Kosovo, but that summer was a golden time, with my diary all but empty, and the lessons offering a sense of progress and engagement in a world that I wanted a better grammar for.

Gazi guided me through the crazy inflections of Albanian, where nouns, for example, change their form not only with singular, plural, gender, case, but also exist in both definite and indefinite forms – so the word for 'the café' is different from the word for 'a café'. It was he who explained to me the crucial difference between the Kosovo and northern Albanian Gheg dialect and the southern, and now standard, Tosk dialect. Albanian has only had an official standard since a conference in 1972 when the dialect of Albania's despotic ruler, Enver Hoxha, from southern Albania, was tactically and tactfully adopted as the standard. Gazi is an advocate of (and has his own publishing house to support) Gheg Albanian being used for literary as well as street purposes. As I studied with him he always gave me the Tosk and Gheg versions of words or structures, when they differed (they could do significantly – 'I will go' is *kam me shkue* in Gheg, *do të shkoj* in Tosk). I was keen to start learning the language that would enable me to embark on Albanian literature – I had as a benchmark the novels of Booker prize-winner, Nobel candidate Ismail Kadare – but also pleased to be learning the language as I could hear it being spoken around me in Kosovo's cafés and bars.

It was also Gazi who was interpreter for me of Kosovo's culture and – since we were meeting in *kafeneja, the* café – Kosovo's cuisine. Through him I learned that the satisfactory but uninspiring pizza and pasta served at the restaurants that were easy to find in central Pristina were not the true tastes of Kosovo. I learned about small restaurants in back streets, and about the things to ask for that might not be on the menu.

He told me that the name of the café where we met at translated

as something like 'the fairies' shelter'. Any ideas I had of an underground gay rendez-vous or delightfully fey enchanted castle were dis-
pelled when I was told the sassy reputation of Albanian fairies – huge
women with hair down to the ground, who suckle Albanian heroes at
their breasts, and live entirely on honeycomb.

And it was Gazi who suggested I tried some honey with the
'llokuma' that was on offer on the café menu. I had a vague sense that
'llokuma' was part of the word for what we call Turkish delight, but he
assured me that these were different.

So in one of our lessons after a few weeks of confidence-building,
I caught the waiter's attention. Slowly (laughably slowly, especially given
the idiomatic English he had spoken to me before) I ventured in
Albanian, 'I would like... please... some *llokuma* [feminine, indefinite
plural, accusative].' Gazi smiled indulgently as I reached the end of the
sentence, and we both held our breath to see what the waiter would
come back with.

They are difficult to describe, these deep-fried puffs of dough.
Calling them doughnuts makes them sound denser and yeastier than
they are. It also suggests a sweetness which they don't have on their
own, being neutral in flavour, and served with a range of tastes including white cheese, jam, chocolate spread, something like tzatziki – and,
best of all, honey. Like so much of my engagement with Albanian, the
name for them loses something in translation. As I learned, you're better
off making and tasting it for yourself.

Llokuma are an every-day treat – something that is relatively easy to
prepare, with ingredients you're likely to have to hand in your kitchen,
but served to make a day feel special; a perfect Sunday breakfast. Served
with the yoghurt and garlic dip they are also the perfect hangover cure.

In traditional Kosovan weddings when the bridegroom's party of
male friends (minus the groom) has set off to collect the bride from her
home, superstition says that they must return a different way from the
route they took to her house. On their journey, they stop off at friends'
who will serve them *llokuma*. *Llokuma* are also made when a baby is
born.

I wrote the recipe down while I watched Shpresa making them for breakfast for us one morning when she and Rob and I were on a trip away from Pristina, near the mountains. Once I'd learned it, I reproduced it for all the house guests we had to stay – parents, sisters, British friends – none were allowed to visit us in Kosovo without at least one lazy brunch where we sat talking and repeatedly reaching for just one more of these bite-size breakfast treats.

Last time I counted, the recipe made 32 pieces.

Beat 2 eggs in a bowl.
Add a cup of yoghurt.
Add half a cup of sparkling water.
Add 1.5 tsp bicarbonate of soda.
In a larger bowl, mix 450g of plain flour with a tablespoon of baking
 powder and a palmful of salt.
Add the wet mixture to the dry mixture and fold together.
Add more flour if the mixture is too wet – it shouldn't stick to your
 fingers – and then decant from the bowl and lightly roll in flour on
 a surface.
Press out to ½cm thick.
Cut into rectangles 3cm x 5cm.
Put into smoking vegetable oil (at a depth of a little more than ½cm).
The *llokuma* should puff up to four times their thickness in the oil. Turn
 them as soon as they start to brown. Eat immediately.

6.
My b-day

New Albanian vocabulary: *flamur* (flag), *U bëfsh njëqind vjeç* (may you live to 100 – the traditional birthday greeting)

As the honeymoon of that first summer in Pristina turned to autumn I started to make plans for a big day that was coming up. I am always childishly excited about my birthday, and this year I had discovered that I would have others to join in the celebrations with me: one of the first indicators that Kosovo was a place I could feel at home, belong, was discovering a deep connection between my birthday and Kosovo's history.

On our very first morning in Kosovo, being driven to register at the British Office I had seen my birthday being used as a roadname. It turns out that 28 November is a day of significance not just for me, but for all Albanians. On 28 November 1443, the Albanian hero Scanderbeg became head of the Kastrioti region, from which he waged his legendary attacks against the Ottomans. On 28 November 1912, the Albanian flag (Scanderbeg's double headed eagle) was raised in Vlora and Albania came of age. From then on, the date was celebrated as Flag Day. Accordingly, the guerrilla Kosovo Liberation Army, the KLA, chose 28 November 1997 to first appear in public.

This year, my birthday was going to be a very special one. After all, a whole country would be celebrating with me. In fact, it was also going to be the starting point for this book.

Walking home on the evening before my birthday, with my head full of treats and presents, I realised that this was how a child – perhaps a pampered princess – might plan their birthday. The town was decked in Scanderbeg's flag, and there was a holiday atmosphere everywhere. Like a child, I couldn't help myself blurting out to everyone I met in the shops that it would be my birthday in the morning.

I woke up with a great sense of anticipation. I am used to being spoiled with a small pile of presents from Rob. I sat up in bed and

smoothed down a space in front of me. Rob saw what I was doing and smiled indulgently. 'This birthday you have one present from me,' he said, and handed over a small, hard heavy parcel. Inside was a pot of amber honey.

I think what I said was, 'oh!'

As he knew, I do love honey. My appetite had only grown during my introduction to it on *fli* and *llokuma*. And from the look of it, this was good quality honey that would be great to spread on toast. Maybe he had also bought me some bread, and we could celebrate my birthday with a sandwich...

Then Rob showed me a photograph. It was of a weathered old wooden box like the ones I had seen from the car, against a deep landscape of uninterrupted hills. 'This is your hive,' he explained, 'and this is the honey that came from it.'

It was the perfect present. Not only was Bee my family nickname, but the world of the hive had always been a fascination for me. Bees had cured me of the glandular fever that had cost me over a term of missed school as a teenager – I had only recovered when a family friend had prescribed me royal jelly, and the bees' nutrient-rich food for their queen had saved my exam results.

I had first dreamed of keeping bees myself a year before, in London, when I read *Lark Rise to Candleford* with the descriptions of self-sufficiency in sweetness from the village hives. This present made that dream come true, but it was a complex gift that also offered me a role in Kosovo, a craft I could learn – a colony I could rule, perhaps, while Rob tinkered with the bizarre politics of human beings. I loved the fact that it would bring me into deeper and more meaningful contact with life in Kosovo's countryside.

The day's activities crowded in on us after that early morning quiet view of the hills in the photograph. Rob was busy writing a speech for the Prime Minister for Flag Day. And, buoyed up by the sense of celebration, for the first time in my adult life I was hosting a birthday party.

I had found a fairytale setting for it – the eighteenth-century house which is now part of Kosovo's Ethnological Museum. The house is my favourite place in Pristina – indeed, I am the founder of the seventy-people-strong Facebook group 'The Emin Gjiku House/Ethnological Museum is my favourite place in Pristina.' The building is made of

wood, with elaborate shutters, and the two entrances typical of homes in Kosovo – one for guests and one for the family. The civilised life led by at least some of its inhabitants is evident from its design – the *çardak* suntrap where meals could be eaten in spring, the beautiful carved woodwork of its *oda* or living room (the word is Turkish and it is from this that we get our word *odalisque*. I have a strong urge to offer my services as an odalisque whenever I walk into the seductive luxury of this old house). The room is carpeted in rich red colours from rugs that cover the floor and the *minder* – a seating construction running the length of the room.

In front of the seating area is a *mangall* – a metal bowl with integral stand that would have been filled with coals. These offered heating, could be used for lighting cigarettes, and – most importantly – for making coffee for guests. Coffee-making and hosting guests was men's work, and as such was done in the elegant quarters of the *oda* rather than the stone-flagged kitchen, the women's domain.

For my celebration I would be breaking with this house's tradition of hospitality, then, as the party was going to take place in the kitchen. This was my choice, fretful about the beautiful rugs of the *oda*, the crumbly cake I was going to serve, and the possible clumsiness of sixty guests carrying glasses of red wine. No-one at the museum seemed worried, so in the end I brought my own fire extinguishers and made my own notices about guests not taking their drinks into the carpeted areas.

I think I was the first person to have used this as a venue for a birthday party (with the exception, I assume, of the family whose home it was until it became a museum in the 1950s). The success of it as a place to celebrate was reinforced six months after my party when a high-profile high-society party was held there to celebrate the birthday of former Prime Minister, Ramush Haradinaj. He was unfortunately unable to attend himself, as he was detained in The Hague facing war crime charges at the time.

But on 28 November 2006 the party being brought to the old house was a new idea. In fact, when I turned up at 3pm to start to organise the event, the building was locked up and the policeman on duty outside said he knew nothing of the evening. There was temporarily no electricity and no water.

A place to party: the *oda* in the eighteenth-century house which is part of
Pristina's Ethnological Museum

The museum guides turned up shortly afterwards, and we formed ourselves into an impromptu party preparation team, joined by the policeman whose initial suspicion was transformed into the telling of incomprehensible jokes and the consumption of cake. By the time the guests arrived at six, the cold old building had also been transformed. Wine was mulling on a portable gas stove set up in one of the outbuildings, flowers glowed in the hearth of the old kitchen and tables of food stood ready, including eight sponge cakes which Rob had smuggled in, nervous lest any of his former KLA fighter colleagues should get to hear of his baking prowess.

The weather was foul with a freezing fog that made it unappealing to be outside. However, we lit candles to show the way from the museum's high wooden gates, and they flickered entrancingly through the haze and led people up the dramatic path, through the frozen gardens to the house itself. Despite the fog, people came – many seeing the museum site for the first time – and laughed, and ate and drank. It was a perfect evening and the photographs show me always smiling and always a little pink, in the giddy warmth of new friendships.

In Kosovo's strange slow courtship of me, that night marked a significant stage. I have a theory about making home in new houses – that they won't feel completely yours until you have done five things in them: prepared a meal, used the toilet, had sex, returned there after a break away, and hosted guests. Hosting so many warm, generous people in this most Kosovan of settings, whatever else I did not do there, was a powerful experience. I was beginning to feel like I belonged somewhere at this end of Europe. And thanks to my birthday present from Rob, I now felt a meaningful connection beyond Pristina, with one small corner of a foreign field that was really mine, busy with my bees.

7.
December: 'The colony is checked only by looking at the hive from outside' – *The Beekeeping Calendar* by Z S Muçolli

---

New Albanian vocabulary: *koshere* (hive), *çeiz* (trousseau: in fact, this word is not Albanian but Turkish – just as the 'English' equivalent is borrowed from our own former occupiers and bringers of fancy ways and ideas, and words)

I couldn't wait to meet my bees. We were in our sitting room talking about practicalities. Rob waved a hand at the view out of the window – at the concrete and glass aspirations of the Ministry of Education next door, the post office building towering over rooftops, the dusty road outside where nothing bloomed in the verges except occasional road-kill; my bees wouldn't thank me if I brought their hive to the city. Rob explained to me he had come to an arrangement that they could be left on the land belonging to Adem, the man he had bought the hive from. I could go up and work on it whenever I had spare time, and be apprenticed to Adem as I learned my new craft.

So we set my first meeting with the bees and with Adem at his home on the first possible weekend after my birthday.

It had been through the father of one of Rob's colleagues that he had been put in contact with Adem to buy the hives. In numerous subsequent phone calls Mr Velija had asked Rob whether I was happy with my present, whether Rob was happy with the arrangement, whether we were sure that we didn't want to move the hives to be with someone who was less of a... villager? Mr Velija owns land near Adem so Rob finally suggested that he could come with us on our visit, and he could see for himself that everything was *tamam*, just so.

We started off through the northern suburbs of Pristina. I'd been told that this part of the city has the highest crime rate, so I eyed the streets with suspicion. But it was the usual Kosovan Sunday scene –

pixie-faced boys in faded sweatshirts playing ball by the road, shop-keepers twitching at the display of their goods outside, over-filled cars with wedding songs wailing from the stereo, weaving along in good-natured chaos, young women in tight jeans sweeping their front steps or banging rugs out of upstairs balconies, while their mothers-in-law in baggy Turkish-style trousers stood watching them.

The houses thinned out and soon each one we passed was set in its own field. By this point in the year the haystacks were dwindling, the single stick which supports each one in the middle was showing – they seemed munched through to the bone. Lean cows tethered in front yards gazed at them sympathetically.

And then there was hardly a house to be seen. We were into the wild hills, uncultivated and impenetrable. There were still landmines in Kosovo off major roads, and I thought of them glinting in the under-growth. I thought of the pixie-faced boys scrambling after their ball.

I had never met Mr Velija before, but on the road we made con-versation – stilted through lack of familiarity and lack of vocabulary.

'My family have always lived in this region,' he told me, and he offered us vignettes of its history, which was also his history. He gestured at a hill to our right. 'Below that are the remains of an ancient city'. He is a founding member of an organisation for the promotion of the economy and culture of this part of Kosovo, and he was working on fundraising for an archaeological dig to uncover the city.

My British mobile phone bleeped in my bag. A text message said 'Welcome to Serbia.' It was ironic – the Belgrade government would claim that I had been in Serbian territory from the very start of my journey in Pristina; here we were only a few miles from the 1999 border. Mr Velija acknowledged what I said with another bit of history. It was on this road that his family fled in 1999. He talked about the roadblocks, the sadism of the paramilitaries who had set them up. We drove on in silence, and I thought about the pixie-faced boys again.

It was only half an hour's journey to the farm. The road had dete-riorated into potholes, and for the last mile was nothing more than mud. Pulling up the hill we could hear the tyres spinning, and we slithered and sprawled to a halt on Adem's land.

I got out of the Landrover and looked around. To the left was the view I was familiar with from that photograph that Rob had given me

for my birthday. Set on the slope, to catch the low slanting winter sun, was the small wooden box of my hive. It stood in a row of perhaps a dozen others.

To my right was a low cluster of buildings: a barn draped in a UNHCR-marked tarpaulin of the kind that were issued to refugees, another outbuilding with a wolfskin nailed to it round which hens picked daintily, a smaller hut with heavy tools hanging off it and a dog tied up below, whimpering when I got closer, and a low stone house, down the steps of which a man was coming forward to greet us.

Adem's face was the colour and texture of a man who is out in all weathers. He looked about my father's age, but of great physical strength. Perhaps, as I'd found with Shpresa's parents, I wasn't good at judging ages in Kosovo. His hand was rough when I shook it, and his smile was enormous, and slightly lopsided because so many of his teeth were missing.

I was shifting and fussing, introducing myself, thanking him, asking after his health, his wife, thanking him again, catching myself in grammatical mistakes, uncertain how this relationship was supposed to work. My shoes had sunk into the mud of his yard and I wished I'd worn something more practical. I wondered what he thought of me.

In the midst of this motion and vacillation, Adem stood still and comfortable. Rob greeted him, and so did Mr Velija, and then when I had finally twittered myself into silence, Adem turned to me 'O Elizabeta,' he said, in welcome. '*Hajde!*' He was ushering me into his house. He had addressed himself to me, not to either of the men, not to Mr Velija who was a generation older than both Rob and I, not to Rob who had paid for this treat. It was a gentle and nicely-judged form of respect and I liked him for it immediately.

The men stood back as Adem steered me up the steps into his home. We took our shoes off at the entrance and stepped into the front room. It was fuggy from a wood stove burning to one side, and it smelt of fried peppers. Standing to greet me was Adem's wife. He nodded at her with one word, 'wife'. I had read Edith Durham, the Edwardian traveller to the Balkans, saying that there was a superstition that couples shouldn't use one another's name; I hadn't known that the tradition persisted.

The woman I subsequently discovered to be called Xhezide wel-

comed us formally in a bird-like voice. She was shorter than me and had to tilt her head to talk to me or the men. She, I could see, was as unsure about how to handle this situation as I was.

'Sit, sit,' Adem invited us, and we sat down on the long upholstered bench that ran along the edge of the room. The children, Mirlinda and Lavdim, were called in – two teenagers who shook hands respectfully before going and helping their mother. Xhezide busied off to the stove and started making Turkish coffee in its special enamel pot. I saw her looking at us as she waited for it to boil. I smiled at her and she looked confused and turned back to her coffee. Adem pulled up a low wooden stool opposite us and offered us cigarettes.

'How are you?' he asked. 'And your family? Your health?' A Kosovar told me of a superstition that bees won't stay on the land of an unhappy family. So maybe these conversations were of agricultural as well as social importance. I could tell that Adem had slowed down his questions for our benefit and I was grateful. This region of Kosovo is known for its quaint vowel sounds and it was hard for me to make sense of them. More than that, I had the sense that Adem was slowing down this ritual – the greetings, the welcome, the cigarettes, coffee, routine questions – to teach us how it was done, to reassure us that we were in safe hands. I felt that I would enjoy learning beekeeping from a man like this.

I tried a few British hospitality rituals of my own. Looking around the room I found things to admire. Xhezide had just put an embroidered table cloth on the table in front of us. 'What beautiful work,' I congratulated her, adding the Albanian formula, 'may your hands be praised.' With everyone pitching in to help with providing a translation she told me that she had made it herself as part of her trousseau. Looking around the single kitchen, dining, entertaining area I realised that all was hand-stitched, hand-carved, hand-cobbled-together.

As we drank our coffee together we all relaxed a little. The family were friendly but seemed confused and maybe even suspicious about us. It takes some explanation – we were obviously not 'villagers' and were people who could buy as much 'Industrialised, Homogenised' honey as we wanted from the well-stocked shelves of Pristina's shops. Instead we were going to be travelling regularly out of the city to bring back the odd jar of honey with a few stray insect wings still stuck to it.

Adem

Nevertheless, Adem led me out to the hives. He explained that we couldn't open them because it was too cold. But the bees were in there, he assured me, and suggested that we tap the box to rouse them so I could hear the sound of them fanning their wings.

I duly knelt on the wet grass with my ear to the wooden box, and knocked against the side. I couldn't hear anything.

I looked up, and Adem was smiling encouragingly at me. 'Do you hear them?' he asked. I didn't know what to say. I thought of new mothers who have told me about the confusion of staring at the ultrasound scans and trying to see the baby the doctors are showing them there. These bees were my first real commitment to Kosovo and I couldn't even be sure they existed. Adem saw my uncertainty, and rapped at the box again. There was a sound. But I thought it might be the noise of my hair rustling against my ear.

I tried one final time. It was becoming embarrassing to be squatting in the mud trying to listen to the bees I'd been given as a present. I thought I could hear something. Perhaps it was the hum of my own blood circulating – this was very like listening for the sound of the sea in a shell. 'It's very faint,' I said sheepishly, and got to my feet.

Maybe there were no bees in my hive, but I didn't dare ask anything more.

Back inside, Xhezide served us tea with honey stirred into it. I cupped my hands around the little glass. It had been bitterly cold outside, but the small room was warmed deliciously by the wood stove where our tea was boiled up. I was reluctant to leave.

That evening I did my first piece of writing about Kosovo. Up till now I had felt that the repeated patterning of Albanian verb tables, the acquiring and playing with new vocabulary, had filled every space for words in my head. But the knocking on the side of my hive had got something stirring.

8.
Kosovo's Chequers: honey in a recipe for social success

New Albanian vocabulary: *thes* (hessian)

I had never received an invitation from a Prime Minister before. Rob had now had six months of working for the man and was blasé about these things, but our invitation to Prime Minister Agim Çeku's house in the country for lunch one weekend put me in a social spin.

Neither had I ever received an invitation from an ex-guerrilla general before. Agim Çeku's past didn't make me feel any more at ease.

To start with, what is the etiquette for a gift to take for the war hero premier of a Balkan country when he is hosting you for lunch? A box of Ferrero Rocher didn't feel quite right.

Eventually I hit on the idea of taking some honey. Decanting a generous but not vulgar amount of the honey made by *my* bees into a new jar, and with some fancily-scripted Albanian announcing it to be 'Elizabeth's Kosovan honey' I felt that I had created the ideal person-alised, patriotic luxury item.

My next worry was about what to wear. I went through my wardrobe, looking for something that would combine paramilitary chic with diplomatic cool, and yet be practical enough for a country weekend in December. Does Albanian *Vogue* have an advice page for this kind of thing?

Until we went into the house, I was very pleased with the outfit I'd finally chosen. At a crafts fair earlier that year I had met a young designer who makes clothing and accessories from old coffee sacks. If there actu-ally is an Albanian *Vogue* then they should do an article on him – the clothes are funky, with their stenciled export destinations running down one side of a skirt, or along the pocket of a jacket. I have one of these hessian skirts with accompanying bag, stenciled 'Kosova'. The playful jingoism of this felt just right. And I had a chunky knitted long cardi-

gan to keep me warm, and a fancy silk scarf, plus some boots that co-ordinated with the scarf. I discovered that I didn't have any tights without holes in them, but I found two pairs with holes in different places, which I could wear together – no bad thing anyway in these freezing temperatures – and I was pleased to discover that the small revealed stretch of tights between bottom of skirt and top of boots was entirely hole-free. I was ready for lunch.

We arrived at the PM's house and he strode out to greet us. He was familiar, of course, from television and newspaper articles – the long legs, shaven head, ears that you could always pick out in a crowd. He's an imposing man, but by no means an intimidating one, especially here in jeans and jumper.

His house shares a site with houses belonging to other members of the family. It's set in fields, and chickens pecked alongside the drive as we walked up together onto frozen mud. It is not quite Chequers; a long way from Camp David. As he would later tell us with genuine pride, the Prime Minister is from a very simple family, and before he won his scholarship to the Yugoslav Military Academy in Belgrade as a teenager, he was looking forward to a career consisting of taking the family's surplus vegetables to market every week. After that scholarship, things changed for the family in so many ways. He was based in Croatia when the war began there between Serbs and Croats, and he deserted from the Yugoslav army to offer his services to the Croatian army. When violence broke out in his own country, his professional soldiering was indispensable to the KLA with whom he became Chief of Staff. The position cost his father his life – unable to hunt down the son, at the height of the conflict in Kosovo, Serb police came to the family home here, where the chickens were pecking around us today, and took the father.

This prime minister is not an uncontroversial figure. When I told a friend in England who it was that Rob was to be working for, she said, 'isn't that the war criminal?' Some internet research showed me what she was referring to – actions in the war in Croatia which the Serbs allege to be war crimes. But googling 'Agim Ceku war crimes' also brought up an article about General Jackson, the British general I had only heard of with respect; the man who had ignored the NATO HQ order to engage the Russians at Pristina airport, and who was therefore credited with

having avoided World War III. (I had heard of him, too, because of the oft-repeated family story of how my father had once acted alongside him in a school play.) The internet article declared Jackson a war criminal for his actions on Bloody Sunday. My internet research shook my clear sense of right and responsibility. I was less bothered by the possibility that these apparently good men might have done terrible things, but by the sense that if these men could do – or could even come close to doing – these things, maybe anyone could. It reinforced a sense of the luck I had to be sheltered from such experiences, my civilian ignorance and inability to understand, let alone judge, the way decisions were made in the heat and fear and confusion of battle – bone and blood, smoke sifting over unfamiliar landscapes, men far from home, isolated in their bivvies and in unnatural systems – so far from Radio 4, from Google, from the terms by which they would be judged.

They were issues that dogged me for months in Kosovo. Rob and I stayed up late arguing: what – who? – was Right for Kosovo? We never found a resolution. In the end we just got on with now, and with the future. It was the approach that most Kosovars seemed to have taken – the dead were dead; whether that was the dead they had killed or the dead they had had taken from them. I couldn't decide whether it was cowardice or bravery to move on like that.

Çeku led us over to where one of his brothers, or maybe his cousin, was making grape *raki* at a still in one of the barns. *Raki* is a national tradition, dating back to the time before Kosovo's Catholic or Orthodox inhabitants were converted to teetotal Islam by the Ottomans. The extent of that conversion was debatable even in the fifteenth century – many heads of families converted 'for tax purposes' (non-Muslims were liable for a hefty tax) while the rest of their families continued worshipping more or less openly as Christians. Today, the standard *raki* drunk for breakfast by many men combines with the pepperoni on pizzas offered in Pristina's restaurants, and the uncovered heads of its fashionable and often scantily-dressed young women as evidence that Kosovo is not as you might imagine a Muslim country to be.

The common epithet for a good *raki* seems to be 'clean'. To my mind, *raki* is clean in the same way that bleach is clean. So to my limited imagination and palate this *raki* did the only thing it was fit for, and warmed us up wonderfully in the sub-zero December chill. The com-

plicated process by which it was made was explained to me, and I tried several times to understand it, before the Prime Minister, his brother – or cousin – and myself all gave up, embarrassed.

And then it was suggested that we should go inside. We didn't initially go in to the main house, but to a room that seemed to be a common entertaining area, shared by all the family houses. It had a little bar in it, and a roaring fire. In common with all homes in Kosovo we were gestured to take off our boots before we went in. I had forgotten that this would happen.

The usual hospitable muddle of slippers lay just inside the door for us to replace our footwear, but the slippers only covered my feet, not my lower legs as the boots had done. To my squirming discomfort, I therefore spent my day with the Prime Minister of Kosovo showing off not one but two pairs of holed tights, and dangling at the end of my inelegant legs some enormous carpet slippers that had been offered when my boots were off. I was only slightly comforted by the fact that the Prime Minister of Kosovo himself was sitting in a pair of enormous carpet slippers – but he could carry them off better than I.

In the end there was only one part of this extraordinary day where I triumphed. Despite their vegetables and their cows and their *raki* still, the Prime Minister's family doesn't have any beehives of their own. As we stood drinking, and Rob was coaxing his favourite war stories from his boss, I had found it hard to know what to say to this man whose life had been so different from mine. Even if the Prime Minister had never won that scholarship to the military academy, my conversational topics would have been limited. I am not easy in smalltalk with subsistence farmers.

But I had just taken a tiny step into this unfamiliar fraternity. When we all moved into the Prime Minister's house to eat, I was able to present him with his jar of personalised honey. What's more, he and I had a brief discussion about beekeeping – the kind of year it had been for the flowers, for the honey stocks. I knew some of this routine from having listened carefully to Adem; I had learned some of the formulae that he had used in his conversation with Mr Velija.

And then we were invited to sit down at the table for lunch, and I sank gratefully into a chair from which my legwear was not visible to anyone.

Lunch included delicious bread, and I subsequently got the recipe for this *pogaqe*:

Ingredients
A cup of set yoghurt
1.5 teaspoon salt
4 tbsp oil
3 cups flour
1 tbsp baking powder
1 egg
Sesame seeds

Put all the ingredients except the white of the egg and the sesame seeds in a bowl and mix with a spoon until you have a compact dough.
Put the dough on an oiled baking sheet and with oiled or floured hands flatten it a little. Make two incisions on the top and cover with egg white and sesame seeds.
Put in a 190 degree oven for 30 minutes.

9.
Tomatoes with honey

New Albanian vocabulary: *ram* (frame; the word comes from Serbian), *tymës* (smoker), *me lëshue* (to swarm), *ama* (queen, literally 'mother' bee; I don't know what the differences between the anglophone and Albanian concepts of this bee say about English queens or Albanian mothers)

My phone rang. It was a number I didn't recognise but when I heard the voice on the other end of the line I knew exactly who it was.

'O, Elizabeta,' growled Adem. I asked after his health, his family. Was he tired? And how were the bees?

He said that the weather was now good enough to open the hives. 'So can we come this weekend?'

'*Hajde...* Come on, let's get on with it...'

It would be my first chance to see, rather than just hear, my bees. I didn't quite know what to expect from inside my hive. I once read some research into young children's formation of the scientific concepts of human biology, where children of perhaps six were asked to draw what they thought was inside their bodies. The images they drew were of human-shaped sacks filled plump with blood, in which floated a few femur-like bones, and a Valentine's heart magically suspended in the middle. That's pretty much the level of understanding I had of the inside of a hive – the inside swirling with furry yellow bumble bees (a cloud of maybe a hundred, I guessed) who built chunks of wax comb (stuck perhaps to the edges?) which they filled with honey.

Before gazing into this new world, I learned I had to get used to new ways of seeing. Unless you are very brave, any view inside a beehive is in fact multiple small images blended together to a picture of reality – each tiny image framed in a black mesh square, as you look out from your hood. The bees and you look at one another, compound eye to compound eye.

I wasn't yet kitted out as a proper beekeeper with my own white

hooded cape, but Adem lent me his. I felt strange, and other-worldly, as if I was wearing a space suit. He looked at me carefully, and gave an instruction to Xhezide. She rushed inside and came out with a pair of his old nylon trousers for me – I hadn't realised my bare legs were a risk.

'I don't want to be any trouble,' I apologised, wishing silently that I had thought more carefully about preparing for this visit, or read more about this new craft I was learning.

'You must, you must. No trouble,' insisted Xhezide – she said she had been stung herself recently and she didn't want me to get hurt. She patted my arm, and watched me walk down to the beehives with Adem.

When Adem lifted the lid on my hive, it looked nothing like the cross-section of a Crunchie bar I had imagined, with gooey clumps stuck round the edges. It looked more like the drawer of a filing cabinet. This is what I discovered was called a Langstroth hive – the revolutionary design of an American clergyman in the 1850s which enabled beekeepers to retrieve their honey without destroying their hive. What in a filing cabinet drawer would be the suspended pockets for storing documents are, in the hive, vertical wooden frames hanging from ridges high on opposite sides of the box. They are organised far better than any filing cabinet I have ever been in charge of – Adem levered out the frames and showed me what was in each. The colony stores honey in some areas, and leaves others for the laying of eggs and the raising of young bees. Honey dripped out as he held the frames up to the pale sun.

As he worked slowly and carefully through the hive, pulling out frame after frame, he was calming the bees all the time. He had a metal jug-and-bellows in which a piece of wood was being burned, and from which, with each puff of the bellows, smoke came out to confuse and sedate the bees. A large component of bee communication is apparently smelling the chemical signals they send each other, and smoke interferes with that process, jamming the radios of the guard bees whose job is to raise the alarm when large human beings hove into view.

I was glad that I had Adem and that he had these precautions – the bees were blacker and more sinister than I'd visualised. They aren't bumble bees – I have since learned that it's not possible to cultivate bumble bees; their hives are messy and usually underground, and they

store only a few days' honey at a time. These were *apis mellifera carnica*, bees originating in the Balkans but now the dominant race of bees across all Europe.

And there were a lot, lot more than a hundred of these creatures. The hive was full, and I now know that a full hive may have over 100,000 resident bees. Looking at mine, ranged along the hillside with the other dozen hives belonging to Adem himself, I realised that I could see the dwellings of almost as many bees as there were people in Kosovo.

As would probably be the case if you lifted the lid on the homes of all the people in Kosovo, when we opened the hives, the sound was staggering. I had expected the familiar sound of one bee, multiplied and amplified. But this was an entirely different voice – as different as listening to one person chatting is from listening to the sound of a Wembley crowd. The noise was less like a buzzing than a throbbing or vibration, or like a note on an organ. With this, the smoke and the man presiding in his special robes, I felt like I was in attendance at a Sunday service.

Adem had been listening more expertly than I to the noises the colony had been making. And apparently this was the sound made when a new queen was born.

'They're ready to split. There can only be one queen in the hive so soon half the bees will take off with the old queen.' I asked why she would leave. 'If they stayed as they were, eventually there wouldn't be enough space or food to go round. They're wise, bees' – Adem tapped his head respectfully.

But Adem may be wiser still – he told me he hoped to be able to catch the bees at it as they swarmed. He took me to the shed and showed me the old-fashioned hives hanging there – teardrop-shaped skeps of wicker, a couple of feet high, and covered in cow dung to block up the gaps between the withies. Before Langstroth's invention, these were what beekeepers offered as long-term homes for their bees. But when their honey was ready to be harvested, the wicker was slit open and the honeycomb cut out like the flesh from a fruit. Then both the bees and the beekeeper had to start work again on building a new home for them.

So Adem doesn't use them as long-term homes for his bees any

more, but he keeps the skeps to use when the old queen, with her coterie of followers, takes off from the hive. She will land on a branch somewhere close (he pointed at the cherry tree nearby that he thought offered a likely resting place) for perhaps a few hours while scouts go off to find a suitable new home for them all. This is a risky time for the swarm, unsure where their next meal will come from. They will have eaten three days worth of food just before they set off, but that needs to last them until they have found a safe new home where they can store pollen and refine their honey.

Adem showed – gently, as if he were calming a frightened animal – how he would then ease the skep over the mass of absconding bees and shake them into a Langstroth hive. Thinking back to the seething mass of little black bodies in my hive, what Adem was proposing seemed brave. I wished I didn't have to go back to Pristina – I would have liked to have seen this little piece of theatre.

Xhezide with her daughter, Mirlinda

'You'll have another colony if we get it right!' he said proudly. It was a good time of year to catch a swarm – as the old English rhyme tells you, 'A swarm of bees in May/Is worth a load of hay;/A swarm of bees in June/Is worth a silver spoon;/A swarm of bees in July/Isn't worth a fly.' Adem told me that I could expect almost double the harvest of honey next year. As a trailer for what that might be like, Xhezide came out at that point and invited us to sit down to lunch. I had spent the morning doing 'man's work' – it is symbolic that I was lent Adem's trousers while I was with the hives. And while I had been out with my fellow men, Xhezide had been preparing lunch.

We sat down to eat it, feeling more comfortable with one another. Xhezide was less wary of us, Adem seemed convinced that I was really interested in learning about beekeeping and didn't mind getting my hands sticky. They remembered what we'd told them about our families – they didn't just ask about 'familja' but about my sister, our nephew and niece. It was almost like we were friends.

The meal itself reinforced a shift in our social relations – where before we had been offered only drinks, this time we were not only invited to lunch, but to eat *fli*. It was served with homemade cheese and sweet home-grown tomatoes (red ones, not the green tomatoes which are traditional here. I learned that it was only in the 1950s that attitudes to red tomatoes changed; before that, red tomatoes were treated as rotten versions of green tomatoes). When our plates were fully loaded, the honey jar was brought out. Honey was drizzled over the whole lot – *fli*, cheese and tomatoes. I felt luxuriously steeped in the stuff.

10.
Queens of the May

New Albanian vocabulary: *dyllë* (wax)

Our beekeeping fraternity was growing. We had got to know Rob's colleague, Dardan, through whom Rob had found and bought me my hive. Mr Velija, who had accompanied us when I had first visited Adem and Xhezide, was Dardan's father, and when Dardan heard about the clean air and the sweet and abundant flowers where my bees pastured he said he was going to buy a hive of his own and keep it next to mine on the smallholding. Unlike me, Dardan didn't need Adem's expertise as well as his land – he knew something about beekeeping already, learned from his experience living with a beekeeper while he was hiding out during the days of NATO's bombing campaign in March 1999.

Sometimes we drove out from Pristina together with Dardan – always in our Landrover, because Dardan said his BMW would get damaged on the rough tracks at the end of the journey to Adem's house. Sometimes on our visits Dardan – American-university-cocky – and Adem, quietly unmovable, would debate approaches to beekeeping. I never heard them contradict one another – Albanian debate doesn't work like that – even when they were in complete disagreement. It was a careful flight alighting gently on the flowers of proposition and counter-proposition. For me it was also a masterclass in beekeeping.

When Dardan heard what Adem had said about the chance that my colony was going to separate, and the need for a new hive he was excited for me.

'I've got some old hives at my house. If you're willing to clean them up with me you can take one and hope to get them to Adem in time to be used for when your bees swarm.'

So on a quiet afternoon on the last day of April, I put on my oldest clothes and went to Dardan's house in the suburbs of Pristina. When I arrived, the family – Dardan, his parents and paternal grandfather – was

sitting outside on a balcony enjoying the sunshine and a lively discussion about religion. I gathered that Dardan and his father didn't agree with the old man's take on things.

'You knew what my grandfather's views were, I guess,' shrugged Dardan.

'No?'

'You can work it out – it was he who named my father "Islam".' Well, that figured. I was interested to think about the name that Dardan's father had given his own son. Dardania is the ancient Albanian name for the area covered by modern-day Kosovo – Islam seemed to have been replaced by nationalism as the generations passed.

'What would you call a son of yours then?' I asked Dardan.

'Something short – something that wouldn't be mispronounced by a non-Albanian. A son of mine will grow up in the international community and I'd want him to fit in.' The three generations of the Velija men were a history of Kosovo in miniature.

Dardan's own attitude to Kosovo's history had been a point of controversy between us before now. During the autumn he had called up to suggest that Rob and I could go for a walk with him in the huge park of Gërmia just outside the capital. We all walked companionably together through my favourite season, chasing falling leaves and breathing in woodsmoke. As we turned a corner on the path that led upwards, we passed a half-destroyed building – concrete powdered to rubble and reinforcing rods twisted to graffiti across the sky.

'What's this?' I asked.

'It was used by Serb forces as a hide-out during the bombing,' Dardan explained.

'Were there people inside it when it was blown up?' I asked.

'I hope so,' Dardan replied.

Naively, I was shocked. I'd never had a glimpse of these attitudes lying below Dardan's urbane surface. His face, his conversation, had always been set forward, to the future promised him by his Western education, his imported car. But the officers in this police station had, of course, been the police who executed his uncle in front of his family, the regime who made him live for a large portion of his life under something like apartheid. I didn't know what to say – so I said nothing.

Some weeks later Dardan had come to lunch at our house. The

date was 5 November and I was feeling more homesick than at any time since we'd moved to Kosovo. In every year of my life so far 5 November had meant fireworks. Childhood memories of my gloved hand being held reassuringly by a parent, hot soup and baked potatoes, gasping in unison at magical shapes shimmering in the sky... not only did I have none of these this year, but there wasn't even anyone to understand what I was missing. It was my first taste of cultural dislocation. So I had been feeling vulnerable anyway, when the subject of the bombed Serbian police station came up again.

'You didn't like what I said to you that day,' Dardan had said when we talked about it during that lunch.

Again I didn't know how to answer.

'I told a friend about it and he said I should never have said something like that to an international.'

Ouch. I didn't know what upset me more – Dardan's attitudes, or his sense that he shouldn't share them with me; that I was an 'international' – and presumably nothing more.

Still I said nothing. But when our lunch guests had gone, Rob gave me a long long hug.

On this early summer day, November seemed a long way away. This was one of those days that even the atheist wants to say are blessed with sunshine – as I squatted with Dardan on the driveway alongside buckets of water to clean up the hives and the frames, sun glinted on the water, and dried the frames that we stacked around the garden. It was a rarity still at that time of year – something that we might have strolled through without thinking a few months later, but we were still savouring it on that day.

But our November conversation still rankled. And so did the fact that I'd said nothing – nothing to challenge or explore the attitudes, not just to the Serbs but to me as an 'international'. Taking a deep breath, I said, 'Do you know how much it upset me that time you called me an 'international', and suggested you should have censored what you said to me?' Dardan knew exactly what I was referring to. He's a thoughtful person and he paused before he said carefully.

'Yes, I can see why it might. I'm sorry. You're not like the 'internationals' who make decisions about this country without taking the time to try to understand it.'

The incident that had been niggling at me as I tried to get close to this country with its unexpected prickles, had been transformed into something positive. We smiled at each other, and got on with the frames.

I do manual work rarely enough that the work was a treat for me – the gentle rhythms of sloshing water, wood emerging fresh from its dust, and my muscles awakening from their slump, as I carried and lifted and stooped. The frames are each fitted with two wires that should be strung taut. It's onto these wires that wax sheets are melted – the sheets serve as a foundation for the bees' honeycomb building. But the old frames in Dardan's yard had strings as slack as the old musical instruments at the Ethnological Museum.

Conversation was freed up now. We discussed sex, politics, war. Dardan told me about his time during the NATO bombardment – attempts to join the KLA, and how 'they stayed put while Rob's army did the work' as he said without apparent bitterness. I tried to get a sense of what those days must have been like, and was surprised to hear them described as days of hope as well as fear – at last Kosovars were really *doing* something to seize their destiny. Talking about the frames he had had the task of making for the beekeeper he was staying with, you got the sense of a younger Dardan poised for bigger action, a Dardania feeling itself on the brink of historic independence.

I was experiencing my own small liberation as we worked too. I realised that this was the first time my beekeeping identity had extended beyond Adem's land. Still under apprenticeship (Dardan directed me and pointed out the wax moth cocoons stuck to some of the hives which would make them impossible to use again – 'the bees will never store honey in a place that's been infested before') but this was how a real beekeeper might spend an afternoon.

It felt a significant day, one for new identities, the turning of the seasons.

'Well, tomorrow is 1 May,' said Dardan, 'look.' He gestured beyond his house where billows of foul thick smoke were tumbling from the tops of the hills. I thought about the NATO bombing and shivered. 'Kids burning stuff. They used to burn wood on the eve of 1 May, but now it's tyres.'

Whatever your mode of expression – the slow process of working together to magic streams of honey from the frail blooms just butting

up through the soil, or the summoning of toxic fumes from molten rubber – this was a day when everyone marked new cycles beginning, ushering in the reign of a new queen.

11.
Golden circles: my own bee-skeps

New Albanian vocabulary: *shportë* (basket), *bukë misri* (cornbread)

The teardrop-shaped skep that Adem had in his shed for catching absconding bees had done its job, and the swarm had been successfully tipped into the new Langstroth hive; I was now the owner of two colonies of bees. Adem offered me his congratulations – and I felt the way that I often did here, when Albanians heard that I was English and wanted to thank me for NATO's campaign which removed the Serb forces. 'It was nothing to do with me!'

There is something very beautiful about the shape of these baskets, and I like the fact that they're made locally from natural materials. They are different from traditional British skeps that I was familiar with from the Gale's honey label. Where British skeps are woven spirals of fibres coiled into a bell shape, the Kosovan models are made with vertical supports around which pliable branches are woven. If I wanted one of these then this country would be the only place I could buy it.

So when I saw one of the skeps for sale at the side of the road while I was in the car with some friends, I shrieked at the driver to stop. My friends were indulgent, screeching to a halt and waiting, even though we were running late, as I skipped back to my skep-seller and started to haggle. For no reason that I could understand, I bought two of these strangely elegant cones, bundled them into the car, and we continued on our way.

It was an auspicious day for Kosovan traditions – we were driving to the festival in Gjonaj which is held every year to showcase local dancing, costumes and baking. Gjonaj is in the steep hills near the ancient cobbled city of Prizren and is in the centre of Has country, a region of Kosovo with its own distinctive costumes. Even the older Has women wear their hair long, and dyed a startling black. More startling than this, however, is their unique skirt which includes a yoke of wood around the waist, used for balancing babies, buckets of water, or baskets

of produce – particularly useful for women negotiating mountain paths in this rugged part of Kosovo. I never saw a young Has woman wearing the traditional costume, but I was delighted to hear about a UK company who have recently started marketing to her modern British counterpart something that would look very familiar to any Has girl. In England you can apparently now buy a rigid shelf attached to a strap to be worn around the waist, for taking the weight of toddlers when they need to be carried on the hip. I imagine that the young women of Prizren would never entertain the idea, but Islington's yummy mummies will be all over it.

We wove higher and higher up the hillside, the air noticeably chilly now, and our journey getting slower not only because of the strain on the gears but because of the weight of traffic. Everyone was heading for the festival, and everyone must have been running late. The views and the driving were breathtaking as cars tried to inch past each other, with the mountain falling away sheer to one side. I concentrated on the spectacular panoramas.

When the car had slowed to less than a walking pace we stopped and got out to go the rest of the way on foot. We had less than twenty minutes to walk, but as we got closer, we were joined by more and more others, all like individual notes coming together in a great orchestral crescendo that built until we reached the loudspeakers that were blaring over a temporary stage erected at the end of a basketball court. We wriggled through to a point where we could see the stage. The performance had started and on tiptoe, jogging my head from side to side as the people in front of me jogged theirs too, I watched one troupe after another come out onto the stage. Each was greeted by their claque in the audience, and as the whooping and cheering vied with the music, girls skipped and twisted, bounced neatly across the stage in well-practised dances. They flirted politely with lithe young men in their white Elizabethan-style smocks, multicoloured woven sashes, the baggy white woollen trousers with thick black seams making geometric shapes across the groin and seat. Somehow the men managed to look smouldering and athletic despite these encumbrances.

Most smouldering and athletic of all was the 'eagle dance' of the Rugova valley – the stately, stealthy prowl, pounce, swoop, and leap performed by elegant men with poise and excellent thigh muscles. The

line of men have their arms around one another's shoulders so it looks like a can-can, but a can-can that is painfully, stunningly slow so that the dancers' control over their scraping, dipping, is the main display. As the men hover and glide in unison there are moments where you can almost believe that it's not muscles but the thermals of the air high above the mountains which sustain this flock in flight.

Throughout their dancing they are serenaded by a musician who keeps pace with them, moving with them, maintaining eye contact with them, bending low when the dancers bend low, straightening as they soar upwards; but this musician is no violinist, this no fragile lark arising, but a pounding martial drum beat inciting the dancer to fight.

With the early summer evening chill from being high in the hills, and the throbbing music, heads dipping to and fro to see the performers, there came a point when I was ready to leave the outdoor performances. My friends and I retreated into the small Culture House behind the stage. We must have been conspicuous – we had been the only non-Kosovars in the audience – and were offered a guided tour of the display which had been laid out in one of the rooms to show the baking for which this region is famous. A conscientious young man from the municipal headquarters led us to the exhibition and gave us a tour of the tables covered in an untouched, untouchable banquet of *tepsis* containing local dishes. Every combination of corn and wheat, dough and batter, yeast and yogurt seemed to have been prepared in an endless succession of golden circles. Some of the breads and cakes I recognised (*fli* and *pogaqe*, cornbreads and *pite*), others were new to me, but this was an exhibit, not a meal, and without being able to sample any of the models laid out it was a tantalising demonstration of plenty. Surely only someone who deep down didn't really like food would put on such a frustrating show, I thought – and then remembered the empty skeps that I had just bought for no reason other than the pleasing shape of them.

When we got back home late that night, I put the skeps in my hallway, either side of the front door. I didn't know what I would do with them eventually but they could stay there for now.

In fact those skeps never moved. When a friend's small and adventurous daughter came to the house she managed to hide herself entirely underneath one of them, and once she had drawn my attention to their

potential as hiding places, I kept my handbag under one, hoping to thwart all but the most thorough burglar. I don't know what this sub-stitution of money for honey says about my developing identity as a beekeeper but with skeps of my own I felt I was moving somewhere.

I later learned to make golden light, rich cornbread circles of my own too. This is the recipe for *leçenik,* given to me by my friend, and museum guide, Alisa.

Ingredients
4 eggs
salt – 2 pinches
200ml oil
800ml yogurt
500g cornmeal
200g flour
6 tsp baking powder
200g mild white cheese like feta

Mix all the ingredients together and put the resulting mixture in a *tepsi* and bake at 185 degrees for 20 minutes.

12.
Learning to live off the land

New Albanian vocabulary: *fshat* (village), *mulli* (mill)

We were being offered a piece of Kosovo. Dardan owns land in the north east, not far from Adem, and said he would give some to Rob and me in exchange for us building a house on it. He told us the land was in his 'village' when he talked to us in English, though he'd warned us, too, that there was 'nothing there'. It's not connected to the water mains, nor to mains electricity, and until last year, had no asphalted roads. He was open about his motivation for his offer of land – the more houses there are, the more case there is for demanding the services he wants there.

The idea of longer-term home-making here had caught my imagination. We were already in the habit of leaving Pristina most weekends to see the bees, Adem and Xhezide, so building a house on Dardan's land would be a natural next step. This could be our *vikendica* – the English word used by Albanians with a Serbian ending was the perfect way to describe the place where some Brits might hole up in Kosovo. I loved the idea of creating our own *oda* – mattresses on the floor around the edge of a room, scattered with cushions. We would have a wood-burning stove like Adem and Xhezide, and we could invite friends down for *vikend* house parties, serve honey *raki*, and play multilingual forfeit Scrabble late into the night. The friends we had made who were artists could come and paint; I would sit and write, and bake, and tend my bees.

Dardan suggested that Rob and I should go with him and visit this 'village' that has 'nothing there' early one Sunday morning before we went to see the bees. We drove off, and I tried to imagine what might be waiting for us – the land which I, like some nineteenth-century indentured servant, was being invited to colonise with my labour. My parents live in a 'village' in the Oxfordshire Cotswolds. It is a clustering of low stone houses, with a pub and a church. There is a noticeboard

where people offer baby-sitting and book groups. In their village, too, people complain about lack of services – there is no post office any more, and for a while there was no internet coverage, and still occasionally no mobile phone reception. I tried to scale down their settlement in my head, and make it speak Albanian and have less disposable income or employment, and wondered whether this was what Dardan's village might be like.

Dardan showed us where to pull off the main road and we headed down the kind of track you need a good bra for – we bounced and bumped and lurched over deep ruts. When we couldn't drive any further, we got out and started walking. The grass and the nettles – and, I thought to myself, probably the snakes – were knee-high. There were young trees everywhere, and a stream, and no path except what I thrashed myself with bare legs. We found tiny wild raspberries – it was the first time I'd ever seen them – which stained our hands and mouths red. Dardan had a plastic bag in his pocket and we filled it with raspberries. Then we found small sweet strawberries too, and added those to the bag and to the murderous mess under our fingernails.

Further on, and as the day heated up, there was the smell of thyme. Crouching down, I found where it was growing and added sprigs of it to the fruit salad in our bag. Later we came across mint, too, and wrapped it round the strawberries like smart little canapés of fresh summer flavours.

I was still not clear where the village was, though, as we wandered in this fecund little paradise.

'How far is it from here to your village, Dardan?' I asked, and he turned to me with half a smile on his face.

'This is my village,' he explained. 'I told you there was nothing here.' I couldn't decide whether he was laughing at my surprise, or laughing with me at how ludicrous it was to call this a village. That's always the problem with foreign-educated Kosovars, and probably with British expats too. They delight in playing it both ways.

'So were there houses here in the past?' I asked, disorientated.

'Yes, thirty years ago there were.' They have all been abandoned now (no mains water, no electricity, no road) although as we walked on down the stream we did see the first sign that anyone had ever lived there once – a broken down waterwheel. That, Dardan said, was on the

land belonging to one of his uncles; the stream marks the boundary.

Rob and he started to talk about the possibilities for building a house here, but I couldn't see it. My imagination was too limited to cut down those saplings, level the bank, install the chemical toilet, and work out where the noticeboard to advertise my book group would go. Dardan saw me frowning.

'OK, would you like to go mushroom hunting while we're here?'

Of course we would! I loved the combination of faint frisson of danger (I thought of all those people who die after a tasty omelette made with the wrong kind of fungus), pastoral idyll and free vegetarian food. So we returned to the car with our fruit bag, and Dardan directed us down the road and into a more established, dark, damp patch of oak wood.

There he pointed out the mushrooms we were hunting – enormous bulging boletus tumours. They had an intense musty smell like old laundry, which made my stomach lurch, and I couldn't decide whether I was still hungry or slightly revolted. Between us we filled a bag with them – Dardan found the biggest, which he gave to us because it was our first time. I remembered the landlord of our house in Pristina, and his pitch to us when we were looking round the place, deciding whether to rent it. He tried in Albanian, in English, and in neither language made any sense to us, other than communicating his enthusiasm and willingness to please. Rob and I had clearly been interested in the house at that point, but what clinched the deal was the portly man leaping down from the steps to a large bush in the garden, and ripping off a rose to present to me. Dardan proffered that luxurious bloom of a mushroom to me with the same panache. But for this property I still wasn't convinced.

It's not far from this village to Adem's house, and the bees. I thought of that other parcel of land (the Albanian phrase translates as a 'mouthful of land' – a phrase that came naturally when I thought about the little grassy patch where my honey was produced) that I had colonised more successfully, and I suggested we might go.

We drove off through the low hills, up slopes covered in beech scrub, and down the other side, with a hazy vista of strip fields and dotted houses laid out for miles ahead of us. Through villages where men walked slowly, with faces showing the gentle contented smugness

it's impossible not to feel when you are on your way home to your family with a weight of deep green watermelon in your arms. I fingered the plastic bag filled with our own small harvest.

When we arrived, Adem and Xhezide insisted on tea before I could have a look at the hives. We sat in their kitchen with our small glasses of tea (with honey). I asked how the bees were, how the family was. They asked about our week.

I was itching to get out to the hives. It was a perfect day to be a beekeeper – or, indeed, a bee, I thought. I wanted to sit quietly near the hive and watch the creatures coming and going, trying to guess the flowers they had been visiting from the colour of the pollen in the so-called 'baskets' on their legs where the collected protein-rich powder bulges to the size of perhaps a matchstick head. I wanted to learn something about their rhythms, their work, the organism that is a hive.

Finally, everyone had finished their tea and I put on my gear and went out with Adem. He brought the smoker and the tool for opening the hive. 'I'll do it,' I suggested. No, no, he assured me, it was fine for him to do it. Maybe he considered that I didn't know enough to be able to do the job properly, I thought. And of course I didn't want to get the process of opening up the hive wrong – insufficient smoke would mean the bees would attack us, which was bad for the temperament of the hive, as well as bringing risks for us, despite our suits. And opening up the hive incorrectly with the metal lever might damage bees that got trapped as the frames came out.

Maybe he was right but I still had a mild sense of frustration as I stood beside Adem opening up the hive. I thought about Dardan laughing at me at not understanding what a Kosovan village was, and about our dashed hopes on building a house here. With the language, the culture, and now with the beekeeping, I was repeatedly reminded by this place of how little I knew, how ill-equipped I was to navigate it successfully. I stood with my big rubber gloves holding Adem's tools and watched through the black mesh of my veil as Adem checked the hives. As he reordered the frames (those at the edges always have less honeycomb built in them because they are the coolest; by rotating the outside frames with those further in, the bees could be persuaded to build and fill more comb) I wondered whether I would ever feel I had touched Kosovo, my own beehives, directly, or whether I would always be rele-

gated to the role of detached observer.

When got home we brought our hunter-gatherer booty to the table on the verandah. I fried the spongy mushroom steaks (a mistake, I think, because they would have kept their flavour better if they'd been grilled) and poured out yoghurt for us to eat with the herbs and fruit that remained.

The bowls of white yoghurt scattered with red fruits and green leaves looked beautiful. I drizzled some of my honey artfully, and felt like William Morris designing a new curtain fabric rather than someone sitting down to eat. I mused that maybe my vision was better for focused interior design than for larger projects building homes and colonising new countries.

A scavenger menu

Ingredients
Bowls of plain yoghurt
A handful of strawberries (wild if possible)
A handful of raspberries (also picked wild if you know where to find them)
A handful of fresh mint (torn)
Fresh thyme, crushed
Honey
Boletus mushrooms, sliced and grilled
Buttered toast

Eat the mushrooms on the toast.

Then combine the fruit and the herbs and the honey as you see best. In my opinion, yoghurt with thyme and honey is a fabulous combination.

Strawberries and mint are also wonderfully fresh together, and the mint sets off raspberries very well too. To my taste, thyme doesn't really combine well with the fruit or with the mint, but of course the honey goes well with everything.

13.
Harvesting the first honey

New Albanian vocabulary: *shkolla e mesme* (secondary — literally 'middle' — school, for students aged 15 to 18)

We had had a call from Adem for help. Mirlinda had finished her final term of 'primary' school the previous month and she and her parents wanted her to continue in the specialised equivalent of the British sixth form. Unfortunately, she hadn't been able to get a place at any of the schools she'd applied to. Adem had explained this last time we were with them, and asked Rob, 'could you get the Prime Minister to write a letter?'

I felt myself stiffen every time I found myself in this situation; this kind of bid for patronage wasn't new to us. Adem wasn't being particularly daring in the suggestion that a Prime Minister might write a letter on behalf of a bee farmer's daughter whom he had never met. If he were in the UK or the US he could go to ask his MP or Congressman to write a letter; Kosovo has no artificial patronage structure of this kind. It's actually possible that if Rob were to ask Çeku to write the necessary letter, the Prime Minister would do so. It's even possible that if the headteacher of the school which Mirlinda wanted to attend were to receive such a letter, she would give Mirlinda a place. It might even be that if that process were to work, none of the people involved would see anything problematic in it, or think any the worse of us. And Mirlinda would get the education that might give her the edge in the fierce, desperate Kosovo job market. It might give her and her parents a reason for her not to marry early, produce children soon afterwards, and spend the rest of her life making *fli* and serving tea with honey stirred in it to her husband's guests. Dardan said, 'this could be the biggest gift you ever gave that family.'

But for us to play our part in such a process would undermine all the democratic structures that we believed we had been contributing to building in Kosovo. We had protested faintly to Adem that the Prime

Minister was a bit busy.

I had suggested the only thing that I would be able to do in the UK. Perhaps I could go with Mirlinda to the school. As I suggested it, I had realised that it was a very British way of showing the pressure that you might be able to bring to bear. I didn't suggest I would speak a word to the headteacher, and certainly no documents would change hands, but the foreign lady (with who-knows-what connections) sitting next to the borderline student might just swing it for Mirlinda's school future. Thinking it through this way, I wondered whether Adem's might be a more honest approach.

And then he called us to come over for lunch at the weekend.

In the end, the discussion about Mirlinda's future was mercifully short. I opened with a reiteration of the offer to go with her to the headteacher. I tried to show I was really ready to help – I told them what days I was free the following week. It was agreed that they would call me when they had decided on which day they could make the trip into Pristina.

'*Hajde*,' summarised Adem, 'let's go and see how the bees are doing. There might be enough honey to harvest today.'

This was big news! My pulse quickened.

'I'll take the smoker,' I offered, with a quaver of assertiveness in my voice. Adem smiled and handed it to me.

Now there were even more butterflies – or some other insects – in my stomach. What if I didn't keep the stream of smoke consistent enough? What if the bees tried attacking Adem. Even him having to correct me would be embarrassing.

I held the smoker steady and made sure the aromatic woodchip smoke was trailing evenly over the frames. Occasionally I glanced at Adem's face, softened by the mesh of his veil. But he was concentrating on his own work. He lifted the frames up and squinted at the dripping cells. The wax starter sheet was hardly visible now – the bees had built honeycomb over all the sheets, and from there had built upwards to create tiny repeated six-sided vats which they were filling with honey.

Adem was less awed than I was. '*S'ka mjaltë* – there's no honey,' he said, thrusting the first frame back in the hive. He was exaggerating: I could see the trickles of liquid seeping out as he held the frames up. But they weren't full.

He picked up another, and repeated himself with a kind of despair.

It was true that Kosovo had had less rain this summer than in any year in living memory; no-one could remember the Mirusha waterfall having dried up before. But Adem's despair upset me. Was the lack of honey something I'd done, or not done in caring for these bees? I sensed that Adem felt he'd let me down.

And then another thought struck me. Was there a metaphorical meaning to his words? A reference to the limited help I'd offered his family's future. I squirmed a bit more.

Eventually we removed two frames from my hive. The bees were understandably even less impressed than Adem at this, and swarmed up to us angrily. I felt my vulnerability as I tried to fend them off with a puffing Billy can; it was the most frightened I'd been by them.

In the absence of any more full frames of honey in my hives, we took more frames from a couple of Adem's and they were slotted into an empty box for transport, and covered with a cloth to hide them from any nearby bees. I knew that we needed to move fast – the honey should be extracted while it's still warm. I carried the golden coffer, swaying with sweetness, back to the house.

By the time I got there, a plastic tablecloth had been put on the floor in the main room of the house where we had eaten, and where the food preparation is done. In the middle of the tablecloth was the new 35-euro centrifuge. I was excited – I had read about this magical process. In the Albanian book on beekeeping, *For You who Keep Bees*, I had read that 'the beekeeper's real poetry is the sound of the centrifuge and jars filling with honey.' The machine seemed disappointingly like a cement mixer to me – the size and shape of a dustbin. But the next-door neighbour had come round to watch, and Xhezide, Mirlinda and the younger son, Lavdim, were all there too. There was a sense of expectation, of a piece of theatre about to begin.

Before we put the frames into the centrifuge to spin out the honey, we had to skim off the wax that had sealed each filled honeycomb cell. For this there is a special tool, like an afro comb, or tuning fork, which Lavdim was using, and after I'd watched him for a while, I had a go myself, scraping at the delicate skin until I was told off by the nosy neighbour for going too deep and scooping up the precious honey as well as the covering. What the hell, at least I was doing it!

I tried to be more careful. When I'd finished, the centrifuge lid was lifted and the frames of skimmed honeycomb set in the brackets round the edge of the centrifuge drum. We took turns at working the handle to spin them. Lavdim was just getting to the age where he cared about the muscles on his slim brown arms; he would have preferred that the rest of us weren't there.

You could lift the lid while the machine was centrifuging and see the threads of honey shuttling out like a golden weft. It was even more beautiful than watching candyfloss being made.

When I had a go, the whole machine started screeching – as if there was an enormous unhappy bee inside; or maybe as if it itself was an enormous unhappy bee. I thought of *For You who Keep Bees*; if this was any kind of poetry, it was rap, and it didn't scan.

Adem was silent at my side. He watched the operations with dismay.

'S'ka mjaltë,' he repeated, rubbing his hand over his chin.

The machine seemed badly designed – the spout from which the honey was supposed to flow started a couple of inches up from the base of the centrifuge hopper. So until we generated a two-inch depth of honey, nothing came out, and there would always be two inches of honey left in the centrifuge.

The spout which allowed the honey to run out had been positioned over a sieve with a bowl underneath it. All eyes were fixed on the spout, which, despite my desperate turning of the centrifuge's handle, was dry as the Mirusha waterfall.

And then the first little golden tongue licked out of the spout. The honey was coming!

The stream thickened, tilted over the edge of the spout, and started spooling into the sieve. There was something sexy and luxurious about this languid, intense amber drool. I was transfixed by the beautiful fairy columns of gold transparency it made as it streamed through the sieve, by the molten golden food spiralling and settling into its jar.

And it was all mine! I could feel the Midas touch of capitalism grip me as I sat watching the precious flow. From those silent bees hibernating on my first visit, elusive despite my knocking, through all the visits to check, medicate, tinker, clean the colonies, this was the result.

It required much scooping of the honey from the bottom (Mirlinda

and I up to the armpit reaching into the centrifuge) and tilting of the whole machine by the men, but in the end we got five jars – one per frame. I felt like I had been present at a display of alchemy. And this time I really had played my part. I was grinning as we wiped down the jars and screwed on their lids.

Before we went, Adem wanted to show us the family's well. All around, the ground was dry and yet on Adem's abundant land there was a cool place where you could dip your zinc bucket in the ground and from deep, deep below, bring up sweet cold water. This must be how the bees had managed to produce the stores we had seen trickling into the jars earlier, despite the drought.

We were saying our goodbyes but Xhezide took my arm and steered me into the temporary polythene greenhouse they had set up to grow peppers and cucumber. The vegetables were blood temperature from the unnatural warmth, and she cut some down. She presented me with a bag as heavy as a small child, for me to take home along with my – my own – jars of honey.

I really really hoped Mirlinda could get a place at school.

14.
Holiday souvenirs: my own bee-suit

New Albanian vocabulary: *duvak* (veil – the word used as in English for both beekeepers and brides)

When I travelled to live in Kosovo I hadn't realised that I was travelling to a place that would be a launchpad for so many other journeys. From Pristina Rob and I had explored in our lumbering Landrover all the other countries of the former Yugoslavia – the vast grey structures of Tito-era Belgrade and the whimsical art deco of Subotica in Vojvodina; the enchanting lakes of Macedonia by sunset; war-scarred Bosnia, where I realised what Kosovo had been spared; Slovenia, startlingly efficient with a quiet Habsburg, EU-member pride and a deep love of bee-keeping; the islands and old cities of Croatia where we ate supper in piazzas around which swallows dived and saxophonists busked and it seemed impossible that this place could have ever been part of the same country as Kosovo.

We had also had a number of trips back to the UK for work, friends and family. These visits were significant as chances to see people we cared about, and to stock up on cheddar (on one occasion we ended up paying the £60 excess baggage charge because of our cheese, and considered it money well spent). I had always found air travel exhilarating, and even with the increase in frequency of my trips, I never lost the adrenaline rush of take-off and landing. On one trip, as we circled low over my homeland, I was caught unawares by a new emotion – flickerings of recognition, but also something like regret. For the first time, I had an instinctive sense that being *here* was preventing being *there* – and that that was something I missed. It most closely resembled a feeling I had only had previously for people rather than places. After Rob and I had known each other a while I realised quite suddenly that this person I knew I was fond of, whose habits I liked and company I enjoyed, was actually someone with whom I had fallen in love. As the wheels bumped over tarmac at Gatwick, I understood with the same sudden

clarity that Kosovo was not to be a one-year stand for me. This was something that would, in some form or another, be a permanent relationship.

So travel really does broaden the mind. But throughout August as our friends in Kosovo were jumping on overheated coaches or into the chilling air-conditioning of 4x4s, to get to crowded coastlines abroad (Croatia, Albania, Montenegro), we stayed lolling in our sunlit Pristina garden among the rose bushes and the honey-bee pollinated apple trees. We had plenty to read – I was immersed in *The Balkan Trilogy* about a British woman who had followed her husband to unknown parts of the Balkans seventy years before me. I found it comforting to read this elegant narrative of petty gossip around the British Council and struggles to find an identity in an expat circuit where you didn't quite belong, in a country where you were so obviously a foreigner. It made me feel like I was a character in a book. With reading, the bees to visit at the weekends and interesting projects at the Ethnological Museum where I was now working as a volunteer, I felt the journeys I was on were taking me far further than the Landrover could.

But one weekend we decided that perhaps we should push ourselves just a little bit beyond Pristina. We couldn't decide exactly where to go in Kosovo, or even whether to make it a day trip or an overnight stay, so Rob suggested a magical mystery tour.

'Meaning?'

'Well, let's just make the decision on what direction to take when we reach any given crossroads, until we get an idea of a final destination.'

It sounded crazy. The idea of setting off with only a spare set of underwear and a full tank of petrol on a sunny day that we could spend happily in our own garden was rather a risk. It felt like we were making a habit of the spontaneity which had landed us in Kosovo to start with.

And yet we set off, knowing nothing of where we would end up, and certainly not that it would be a stop on my route to competent beekeeper. At the bottom of our road, Rob asked whether we should go left or right. Left would take you into an underpass where there is normally at least one dead dog lying halfway into the road, and always the sense that you might find more cadavers if you looked hard. There are rubbish skips in the roadway and usually some poor soul rummaging them for recyclable metal that could be sold. There is always the

fear of our car running into them in the ill-lit narrow space. Added to all this, the gratings in the roof of the underpass through which a little sunshine filters are gratings in the paving of the pedestrian shopping area which has been created above. Unidentified liquids drip down.

As if it was a decision of Manichean significance, I chose right.

This leads you on the road south. About twenty minutes out of Pristina, this road takes you past one of the new out-of-town super-markets. This particular supermarket sometimes has real French cheese in stock, as well as a bakery that was the only place in Kosovo where you could order fresh-baked French bread and ciabatta rolls. I suggested we stopped there to buy a picnic.

With a good lunch in front of us, we set off from the supermarket car park.

'Right,' I said.

We found ourselves approaching a sign to Gjilan.

'Gjilan?' we said. 'Gjilan!' we said. It is one of Kosovo's five largest towns, and a place neither of us had ever been. I had a vivid picture of it from *Shadow behind the Sun*, a book written by a woman from the town about her life there until 1999 and her frightening flight to Glasgow where she now works with asylum seekers from around the world. Yes, this was a place I should see for myself, so we drove on towards it.

It's a pleasant town, with wide boulevards that give it a different feel from Pristina.

Not that different though – as we drove down the main street I saw someone I recognised. Fatmir is a writer and academic to whom I had taught English in Pristina for a few months. Unlike my other Albanian friends who had been refugees in Germany, the UK, the States, he was a refugee within Kosovo. His family home was in the Preshevo valley, in the ethnically Albanian part of Serbia. The drawing of new borderlines had left this population isolated from its ethnic and linguis-tic brothers, just as it had left the ethnic Serbs of northern Kosovo iso-lated from theirs. There was ongoing debate about what the fate of Preshevo should be – united with Kosovo (and, some would suggest, later with Albania too, to create a Greater Albania which stretched across these current borders, and into some of Macedonia, Montenegro and Greece), or exchanged as part of a deal whereby northern Kosovo's

Serbs were reunited with Serbia? Neither seemed likely any time soon, and as ever, it was the small pockets of minority ethnicity who would suffer in any broad realignment. Fatmir's political activities and the oppression of the Serb regime had not been a good mixture, so he was sheltering in Pristina where he wrote and campaigned for the community he had left behind, and told me stories which haunted me about how his library of books and collection of Albanian ethnological artefacts had all been burned. I was almost ashamed at how it had upset me, in a lesson I'd come to straight from the Ethnological Museum's similar collection of precious salvage, to hear about this destruction. 'They're only *things*,' I'd said, 'it shouldn't matter like people's lives matter.'

'People live their lives knowing that they will come to an end one day. But with the right care, objects can live almost forever.' We understood each other.

I had wanted Rob to meet Fatmir, to hear him talk passionately about history, politics, nationalism – why these things matter. And to hear his enormous and unpredictable laugh, as if he caught himself out sometimes with the realisation that they don't. This chance meeting in Gjilan was the perfect and typically Kosovo-given opportunity. We stopped the car and I rushed across the road to him.

He seemed as delighted as I was. He was on his way to a meeting but of course had time for a coffee – would we join him? He would show us the nicest place to drink it: a café on a hill on the outskirts of town. He would buy us the coffee (Albanian rules are really very strict on this point. The person who suggests having coffee is from that moment the host for the occasion, and it is unthinkable that the other party would pay for their own, or anyone else's share – as unthinkable as if you were to try to pay for a meal you had eaten at a friend's home).

As we drove through the streets to the café he recommended, while Fatmir and Rob animatedly discussed the Cold War (I was right to have wanted them to get together previously), I saw a poster advertising a bee supplies shop. So once we had drunk our coffees (the men sorting out Russia all the while) and given Fatmir a ride back into town, we walked to the shop.

At this moment, more than any other, I felt I had become a beekeeper. Up till then, because of the unusual circumstances through which I had been given my bees, and because Adem was the only bee-

keeper I knew, my understanding of beekeeping had been entirely con-textualised around his small house and plot of land. Walking into the shop and seeing the beekeepers' suits (*Adem's* beekeeper suits) hung up for sale, and multiple smokers (*Adem's* smokers) stacked along the shelf, alongside piles of new frames (just like Adem's frames) was rather like walking into a theatre green room. There was the same sense of a spell broken, and the same sense of a new spell woven. So it wasn't just Adem who could do this magic – conjuring honey from wooden boxes. But if it wasn't just Adem who could do so, then maybe that meant that I could do it myself too.

It was in the beekeeping shop in Gjilan that I bought my own magician's suit, an elasticated top with integral hood and black mesh vizor.

The next day, Rob and I left Gjilan and wandered again around Kosovo, taking arbitrary lefts and rights. We chanced on the spring where our favourite Kosovan mineral water was bottled, and went in the allegedly healing pool there; we picnicked on our French cheeses and played word games in the sun.

I was keen to go back to my bees at my first opportunity – to show them my new suit, and to use it. As with new jeans or trainers, you want to get over the stiff, shiny stage as soon as possible. At the moment my new suit was a glaring white, where Adem's was always blotched with little stains of honey, wax and propolis, blooming like lichens over the soft fabric. My suit smelt new – like a hospital – while his had always smelt like a hive; wearing it, I had felt like a great bee myself.

And I guess I wanted Adem to see how I was growing into my role. We hadn't heard from him for a few weeks, which meant that he hadn't contacted me about my offer of accompanying Mirlinda to her potential new school. With a little nervousness, I phoned him to see if we could come and harvest some more honey.

Of course we could.

'And Mirlinda? Is there any news on her school?' I asked hesitantly.

'Oh yes, she has a place,' he said proudly.

So the system worked without us. I was relieved for a whole range of reasons.

When I put on my new suit Adem looked at it approvingly. We went down to see the bees and found a few more frames in my hives

which had enough honey to harvest – enough to load the slots in the centrifuge entirely with my bees' frames, without mixing them with Adem's. We went through the processes again, and I managed to be more careful in my scraping of the topping wax this time. I wiped things onto my new suit deliberately. I could tell that Adem was watching me.

I was proud of doing this by myself. I think Adem was proud too; when the first kilogram jar was filled from the centrifuge, he picked it up and presented it to me like a certificate.

Practical Xhezide took it away from me and wiped it down with a damp cloth before giving it back, like a midwife at a birth. As other jars were filled, they all needed wiping down, so while Rob, Adem and Lavdim all took their turns at the centrifuge, I stood with Xhezide at the sink helping to tidy things up. It was new, this patterning within our visit of the two of us alone. We talked to each other awkwardly at first. Only once the wiping and sorting settled into a rhythm, did our conversation do so too. I asked a bit about her life before Adem, before this farm.

'I was born in Pristina. It was an arranged marriage. I came here to nurse Adem's mother until she died.'

I had never thought of Xhezide in Pristina – she had always seemed a part of this farm. I realised that I had always spoken to Adem and Xhezide of Pristina in the same way that I spoke about London – a concept I politely suggested they might have heard of. But then to what extent would Xhezide's Pristina be the same city as my Pristina? It had been twenty years ago, and in so many ways, longer even than that.

We went on to harvest more than a kilogram jar of honey per frame this time – my care in scraping off the wax toppings paid off. It takes bees visiting ten million flowers to generate a kilogram of honey, and as the stuff spilled out of the centrifuge I tried to imagine these extravagant wild bouquets we were squeezing into the jars.

There was the same problem we had had on our previous visit, of the two inches of honey lying in the bottom of the centrifuge, below the spout, and only accessible by leaning over the top, and half-diving down into the honeytrap. It was a time-consuming business and as we had a deadline for getting back to Pristina, I suggested that since the family had given us more than our share of the harvest on the previous occasion, the excess from my hives which was lying in the bottom of the hopper could be left for them this time if they didn't mind doing the scooping.

We said our goodbyes and got into the car. As the engine started up, Xhezide ran down the steps of the house, still sticky from the gleaning she had been doing of the excess at the bottom of the centrifuge. In her arms was an enormous jar – perhaps four or five litres capacity – of the remaining honey. She would brook no argument: this was for us to take with us. I felt that I had not yet found a single way to repay my mounting debts to this kind, careful family. The jeroboam of generosity sat on the back seat where the afternoon sun glinted through it, casting pleasing honey-coloured stains of shadow onto my white bee-keeper suit.

15.
Honey and chewing gum

New Albanian vocabulary: *shaci* (Kosovo Albanian returned from abroad to find an Albanian wife)

I was to dip into this huge jar very soon, when we were invited to visit the family of one of Rob's closest colleagues. Vedat is an Albanian-American about the same age as Rob and I. The story of his family, as he'd told it to Rob and me over drinks in a variety of Pristina cafés, is the American – and maybe the Kosovan – dream.

He was born in Kosovo but as a baby he moved to Germany when his father started work there. From there the family moved to New York where his father was employed in construction. 'My dad worked three jobs and saved hard until he could buy his first piece of real estate.' He multiplied this into a family real estate business with careful management, more strategic loans and hard work. 'My dad just worked. Worked and worked. Even now, as head of a successful company, he can't see a job needing doing without itching to get it done himself. I've seen him on building sites in his designer suit, picking up a bucket, tidying lumber away, just making sure everything is done right.'

The business is still thriving – the older brother works there now alongside his father; Vedat's parents, with his brother, sister-in-law and their children, have just bought a phenomenal property in Westchester County, complete with landscaped gardens and tennis court.

Vedat worked as a lawyer in the States, and then had the opportunity to come to the newly liberated Kosovo to work as legal advisor, first to the Deputy Prime Minister, and then to the Prime Minister himself. It's a civilian version of the 'Atlantic Brigade' – ethnic Albanian Americans who came to fight in the KLA in 1998. It's a different way of joining the struggle for independence; everyone acknowledged that whatever the heroism of the Brigades in 1999, until Kosovo had in place a democratic infrastructure, including the laws that a state needs to function, the international community wouldn't

be persuaded to support the country's independence. Vedat is passionate about his country and his family; he is a bright, extremely funny raconteur, and a composite of Kosovo and the United States that makes me love them both.

His parents still keep a house in the west of Kosovo, the place where Vedat was born. They come back every summer, and one weekend we were invited to go and visit them there, along with Vedat and his girlfriend. It's a dramatic part of Kosovo, near to the city of Peja, nestling beneath the sheer rise of the so-called 'Accursed' Mountains. I felt excited about the prospect of a trip out of baking Pristina, into greenery and the cooling presence of high mountains, and I was curious to get to understand *the diaspora* better.

Members of the diaspora are the ghostly figures alluded to in almost any discussion about Kosovo, especially any discussion of economics. The Albanians abroad are alleged to be the unseen force that shapes Kosovo, through the money they send home. During the years of Milošević's oppression it was the unofficial tax on diaspora income, levied by the Kosovo Albanian government in exile, which funded the parallel (unofficial) services in Kosovo. More than US$125 million was collected from the diaspora to fund medical care and schools which kept Kosovo Albanians alive and thinking. It was also the diaspora who largely funded the KLA.

After the war, the diaspora continued to pour money back into Kosovo to rebuild it, both literally and figuratively. A report I'd read researched some representative Kosovan villages to assess the impact of the diaspora. In one village, of 97 households who own a tractor, 91 said that money for its purchase was earned abroad. Of 147 households there who owned a car, 137 bought it with money transferred by family members abroad. The government recognises the way this informal safety net operates – those with a family member abroad who were able to work are not eligible for benefits.

So the diaspora are unmistakably still a part of their homeland – in the tractors and foreign clothes that stand out in shabby villages, even in the daily newspapers' regular slot, after the Kosovo and regional pages, which gives the latest on diaspora issues. They are only physically present themselves during the summer, when they return in their thousands, with something to prove, as is shown by the Mercedes that they

drive down from Germany and Switzerland. Like bees returning to a hive, they descend on Pristina, where the young men sit in holiday mood in the most recently opened cafés, checking out Kosovo's beautiful girls on the streets, hoping to take one back with them to London, New York, Zurich. This hobby of the returned diaspora, and the mating calls they make in their new-found language has given them their nickname of either 'honeys' or '*shatzis*' depending on whether the endearments they've learned to holler at passing talent are from English- or German-speaking lands.

Some people claim that the diaspora have been a brake on development in Kosovo because remittances have substituted for the lack of any effective development policies. But the dynamo of Vedat's family could never be described as any kind of a brake. Of course, they are not a typical diaspora story anyway, because the whole family moved abroad together, in distinction to the traditional model where unmarried young men migrate in order to send money back to the family they have left behind. This family, who crossed the world together and have crossed back again to remind themselves of what they left, were wonderful to spend time with. They were enthusiastic at being back in Kosovo, and just as enthusiastic about the lifestyle they have created in the United States. We were invited to watch a home video – literally, a video of their new home – by Vedat's mother. She is called Hate; each letter is pronounced, as in most Albanian words, so the name would be pronounced something like Hatty in English, but Vedat does acknowledge that as a kid growing up in the US it raised some awkward social, not to say Oedipal, questions having a mother named Hate. I suggested he could have had her name tattooed on the knuckles of one hand, with *love* on the other.

As Hate talked us through the video, she used Albanian – until we reached the bumpy footage around the outside entertaining area and she wanted to tell me about her *deck*. Her mother-tongue failed her – perhaps there is no Albanian word for this very Westchester County concept – but once she had explained in English what they had done with the patio, she continued speaking just like any woman from Peja would; or at least just like any woman from Peja with multiple garaging and swimming pools.

We sat and talked in the front room for some time, ranged around

the enormous upholstered seating unit which ran the margin of the room and which is the modern Kosovan equivalent of the *minder* of the Ethnological Museum's eighteenth-century guest room. I noticed that as the family sat down, they ordered themselves as the eighteenth-century family would have done too – the father with the place of honour and then Vedat as the older of the brothers present, followed by his younger brother. Rob was offered space to the other side of the household head, as the senior (=male) guest. I got to sit next to him, which I'm assuming wouldn't have happened in the eighteenth century.

I guessed right that in visiting this family, some traditional hospitality rituals would be appropriate. Where my Kosovan friends arrived at my house with homemade food or cuttings from their garden or produce from their families' smallholdings, I had felt myself unable to compete. My equivalent gift of supermarket wine or imported box of chocolates had always seemed inadequate in the context of such a rich tradition. But that day, since we had just harvested the honey, it had seemed like a good idea to take Vedat's mother a pot.

I had a proud sense of getting it right when I handed over my produce. I had repeated the labeling I had used on the pot I brought to Prime Minister Çeku the previous year – the cartoon bee whose flight path spells out the letters *Elizabeth's Kosovan Honey*. That time, it had been honey from my bees. This time I had even harvested it myself. And I felt that somehow with this honey I could now give as well as receive, its golden threads spinning between me and my hosts, in Hate's home as well as in Kosovo more widely, as visible social currency.

Hate dimpled when she saw it, and for a few hours I sat comfortably balanced on the sheet where social capital is accounted. The feeling lasted throughout the enormous lunch we were treated to of delicious baked local trout, and during the hours spent outside, on the family's land. Vedat's father took his sons off, with us trailing behind, to walk the land. He pointed out the boundaries – to us, but also, I guessed, to Vedat and Ekrem, gently reminding them of their inheritance, the names and stories of the neighbours and tenants, in a narrative that had none of the rough edges of a first telling.

When the walk was done, like a kid let out of school, Vedat asked whether he could get the puppy out. He had just bought a Sharr – one of the long-haired flat-nosed fierce mountain dogs that will attack

wolves. Released, the little bundle forgot to be ferocious in its exuberance. Vedat and Rob wore themselves out with balls and sticks and
improvised games, while the spectators giggled, all of us bubbling along
with the puppy with the reminder of the thrill of movement and play.
Eventually the puppy had no more wag left in its little black-tipped tail,
and even Vedat's own puppyish energy was flagging. It was time to go
home.

It was at the end of the visit that Hate pulled a typically generous
Kosovamerican trick on us. Our car was pulling out of the gates when
she rushed out of the house – just as Xhezide had done earlier in the
month – with her hands full. Where Xhezide had brought my barrel of
honey, Hate was carrying the American equivalent – a trick-or-treat
fistful of packs of chewing gum that she'd brought out from New York.
She tipped it through the window at us, and we murmured incoherent
thanks as we drove off. For all my honey on the balance sheet, I was no
further on than I'd been before.

16.
Honey for sale at the Ethnological Museum, Pristina

New Albanian vocabulary: *zanatli* (craftsman), *krabëz* (knitting needles)

I had been making regular visits to the Ethnological Museum where I had held my birthday party. Sometimes I took guests from England, sometimes I went alone, just to soak up its colours and its peace. Rob came to draw in the gardens, and we got to know the guides. The relationship had been forged with them as we coaxed candles to flickering flames in the fog and cut up the cakes together at my birthday party. They were an inspiring group of young Kosovars, with diverse reasons for working at the museum: Alisa, the artist, inseparable Valon and Bekim the serious young 'etnologs', quiet Ilir who brought me his mother's quince jam recipe when he heard I had never cooked these strange subtle fruits before, pretty, bright Arberita, and Besnik who had been the late President Rugova's bodyguard, and thus had impeccable party connections.

They taught me about Kosovo's history and traditions, glossing the ethnology I had first tasted at Shpresa's family home, a study I had developed in Adem and Xhezide's sitting room. But I had begun to realise how unusually privileged I was in these glimpses of Kosovo. Many of my friends who, like us, were part of the international community in Kosovo would grumble regularly that Kosovo had no culture, that there was nothing to do here. It hurt me for everyone's sake to hear these kinds of complaints: I felt sad that friends were missing out on the wonderful experiences that Kosovo had offered me, and frustrated for Kosovo that it was misrepresented.

I had talked to the guides about what more could be done in the face of this mutual misunderstanding. They felt it too – the low visitor numbers at the museum were both a professional and patriotic challenge to them. 'But what can we do?' they asked. 'There's no tradition

of museum-going in Kosovo. Especially if you're not a Serb, you feel that museums have always shown other people's history in other people's language.' It was perhaps ironic to set up a museum of Kosovo's traditions, when those traditions excluded museums. And of course there were still challenges in representing the varied multi-ethnicity of Kosovo's history in the museum. The collection did include Serbian, Gorani, Bosnian artefacts, but there was no escaping its Albanian emphasis, or the Albanian ethnicity of all of its guides, despite the fact that some of them spoke Serbian and they told me how groups from Serbia had come and been welcomed at the museum.

One idea we came up with was a programme of promotional events on summer Saturday afternoons. As my own introduction to Kosovo's hospitality had done, the programme started off with that *fli* being prepared outside in the typical way over an open fire. The dark haired smiling young woman who cleaned the museum was known to be a good *fli*-maker and she had been invited to come and wear some of the clothes in the museum's collection while she cooked. English Heritage would no doubt have had a fit at the impact of such an approach on conservation, but when Shuki was dressed in the outfit we knew we had a photo opportunity that the newspapers and TV stations wouldn't pass up, and which would attract visitors hungry for culture – and traditional carbohydrates – to the museum gardens.

Shuki literally brought life to the clothes which were usually laid out in the museum. The woven loose cotton shifts seem unfeasibly long when they trail like ghosts in the museum display cabinets; it was only looking at Shuki's outfit that I understood that the shifts are designed to be hitched up over a belt. Seeing the clothes worn also made sense of the ornate little waistcoats I'd seen pinned like exotic butterflies inside the museum. The waistcoats are so small that when they're on display visitors often take them to be children's clothes. But Shuki wore the waistcoat unfastened so it came scarcely further than her armpits, skirting the bust entirely, but this meant that the intricate design on the back was fully displayed across the shoulder blades when you looked from behind.

I had offered to help with whatever I could, and having set up tables in the garden, when the first visitors arrived on the first promotional Saturday afternoon I felt an adrenaline rush. I was really part of this! Over the course of the summer, subsequent Saturday afternoons

attracted hundreds of people. The expats who filled the UN and EU missions, the international liaison offices (they still couldn't be called embassies) and aid missions, came. The few dusty and intrepid back-packers who made it to Kosovo as an original twist on an inter-railing summer found their way to us. Our friends joined us, and friends-of-friends, and people who became friends as we talked together – about Kosovo, about the food. Every Kosovar had a *fli* story to tell – about cooking it in the park on the 1 May holiday, about whose was best, how modern oven-baked *fli* didn't taste anything like the properly-prepared, open-fired traditional dish. There would usually be someone from Gjakova and someone from Pristina arguing over the name for the tool used to lift the lid in between layerings of batter.

For the first few weeks of the programme everyone got a plate of *fli* and honey with their entry ticket. But as we realised that people were coming back Saturday after Saturday we changed the programme slightly every week, offering the sights and smells of different dishes being prepared, added traditional music and crafts. I took responsibility for sending out an email to the mailing list we had built up of people interested in culture in Kosovo so that each week they were alerted to what would be happening at the museum that weekend.

The media had enjoyed the days as much as anyone – during the summer low season for news, the appeal of a story celebrating the national dish of Kosovo prepared by a beautiful woman in national costume was a no-brainer; motherhood and apple pie. The journalists had relished the fact, too, that so many non-Kosovars had come to eat and learn to make these quintessentially local dishes. On one Saturday we had realised that we were going to need two *tepsis* of food in order to keep up with the sixty or so visitors needing feeding during the afternoon, so we made an arrangement with the nearest bakery that they would bake one tray for us while the other cooked in the tradi-tional way over the open fire outside. In the end it was me who had gone to collect the *tepsi* and as I had walked through the wide wooden gates of the museum compound bearing the large steaming tray, the television cameras had caught me. The story that night on the news was 'foreigner thinks *fli* delicious' along with soundbites from others of the multi-national group of visitors all agreeing that this odd dish dripping with honey was a wonderful treat.

It was part of the special treatment frequently offered to me and other foreigners by Kosovars. When I went shopping, of course people recognised that I was foreign. As far as I ever found out they didn't charge higher prices – if anything, they were likely to throw in an extra nectarine, and thank me for everything my country had done. What does one do in a situation like that? Throw back the nectarine and say you don't want any kickbacks? Accept graciously. One day I was at the post office when it suddenly started raining, in one of those angry showers that make it impossible to travel more than a few steps before feet start slipping inside shoes, clothes chafe, hair sticks to your face. On my way out of the post office I found a gaggle of perhaps fifteen Kosovan men and women, most older than me, sheltering under the entrance and waiting for the weather to pass. I took my place among them when the woman who had sold me my stamps came hurrying out from behind her desk. 'Take this,' she offered, holding out an umbrella.

Why should I take it? Why not the seventy-year-old man who looked arthritic? But it was not mine to pass on. I gestured at the others. 'Take it, take it,' the woman insisted, so I mutely accepted it and set off through the storm, leaving the others waiting, with guilt squelching at my every step home. It was a literal representation of a layer I felt being imposed between me and my experience of Kosovo.

What were the reasons for this excessive care shown to me? Respect? Hope of some return? Gratitude to my country, of which I was the only ambassador the stamp-seller had perhaps ever spoken to? A lack of understanding of the kind of engagement I would prefer? Shpresa suggested that it was because of my attempts to learn the language. This is depressingly rare – at one point I was invited as studio guest to a Kosovan TV show whose theme was 'foreigners who have learned Albanian'. There were three of us on the panel.

The guides shrugged when I complained about the photos of me with food at the museum. 'At least it's publicity for us.' But despite our work during those summer Saturdays, the museum remained Pristina's best-kept secret. I'd read in the ESI think tank's report, *A Future for Pristina's Past*, about the socialist era determination to 'destroy the old, build the new', creating a brave new capital, and removing the rough edges of natural material, the fussy details of history. From the stall-holders selling secondhand books outside the grim 1970s Grand Hotel

I had bought books from one or two generations back, their garish technicolour showing off a migraine vision of Modernity. The concrete manifestations of that vision now stand skid-marked and stained on the ruins of former Ottoman-era elegance, and the Ethnological Museum is the only place in the capital where you can see what an eighteenth-century Kosovan home would have looked like. But still people didn't know about it.

Clearly, we needed some new strategies. And the people who visited the museum seemed to be our best ambassadors. I thought about the 'waggle dance' of bees – the sophisticated language of dance used by bees to share information about sources of nectar they have found. I'd noticed the strange movements of bees at the entrance to my hive and had looked up some information about what the motions mean. The waggle dance is a figure of eight; its angle from the sun indicates direction while the duration of the dance, which can be repeated over a hundred times, shows distance. In a well-networked place like Kosovo where one person links to an extended family, often in the same house or compound, we needed to give people a reason to communicate about the museum with one another, to do their own tongue-waggling information-sharing about us.

When people do come they are always impressed. I have never seen a visitor leave after a cursory glance; never heard any criticism of the museum – other than how difficult it is to find. The visitor's book is covered in comments from people for whom a visit has clearly been an epiphany:

> 'I am so pleased that I came here and that you have managed to explain Albanian culture and traditions, even more so for those of us *në gurbet* [this word means something between emigration and exile]. Enormous significance for me. Thank you very much from an Albanian Swedish soldier.'(In misspelled Albanian)

> 'This day will stay in our memories for a long time because of what we've learned about our centuries-old traditions' – class 8 (the 14-year-olds) from a local school.

> 'The most beautiful museum in the world... oh, how wonderful it is to be Albanian.'

'I am proud to belong to this people – who could not be proud
on coming here? Protect our cultural treasures and values; this will
make us civilised and European.'

We liked the idea that the museum could be seen as an inspiration
for ongoing creativity in the worlds of art and design, and not just a
closed display case of things created long ago and no longer used. So
the guides and I wrote a proposal and got funding for a creative 'resi-
dency' week. Craftspeople were invited to come to the museum during
the week, to demonstrate their work, and then on the final day to sell
their products in a fair that was to take over all the rooms of the
museum.

The week brought us more than 600 visitors. Women's groups
from communities across Kosovo – Serbian, Roma, Bosnian, Albanian,
Gorani – sat among the exhibits and created new and beautiful things.
They knitted, they crocheted, they sewed, they did something called
'*oia*' which magicked fine edging and fragile flowers from knots in
simple cotton thread. Watching them, I felt like an illiterate might do
observing people writing. They seemed to be simply looping and
twisting, knotting and stabbing with some very basic tools and raw
materials. These loops and knots hold no meaning for me, even
though I understand that the finished product has meaning. And when
I tried to replicate them, I was left with loops and knots but no
meaning or finished product at all. I sat in awe to watch them work
in the sun-filled *çardak* as their predecessors must have done before
them.

Men came, too – woodcarvers, hatmakers, filigree jewellers, potters.
And on Saturday the accumulated production of the week's creative
profusion was displayed. This was the chance for honey to have its day.

I had recently found skeps being sold in Pristina and asked the shop
whether they would be able to come to the museum on Saturday to sell
them – both full-sized, and a small ornamental variety. I suggested that
they might bring honey too. So as the throngs of people left the
museum that Saturday with hand-knitted socks, pots, earrings and the
typical white felt *plis* hats, many also had tucked under their arms a traditional teardrop hive. Even more of them carried honey. As they buzzed
off home, I hoped that they would act as pollinators for us themselves,

carrying the news of the museum, sharing out leaflets – doing the more decorous human equivalent of the bee dance to show the location of the best nectar, the richest flowering.

Ilir's mother's recipe for quince jam, *reçel*

Wash and peel the quinces.
Cut into small pieces.
Put into a heavy-bottomed pan 1.2 kilograms sugar for every kilogram of quince, and enough water for it to be wet through.
Slowly add the pieces of quince (note: quince spatters as it cooks so you might want to consider using a long spoon or wearing rubber gloves to protect your hands as you stir).
Boil until the quince has turned to amber and softened.

17.
The axe that fell in honey

New Serbian vocabulary: *sekira* (axe), *med* (honey)

After a year of Albanian lessons, I decided it was time to do something structured about being able to speak to the other eight per cent of Kosovo's population. Working on a bilingual education project with an international charity, it was becoming increasingly embarrassing with the multi-ethnic team in the office, or at coffee breaks in the training sessions I ran, when the interpreters were at rest, and I chattered away in my enthusiastically flawed Albanian to the Albanian-speakers while miming '*dobro*' and '*hvala*' with incompetent smiles to the Serb-speakers.

I knew from the well-thumbed Albanian book in my bag that the first thing I needed in learning a language was a dictionary. When a friend heard I was interested he put me in contact with Kujtim, the Samuel Johnson of Kosovo, a man who had produced a bizarre Kosovan achievement – a dictionary in six languages, including all those of communities in Kosovo.

Kujtim is Roma – one of the smallest and the most desperately alienated minorities in Kosovo. Whether it's the official statistics on girls dropping out of school to get married, or the figures you see scrabbling in the city's skips for metal to recycle, it is clear that the Roma are frighteningly vulnerable. We spoke on the phone and he told me how his privileged experience as a Kosovan Roma at the Sorbonne made him want to do something in his own field of expertise to help his people. We arranged to meet so I could see the result of his labours. When I got to the café, I had no problem working out which one was Kujtim, with his dark skin and professorially wild hair.

He showed me the six-way dictionary he had compiled. It starts with a history of the Roma language in Roma, translated into English, Turkish, Albanian, Serbian and French. From there it offers some charming phrasebook nonsense ('I'm sorry we have no bread/money/guitars,'

'Tomorrow is the circumcision of my brother's son') and then a picture dictionary where words are listed alphabetically – in Roma.

Some weeks later I was desperate to ask for butter in a Serbian hotel we were staying at, and found myself flicking through the pages of Kujtim's dictionary looking for the picture of butter, and wondering whether I'd have to learn Roma for reference purposes before embarking on any other languages round here. The waiter had come and gone, and Rob had finished his dry roll before I discovered the dictionary's line drawing of something greasy in a pat, and triumphantly pronounced the word written next to it. Treasure trove though the six-way Kosovan dictionary was, maybe it would be better to find another way into Serbian.

The next thing I learned about Serbian was how difficult it was to find someone willing to teach it to me. I can't say what part of that was because I was British, and the Brits were loudly and forcefully calling for a resolution of Kosovo's final status to include independence from Serbia. Equally, many Serbs were reluctant to come into Pristina – a factor of the perception of risk that was impossible to counter. If Serbs didn't believe they were safe to move freely around Kosovo, then who was I, or an Albanian, or the international military presence, to assure them that they were? Some Albanians offered to teach me – anyone over a certain age had needed Serbian for education and work and many spoke it fluently – but I rebelled against that idea. Language is politics, and learning Serbian was more than acquiring a picture dictionary or even a cluster of nouns. For me it was some kind of commitment to Kosovo in all its variety, not just to the Albanian-speakers who had become my friends.

In the end, I was introduced to Ana, and her cousin Zorica who acted as her driver. Stout and bottle-blonde, they were unlikely heroines, but for me they achieved that status for their bullish determination – in remaining in Kosovo with their children, in driving freely between their little Serb-only village and Pristina, and in speaking Serbian loudly to me through the car window when I met or left them outside my house, under the gaze of groups of fit young Albanian men who dominated the passing traffic on every Kosovan city street.

I never found out why Ana didn't drive herself – perhaps, like me, she was simply terrified of all Kosovo's swerve-inducing potholes, the

impulsive overtaking, compounded in the hours of darkness by the unlit horse and carts and the power cuts that take out all lights, including traffic lights. But none of these things – indeed, very few things in the world at all – seemed to scare Zorica. Usually she would collect me from my home and drive me out to the village, past the Albanian-language signs, the posters urging votes for Albanian politicians, the defiant Albanian black eagle on its red flag flying from most shops. The drive, looking out through her windscreen at this country, was a lesson for me in so many ways, translating Kosovo into a different syntax. Zorica used to be the deputy leader of Pristina municipality – in the days when Serbs did that kind of thing. In the days before Albanians did that kind of thing. She told me that she has Albanian friends. She tried to speak English occasionally, and often mixed her English words with Albanian which she had never admitted to knowing. I liked her. I hope that people like her stay in Kosovo.

And I hope that Ana's little house and the Serbian houses like it stay in Kosovo. It was the first time I'd been to a Serb's home and when I first started tuition there, the weather was still good enough for us to have our lessons in the garden. Chickens clucked around our feet, the neighbour's cow bellowed from the next field. On one occasion, Ana mistook it for her choleric husband calling, and tried to answer it, until she realised her mistake and we both fell into awkward giggles. Ana's bristly mother-in-law sat in the shade stripping peppers for the sweet pepper chutney called *ajvar*. To reach the table where our lessons were held you had to walk through the orchard, avoiding bumping your head on the plump apples on the loaded branches.

Ana's family eats mainly homemade and home-grown. As such, it is the bounty from their backyard – not the Bounty from the corner shop – that is their main source of treats. Honey – yes, they also keep hives – is therefore a synonym for luxury and indulgence. Sitting in the hum of the bee-loud glade with my textbook, it seemed very appropriate when we covered the chapter on 'Serbian idioms' to learn that when someone has unexpected luck, in Serbian you would say *his axe has fallen in honey*.

I understood how honey could be used to mean sudden fortune, but the axe didn't make sense to me. Did it suggest fortune so sweet that even the most brutal of weapons, most vicious of tools, was no longer

destructive? As so often with folklore, I tried to imagine the circumstances that could have led to this saying, and failed. A wild hive revealed as you are cutting down a tree so that your blade drips with honey, perhaps? In the context of manual work around trees, it would be the weary woodcutter's version of the tired fruitpicker's *windfall*. But if your axe fell in honey, wouldn't you just be annoyed – the honey would get sawdust in it, and the axe would need a lot of cleaning?

Ana couldn't see what my problem was with the expression, so I let it go. Perhaps it had lost something in translation. On our way to the garden gate at the end of the lesson, she cupped a hanging cluster of grapes and offered them to me. I should take them this week, she explained, because the family was about to harvest all the grapes for home-made wine. It was an unexpected bonus – a windfall, a sticky blade.

Recipe for *ajvar*, sweet red pepper relish

Ingredients
2kg red peppers
2 cloves garlic
2.5 tbsp salt
Pepper to taste
225ml olive oil
110ml white vinegar

Preheat an oven to 190 degrees. Roast the peppers until the skin is black on all sides.
Place the roasted peppers in a large pot. Cover and leave for two hours. When the peppers are cool, peel the skin off and remove the seeds and stems.
Mash the peppers to a pulp. Transfer to a large cooking pot.
Add crushed garlic, salt, pepper, olive oil and vinegar. Cook for three hours at 190 degrees.
When finished cooking, let it cool. Fill jars almost to the top.

Makes just over half a litre of relish.

18.
When blood makes way for honey

New Albanian vocabulary: *gjakmarrje* (blood feud), *pajtim* (reconciliation), *ahër* (stable), *shilte* (foam mattress), *me bujtë* (stay the night)

Following bewildering directions in a midwinter late afternoon gloom, the tyres of our 4x4 span on the muddy streets of Dranoc. All around us were *kullas* built of stone, with as few windows as possible – sometimes none – on the walls that face onto the street or other people's land. Gazi had told me that *kulla* is actually a Turkish word meaning simply 'tower'. The fact that it's used for these old houses reminds you that in a period before Manhattan, when most things were single-storey, a building on three floors must have seemed dizzyingly high. But it's no longer the height that strikes you when you arrive among a village of *kullas*; the book written by Norwegian anthropologist Berit Backer about her experiences living near Dranoc in the 1970s was called *Behind Stone Walls* – it's these bleak, blank faces that stare you down as soon as you enter the village. The single feature relieving these walls are small holes, just large enough for the muzzle of a gun to be poked through.

So we had a sense of being watched, though no-one was about, as we drew up at the large wooden gates with some misgivings. We had come to stay the night in a *kulla* that had been restored by the Swedish NGO, Cultural Heritage without Borders, who were now offering it as bed and breakfast accommodation. Fear subsided slightly as the custodian opened up, welcomed us in, and took us through the low doorway (so that visitors have no choice but to bow respectfully as they enter) to the ground floor of the *kulla*. This would originally have been used as a stable, but now there were tables laid out for a seminar, with a Powerpoint screen covering one wall.

There was a power cut, so we made our way by torchlight up the stairs to the *oda* on the *kulla's* top floor. It was bitterly cold, and we hurried through the wonky door. It opened onto an enchantingly cosy

scene. A wooden stove had warmed the room seductively and candles were lit on a huge round table. I wanted immediately to sink down on one of the covered foam mattresses around the edge of the room, and watch the soft light flicker over mellow woodwork, the special little built-in cupboard for keeping coffee and sugar in, the bright woven cushion covers and rugs.

That's pretty much what we did. We laid the low *sofra* table and cooked a simple meal with a bottle of wine. Then we lolled and chatted and relaxed in the *oda's* simple luxury. I knew that I wanted to come back, and I thought of all the people I wanted to share this discovery with. The *kulla* in Dranoc is a unique opportunity to get a sense of a style of architecture that has otherwise almost completely disappeared. The *kullas* suffered in the 1990s because they were, and were suspected to be, places where KLA supplies could be safely piled. As such, they were targeted by Serbian forces and largely destroyed.

But after Serb forces withdrew from Kosovo following the NATO bombing campaign in 1999, Kosovo's remaining *kullas* were still not safe. They continued to be at risk but now it was from poverty – families without enough money to mend a roof or rebuild a wall found it cheaper either to let the building disintegrate, or to knock it down and build something from concrete in its place. And ironically, the *kullas* that didn't fall prey to poverty instead fell prey to wealth – specifically the dollars, deutschmarks, pounds and francs sent back by the diaspora or families' improved economic situation resulting from the investment which followed the NATO, UN and foreign NGO arrival in Kosovo. It was now possible to buy the Slovenian roof, the modern plastic front door, the fancy balcony that *kulla* owners had been unable to afford previously. I could see the importance of Cultural Heritage without Borders' work in saving this building, holding on to one small reminder of a Kosovo that was being forgotten.

We returned to Dranoc a few weeks later with Shpresa; it was in the *kulla's* new fitted kitchen that she taught me to make *llokuma*. In February we arranged Rob's birthday party in the *kulla*. Fifty people came for lunch that day, and twelve stayed the night with us, playing games in the candlelit *oda* until late.

But each time I checked the visitors' book, I was depressed to see my own name as the previous entry. No presentations had been

screened in the stable, and from talking to the custodian it was clear that what could have been a living, income-generating flagship for sustainable tourism in Kosovo was instead just a cold old house.

I asked the custodian for the email address of head office and contacted Cultural Heritage without Borders, suggesting that a friend and I could work as volunteers to promote the *kulla*. The head of the NGO, a good-looking young Albanian architect, was enthusiastic about the idea. So then I rang my friend, Cindy. Recently arrived in Kosovo from Washington DC, when she and I had had coffee together a few weeks before, she'd told me that she was looking for a project.

Was there something slightly paradoxical about a Brit and an American working to promote Kosovo's culture like this? Well, yes, but as I had realised at Adem and Xhezide's the day of the mushroom hunting, you can still be passionate about beekeeping and honey even if you are rarely allowed to get on with the business of beekeeping yourself. And I was increasingly passionate about Kosovo, without being a Kosovar.

We planned a series of cultural workshops at the *kulla* to showcase it as a space for events, over six Saturdays in October and November. We arranged an art class run by a local artist, a tasting event for Kosovan wine and *raki*, an Albanian language class, a lesson in Kosovan lullabies run by a professional soprano. I asked my friends for ideas for what else should be in the series? One subject kept resurfacing: 'you can't understand Kosovo – you certainly can't understand Dranoc – if you don't understand the Kanun.'

For my first birthday in Kosovo, along with the beehive, my presents had included a copy of the laws collected in this Code or *Kanun* of Lekë Dukagjini. The book's introduction explained that the laws were only written down in the nineteenth century, but have been in existence for at least 600 years, and possibly hundreds more. Flicking through it, I learned about the rules for every aspect of social life: the correct order of precedence at a wedding, the ways that guests should be cared for – or the compensation due if someone's bees escape.

> If someone's bees swarm and fly to the orchard or fence of another person and the owner is pursuing it, the swarm belongs to him, and the owner of the orchard or fence may not prevent him from retrieving it. If bees swarm from the hive and fly to the orchard or

fence of another person and no-one pursues them, the owner of the orchard or fence has the right not to give them to anyone else and to keep them for himself. Bees that are swarming must be pursued step by step and followed until they settle somewhere, and wherever they stop they are collected by the owner.

The *Kanun* also specifies the going rates for a variety of commodities. The cost of a beehive with the insects inside is set in the *Kanun* as fifty grosh. This is the same value as 56 kilos of flour or wine, 19 kilos of meat, 11 kilos of honey, unwashed wool, *raki* or cheese or six kilos of coffee beans.

Whatever the charming glimpses all this gives into Kosovo's domestic economy in centuries past, the *Kanun* makes some more chilling requirements too. 'Woman,' it says, 'is a sack to be hard used.' And it specifies some of the ways in which this is so, specifying that a girl has no right to be involved in decisions about her marriage, though girls would have had fair cause to be interested in what kind of man they would marry – this husband has, according to the *Kanun*, the right to 'beat and bind his wife when she scorns his words and orders'. There was no way out for these women: 'if the girl does not submit and marry her fiance, she should be handed over to him by force, together with a cartridge; and if the girl tries to flee, her husband may kill her with her parents' cartridge, and the girl's blood is unavenged because it was with their cartridge that she was killed.'

The careful specification of the limits of vengeance appears throughout the *Kanun*. The copy I was given had a blood red cover, and I began to realise more than one reason why this might be so. It is this requirement for vengeance that is the connection between *Kanun* and *kullas*. In general the principle is that for any man killed, the life of one of the murderer's relatives must be taken in exchange. Although this was established as a limiting principle (an eye for an eye, a tooth – *and no more* – for a tooth) the consequence was that when the murderer's kinsman (possibly a man who knew little or nothing of his relative's crime – and in some case didn't even know that the crime had been committed and that his own life was therefore at risk) was killed, that family were then eager for further retribution. In this way, blood feuds could go back and forth for generations, and each of those gen-

A village elder, who adjudicates on the basis of the *Kanun*, wearing the traditional *plis* hat

erations of boys and men needed a defensible retreat to keep them safe. This was why the *kulla* walls have holes just big enough to poke your rifle through.

Cindy and I added a study day on the *Kanun* to our list of workshops.

I talked to people more about the *Kanun* – the way that it continued to inform life in Kosovo, but also the elements that modern Kosovars had left behind. Revenge killings, for example, were almost non-existent in Kosovo now, largely due to a campaign of reconciliation during the 1990s, led by a perhaps incongruous figure – a Kosovan folklorist, Anton Çetta.

Çetta was one of the first characters I had met during my immersion course in Kosovan history; two copies of the same statue of him stand in the front garden of a sculptor in central Pristina. I walked past that house to get to the Ethnological Museum and grew used to seeing the twin men gesturing at me with outstretched palm as I passed, the outlines in their blazer pockets showing that they were men of the book. When winter came, the snow settled on their heads, giving them small white hats just like those that the real life old men wear in the streets of Pristina.

During Çetta's travels around Kosovo to collect examples of folklore, he became aware of how paralysed his country had become because of the blood feuds. While the Albanians of Kosovo were being targeted by the Serbian authorities, Çetta could see the importance of solidarity between themselves, and he set about organising enormous formal ceremonies of reconciliation for hundreds of families 'in blood' with each other.

Unsurprisingly, given this rich history, bookings started coming in for the *Kanun* workshop as well as the others we'd advertised. Almost everyone due to attend was from Pristina – a mixture of foreigners and Albanian Kosovars, with a disproportionately large number of the former, despite the reduced rates we were offering for people on local salaries. But Cindy and I didn't want the workshops just to be opportunities for city folk to lumber down to the country in their 4x4s, leaving nothing but tyre tracks in the churned-up mud lanes of the village to show they had been there; we wanted to offer some benefit to the people living in Dranoc.

To talk to the families in the village we didn't have to do anything more than walk through the streets. We looked conspicuously foreign, and when we passed someone, Cindy smiled and I used an Albanian greeting. Cindy would always draw attention, and Albanians, both male and female, are great appreciators of feminine beauty; where English women might snarl, Albanian girls will admire frankly. It was never long before we would be in conversation about just what we were doing in Dranoc; I was confident enough now in my language skills to strike up these conversations with strangers. Almost without exception we were then invited in for coffee and over our coffees we explained more about why we were here. We presented the workshop as an opportunity for people in Dranoc to sell things (and keep all their takings) – perhaps handcrafts, or home-made cheese, *raki*... Honey? I suggested.

It was coming up to elections, and one of our hosts told us that people in this village had nothing to sell 'except their votes'. One wrinkled old man with lively eyes countered that Dranoc might be able to rustle up some women for sale if the people from Pristina were interested. But it wasn't that kind of honeys I had been hoping for.

On our walk we met Syzana, an 18-year-old who lives with her parents and five brothers and sisters in a plasterboard house near the *kulla*. She invited us to supper at her home, where we were met at the door by a pinprick of torchlight in the power cut. It threw strange shadows on our faces, as her parents welcomed us in, and we picked our way through the shoes outside the door into the little house.

Syzana's father apologised for the humble home he was hosting us in. 'Our house was destroyed during the war, when we were hiding up in the mountains.' He gestured to the sheer rock face that forms the border with Albania, rising up behind the village. The mountains' Albanian name means 'accursed'. I looked round the family, at their pretty little daughter who would have been only a baby in the war, at the son who limps; I imagined them all sheltering out there in the night, cowering, listening, hushing the children.

I used the toilet in their house – a tiny bathroom where you had to step over the plastic water bottles filled when there was water on tap, and stored up for the hours, or whole nights, when there was none in the pipes. There were small stickers on the doorways with Japanese lettering – the temporary shelter had been the gift of a Japanese aid agency.

Eight years on, with two additional children, the family was still crowded into it, and no member of the family had work outside the home.

Back in the family sitting room, we were gathered round the only light, a saucer of sunflower oil from which trailed half a dozen short cotton threads that acted as feebly-glowing wicks. After we had eaten, Syzana's mother handed us chunks of her nettle *pite* pie wrapped in newspaper to take back with us – in our Landrover to our centrally-heated house, stuffed with its imported luxury food. And Syzana opened up her suitcase of handicrafts – the poorly-lit hours she had woven together evening after evening in the cold front room into endless fine table mats and pretty coffee cup holders. Before we knew it, three little crocheted doilies were being packaged up for us to take home too. But the family wasn't sure about bringing any of these to sell to our visitors.

The following weekend the first workshop opened at the *kulla*. Two television crews and a documentary film-maker poked the long noses of their cameras round the door to the *oda*, and journalists lolled on the mattresses with their notebooks. As each workshop participant arrived I greeted them and escorted them up the stairs to the *oda*. So I had the chance to relive fifteen separate times that thrill as the door which was hung askew on its hinges swang back to show the room's elegant simplicity, the old wood and weavings, the warm stove.

But not a single person from the village came offering to sell their honey, or anything else. I talked to one of the Americans who'd come to the workshop. 'Elizabeth, the concept of selling surplus is very sophisticated – too sophisticated to be grasped by people who live by subsistence farming.'

When the workshop had finished, I went out again around the village, visiting new houses, hoping to generate some interest in bringing things to sell next week. More coffee, conversation, explanation, offers, and still no suggestion that anyone would take up the opportunity the following Saturday.

Six days later we were back, in the company of a young Kosovar who had trained as an oenologist. Over supper the night before his workshop he told us about Kosovo's previously productive wine industry, despite the vineyards that had been abandoned since the war. He poured us samples from some small vineyards that had been restarted

recently – peppery Merlot and a berry-rich Cabernet. The old state-owned vineyard had been privatised recently and we tried some other good red wine (and some less good white) from there. 'You'll have drunk this before,' Albert smiled. 'Most of it went for export under a Yugoslav label before the war.'

As we set up the glasses for his tasting workshop the next morning, there was a knock on the front door. Syzana was standing outside. We asked how she was, was she tired? In answer, she gestured to the plastic bag she had with her, and pulled out some table mats which she and other members of her family had beaded and crocheted. I could have kissed her.

In fact, I did.

Of course, the visitors to the workshop loved her work. Syzana sold almost everything she had brought, and she asked if she could come back the following Saturday. When she returned the next week, Syzana brought her friends with her. They laid out their handmade beading, their ubiquitous table mats. One brought a brother who had walnuts, homemade cheese, cornflour. And someone else brought honey.

The Mazrekaj *kulla* in Dranoc where our workshops were held and honey sold

The honey was a runaway success and the beekeeper sold out. He was selling it at seven euros a kilogram – cheaper, and definitely tastier, than you can buy it in the Pristina market. If my maths is right, then Lekë Dukagjini would have found it a bargain too: proof, if any were needed, that it's better to live on local honey than it is to survive on coffee, wine – or unwashed wool. And our sales confirmed that even the beekeepers who don't get their hands dirty as much as they would like do still have a part to play in supporting honey production.

Putting the *pite* into hospitality
Although I later returned many times to Syzana's house and ate more of the excellent *pite* I never watched it made there from start to finish. One day, on a flight to Pristina, I was discussing with the Albanian woman sitting next to me how I'd like to know how to make the dish. 'Would you, by any chance, know a recipe?' She was kind enough to dictate one to me as we sat in the clouds a mile above Eastern Europe. Sometimes, when I wasn't clear about the details of what she was describing, she used her airline meal napkin to demonstrate the layers of the pastry, just how you pinch them together. I apologised for interrupting her journey but she waved away my apology. 'It's good,' she said. 'I want my daughter to learn too.' The 23-year-old next to her was her daughter, and it emerged that the reason it would be particularly useful for her to learn the art of good *pite*-making was that she was on this flight to Kosovo to celebrate her engagement. Two months previously she had been visiting Kosovo from her home in Finland and her grandfather had suggested the son of his next-door neighbour as a suitable husband. The couple and their parents met and confirmed that the match would be a good one (I think he is a very lucky man – Ardita is beautiful and also has 'papers' in Finland), so now only weeks later, this plane journey was the beginning of their life together. Ardita will bring her husband back to Helsinki, where she will no doubt, as her mother has taught her, cook exquisite things for this near-stranger. I suggested to her that she was very brave to be starting a new life like this. She shrugged: 'my grandfather knows his family' – as if that was all the assurance any girl needed.

When my friend Valbona heard about Ardita's mother's recipe she was sceptical. Different areas of Kosovo have very different approaches to *pite*-making and she offered to share her version with me. What follows is my combination of the two recipes.

Ingredients
For the pastry
900g plain flour
1tsp salt
approx 550ml warm water
plus 1 tbsp oil to glaze

For the filling
250g nettles – remove stalks
1 small onion
1 egg
125g yoghurt
100ml single cream
salt to taste

Measure out the flour into a deep bowl. Add the salt and water until the dough is the 'right' consistency (when I queried what this meant I was given a simple guideline, which I learned later was not of Valbona's own devising. The mixture should feel like the flesh in your earlobe. Try feeling your earlobe now and you will see what a useful guide this is). Knead the dough on a floured surface (Valbona uses the heel of her right hand while her left spins the ball of dough in a movement I couldn't reproduce however hard I tried). Cover with a plate to rest.

Chop the nettles finely and wash them twice in hot water then 2 or 3 times in cold water. Drain.

Chop the onion finely, and fry to soften it.

Mix the nettles and onions together. Add the egg, creme fraiche, flour, milk and salt, and mix together.

Return to the dough and form into 25 balls a little larger than golf balls. Gently knead each of these using a motion from the heel of your hand down your thumb, and roll each of them out to 10cm diameter.

Take one of the circles you have made and spread oil on top of it. Place another circle on top and drape these two over the fist of one hand so that the discs begin to distend with their own weight. With your free hand stretch the discs further. Repeat this process with new discs, pulling the pile to increase its diameter with each new addition, until you have a stack of 7 discs of 40cm diameter.

Repeat the process to make another stack from the other 6 balls.

Oil a *tepsi* and line it with the 7 layers, making sure they go up the sides.

Cover with the filling.

Place the 6-layer stack on top of the filling and pinch and twist the edges together to seal the filling in.

Spread oil on top of the *pite*. Prick the pie with a fork and place in a 200°C oven for 35–40 minutes.

The *pite* is served in slices like a pizza.

It is often made with spinach and/or the white crumbly cheese, or with pumpkin.

19.
The land of blood and honey

New Albanian vocabulary: *rrugë të mbarë* (Have a good trip)

I had been keeping notes and odd little diaries since the beginning of our time in Kosovo. Leafing back through them, I realised how quickly things pass; some of the notes meant nothing any more. Others were cryptic, but powerful – in my notebook for my first, foreign month in Pristina I had scraps of Albanian written – for practice or to look up later. On one page there were five words in a line – 'I understand', 'I think', 'I am', 'I have', 'I speak'.

If this was how memories could fragment and decompose after only 17 months, I needed to do something to stop the rot. I have been told that honey is a preservative. Apocryphally, Alexander the Great was buried in a honey coffin, and it was apparently common practice for the ancient Babylonians to be buried in honey. Honey is hygroscopic, absorbing water, and leaving none for the bacteria necessary for decomposition, and when it comes into contact with animal tissue, it produces hydrogen peroxide, which stops putrefaction.

So I took my photographs, my notes and scraps of writing and decided to begin embalming my love story so far in a book of honey. To start me off I decided that I was going to buy a ticket to the place where I do my best writing – a train carriage. In the UK with a train journey as part of my daily commute, I had found a way to safeguard writing time, free from interruptions. Having come to Kosovo to live in a city with everything in walking distance, and a country mainly accessible only by road rather than rail, my writing routines had been broken. So I planned a trip along Kosovo's longest piece of track, not in order to get to its terminal in Skopje, Macedonia, but to start to write down some of the bees and some of the impressions that had been buzzing round my head for the past year. It's better to travel than to arrive.

I was standing on the frozen platform at 6am when an old man

approached me. In answer to his question I confirmed there was no-one in the ticket office. The train was due in twenty minutes I believed. No, I couldn't say if the train we wanted was the one standing in the station. We stood close to each other in companionable silence, and waited.

The closeness was a choice. That he had used me as his source of information wasn't: we had the whole station to ourselves. This was the morning train, one of only two a day, which link Pristina to the national capital nearest to it – Skopje in Macedonia. The equivalent in Britain would be waiting for the Eurostar. But we were the only people on the station.

It was sad – and maybe suspicious... All my fears and prejudices began to surface. Bloody railway staff – bloody typical. And had I mis-understood something? Bloody Albanian language. Bloody stupid me. Bloody Balkan timekeeping. If this was England...

And indeed, how different from England. From the other side of the train which was sitting in frosty silence opposite us, someone in uniform descended. I ventured a '*mirëmëngjes*' and the uniform responded politely.

Was this the train for Skopje? Yes, yes, but we shouldn't get on it yet. Why didn't we come inside and warm up in his office.

Once inside and without further discussion, he got out four glasses (a colleague soon joined us) and some teabags, and we sat sleepily over our hot drinks, slurping without inhibitions and thawing pleasantly. I asked about the age of the station building, which is an elegant low structure with a beautiful old clock. Betjeman probably wouldn't have got excited about it – but if Betjeman had lived in Pristina he would have done. If you used only fingers and toes you could count the city's buildings that date from before the Second World War. If current atti-tudes to preservation continue, you soon won't even need your toes. The station manager answered with the precision of someone used to replying to timetable queries: the building dates from 1930.

As we drank our tea, the hands of the attractive clock seemed not to move. The petty adrenaline rush of organising this trip (passport? money? dictionary?) subsided, and I concentrated, as our host had encouraged us, on making myself *rahat* – comfortable, relaxed. Looking up, I admired the clock again and suddenly realised that the hands really

hadn't moved. Glancing down I saw that my watch hands, however, had raced ahead – we had only two minutes before the train was due to leave. Adrenaline, bloody Balkan timekeeping, bloody Albanian language, stupid me. Etc.

In an uptight British way I asked about the train. Reassuring smiles – the colleague who'd joined us for tea was the driver. But yes, why didn't I buy a ticket.

'Where exactly are you planning to go, *kismet,*' the station manager asked, using the Turkish for the will of fate, made famous in Nelson's dying words. Like Hardy, I have to assume that this was what I heard, and not an improper suggestion. It would cost me four euros (£2.40) for this three-hour journey. The ticket I was given was numbered 00010; the railway network had recently been given a facelift but the new tickets didn't seem to be very popular. It was good to see that there was room for expansion though. I wondered whether they would still be serving free tea for passenger 99,999.

The old man got a pensioner's rate once he'd told the official what 'generation' he was. A few days before, someone had asked me how old I was? Seventy-three? Since this had followed the standard 'good day, are you tired?', I had worried what on earth I must be looking like. But '73 was the year of my birth I was being asked about – and here the old man answered '1935'. He was only five years younger than the station. I tried to work out what this country was called when they were both born: I think it had just become Yugoslavia, the 'Land of the South Slavs', from being the Kingdom of Serbs, Croats and Slovenes; no mention of Albanians, or of the French, whose plans, I was told by the station master, were used for the station architecture.

We were hurried up a bit now – I didn't finish my tea, though I had the sense that had I chosen to, the Kosovan code of hospitality would have prevented the driver from leaving until I was done, and the people at the first station down the line would just have had to wait. We were wished *rrugë të mbarë*.

The man-as-old-as-the-station and I got into the same carriage, even though we were still the only passengers. I knew one significant reason for the low passenger numbers on Kosovan trains; it was on this line that Albanians were herded in March 1999 by the Serbian forces. They were kept at the station for 24 hours in the bitter cold (worse

than today – there was snow that March). One woman gave birth during that time, and an old man died. No-one knew where they were being taken or what would be done to them when they got there, but everyone knew what had happened when the Jews had been bustled onto trains.

In fact, when these trains had been filled, they took the Albanians only as far as the border with Macedonia – the exact journey I was making. There, the families were dropped and left to the tender mercies of refugee camps. I had learnt about this from books, and I remember sitting in a Cornish holiday cottage in spring 1999, watching it on television. I had also been told about it by my friend who was transported on one of those trains.

Like most people I'd met in Kosovo, Elmaze's experience in the war is something that came out gently and only after I'd known her some months. I can only guess at the psychological, social and political reasons for this. Like the nose of our train, Kosovo has its face firmly set towards the future.

I only heard about Elmaze's experience because when we were heading out for a drink together one evening, she greeted someone on the street. As we walked on she explained, 'she was a teacher with me in the refugee camp.' I hadn't known Elmaze had been a teacher, and I hadn't known she had been a refugee. I asked her to tell me about it while we had our drink. By the end of her story she was in tears, but she gave me some idea of the conditions in the place, of the educated people like herself who tried to simulate normality for the kids through impromptu classes. Elmaze had trained as an economist so she taught maths. Others contributed whatever skills they had. I still don't have a very clear picture of these places in my mind – where they lay on the continuum between Darfur and a grim Brittany campsite. But Elmaze told me she wouldn't ever travel by train again.

For me, of course, trains have a different meaning. They are Adlestrop and Auden's *Night Mail* and Celia Johnson. So it was here, in the train's huge comfy armchair-style seats, that I sat down to write my story set in Kosovo. I wanted to tell what I had learned about Kosovo, the war zone ('is it very dangerous?' was usually the first question people in the UK had asked me) where Dardan's uncle was killed at the roadside and Milošević's murders were still part of everyone's emotional

landscape; but also about Kosovo, the land of Adem and Xhezide, the land of strong tastes, farmer prime ministers, and Ana's lush garden – the land of honey.

It was only later that I was told that I wasn't alone in seeing this place as a land of such contradictions. In the artists' bar we liked to go to for Bob Dylan and Kosovan wine, and a cocktail called 'Green Stuff', a big guy with a safety pin through his eyebrow and a smile like a baby's came up to me to say he'd heard that I was interested in honey and its history here. Did I know that in Turkish, *bal* means 'honey' and *kan* means 'blood'. The story, almost certainly untrue, goes that when the Turks arrived in the Bal-kans, they immediately saw the potential of a fertile land where you can be happy sipping sweet nectar. Only when they had discovered how hard they would have to fight to subdue, and eventually lose, the territory, did they understand its second syllable. And that is how the region got its full name, the land of blood and honey.

20.
Ana's *slava* baklava

New Serbian vocabulary: *vreti* (simmer), *liti* (pour)

On the drive to a Serbian lesson early in January, Zorica explained that Ana had been busy that week because it had been her *slava*. The *slava* is the family saint day – a day of visiting and eating which is preceded by furious cooking including the baking of a special *slava* cake made with water sanctified by your priest. I knew that this water blessed on the *slava* is very precious for the family – as well as each member of the family taking three sips on the day itself, the water is saved so it can be dabbed on the forehead if anyone in the family falls ill later in the year. In every way, the *slava* is a day for setting the family up, in physical, social and spiritual capital for the months ahead. When the priest comes round, the oldest member of the family is invited to repeat the names of all members of the family, whether present or not, to receive a blessing.

I was sad not to have known about Ana's celebration, not to have taken part, not to have been invited. When we got to the house, Ana told me rather half-heartedly that you don't invite people to a *slava* – everyone knows which your family saint is, and thus on which day to visit you. I didn't know whether she was just making excuses, but I made up my mind to turn up on the day next time, and call her bluff.

But at least I hadn't missed out on the food. None of the special *slava* cake, but there was still baklava to spare, and before I started on the tedious Serbian grammar, I was allowed to indulge myself with one of its better nouns. Baklava is one of the unifying aspects of culture in Kosovo. Of course, it has its own history of conflict – it is originally a Turkish dish, and spread through both the Serbian and Albanian populations only with the spread of the Ottoman Empire after the fourteenth century. Yet it offers hope to a multi-culturalist that there might be a future when people from all communities in Kosovo could eat their celebratory food together: once when running training here I tried

to use my experience of ethnic conflict in inner-city London schools as a starting point with some ethnically-mixed Kosovan teachers. I mentioned the passions that could be raised by children trying spicy Pakistani food for the first time, or racist remarks when white British kids were offered Caribbean goat dishes, and asked the Kosovan teachers how they might handle a situation when a child brought in for a school party, for example, a dish from home that was unfamiliar, and perhaps unattractive to others in their class. They looked at me uncomprehendingly and somebody explained, 'but everyone would bring baklava.'

I have been offered a number of celebratory pieces of baklava here. Some, it must be said, have tasted like tracing paper in syrup. Ana's was fantastic and (because) you could taste the honey in it.

When I asked she dictated the recipe to me, a recipe handed down from her Gorani grandmother. The Goranis are Slav but in religion, Muslim, like most Albanians – and thus either uniquely placed to fit in with both the main ethnic groups here, or uniquely placed to be despised equally by both. They are known as the pastry-cooks of the Balkans and I had visited the area in Kosovo with the highest concentration of Gorani, the dramatic wooded hills and valleys of Dragash. We had stopped on our drive through and bought small sweet pastries in a little fly-blown shop, and driven on along tight hill roads where we caught glimpses of young girls in traditional Gorani dress – long frockcoats covered in sequins. I wished now that I had stayed longer, eaten more.

My version of Ana's recipe, to make approximately 30 pieces of baklava

Ingredients
330g filo pastry for baklava (Ana makes her own; there was no way I was going to do that. I removed the pastry I'd bought from its plastic wrapper, unfolding it carefully like a very old vellum book with pages that might easily tear)
125g butter, melted
230g honey

230g walnuts*, half of them ground, the other half chopped
Juice of half a lemon
Half a teaspoon vanilla flavouring

Preheat the oven to 200 degrees.
Lay out a sheet of the pastry. Slather it with melted butter and then lay
 on another sheet. Slather again. Repeat so the final pastry is 3 sheets
 thick.
Cover the bottom third of the pastry sheet stack with the walnuts and
 then roll all the pastry tightly into a cylinder. Repeat until you have
 used up all the pastry and nuts.
Grease a baking tin.
Cut the cylinder into lengths of 3-4cm and place each small cylinder
 in the baking tin, snuggling them together. Drizzle any remaining
 melted butter between each length and over all of it.
Turn down the oven to 150 degrees and bake the baklava at the bottom
 of the oven for an hour.
When the baklava is out of the oven, put the honey in a saucepan with
 a few tablespoons of water and bring to the boil.
Add the lemon juice and vanilla flavouring.
Pour the syrup over the baklava. Cool and serve.

Having tasted the pastry, I had even more motivation to note in
my diary when Ana's next *slava* would be. It was sooner than you might

---

* I had never tasted fresh walnuts until I came to Kosovo. I didn't even know that
to start with they have soft, bready flesh like a conker, and it is only after this has
been dried that you get the bitter, woody nut. In Islington I had only ever
bought walnuts not only pre-shelled, but pre-chopped. In Kosovo, I was given
them straight off the trees in the Ethnological Museum gardens; I once stopped
the car on the road out of Deçan and handed small change to a young boy with
eyes like coins, in exchange for a net bag of fresh walnuts, and saw as we drove
away how he waved the money at his brother still up the tree picking them.
    At the *kulla* in Dranoc I had even helped with selling walnuts myself,
writing out the labels for bagged nuts when the boy from next-door brought
them over to sell to the visitors at one of the cultural workshops. And it was in
Kosovo that it was explained to me that walnuts are an aid to virility. Certainly,
the boy in Dranoc is one of eight children.

think because every saint, and thus every family, has two separate days of celebration – the 'big' and the 'small' *slava* – each year. These were about six months apart; so, salivating for the sweetmeats, half a year later Rob and I turned up at Ana's house to see what we'd missed out on first time round.

We hadn't been offered an invitation this time, either, and I felt like a gatecrasher as we pulled up outside Ana's house. This would be the first time I'd seen Ana socially, rather than with the heavy textbook under my arm as entry ticket. Walking up her little path I realised that this would also be the first time I'd visited any Serb family socially. It felt like all the months using highlighter pen in that textbook with its inexplicable chapters on idioms were being put to the test today in so many ways. While I was still muttering to Rob, 'maybe we shouldn't have come without a definite invitation?' Ana came to the door and greeted us with an enthusiastic torrent of Serbian and smiles.

The tiny front room was packed. The mother-in-law was there, along with Ana's husband, their daughters, an uncle and his wife, some neighbours, a family from a nearby village. None of the other guests spoke English any better than I spoke Serbian. Ana's husband teaches at a Serbian university in the north of Kosovo and one of his colleagues was there, eager to talk to me about nineteenth-century world litera-ture. His passionate Serbian flowed around me, as bewildering as the *raki,* with only the occasional 'Flobber' or 'Hurter' or other dimly-recalled continental novelist to anchor me.

The table was full of food and we were gestured to fill our plates. There were salads and pies, meats, cheeses and the *ajvar* I'd seen being prepared here. No matter what I took, or how much of it, Ana's mother-in-law was offended. 'More, more,' she urged (and out of the corner of my eye I could see Ana's husband, bottle in hand, saying the same to Rob). Great slabs of cheese pie were ladled onto my plate. There was no chance of saving space for the baklava.

As I struggled through my carbohydrate, I saw Rob turning to kiss his host, Dragan. My heart sank.

But Rob is a pro. And, unlike me, this was not his first *slava,* having been to others with work colleagues. He was being embraced in some version of a loving cup that seems to be a traditional Serbian male toast, especially on *slavas*. Imagine *Auld Lang Syne* and the pose for pulling

Christmas crackers round a table. Throw in alcohol to the value of a Hogmanay's worth of whisky plus a Christmas dinner's worth of wine, and then picture two men kissing each other three times, trying to entwine arms and drink a toast from their own cup. Yes, it's messy.

Ana ignored all this with great determination and was still correcting my grammar as we talked. I asked her more about exactly what was being celebrated that day and she put on her teacher's voice.

'Your family saint is inherited from your father – like a surname.' Like a surname, when women marry they take on the saint of their husband. Within this, there seems to be some flexibility as to which of the saint's days you choose as your 'big *slava*' and which as the smaller celebration. She told me what happened when Dragan's brother decided he wanted his main *slava* to be on the date when the rest of the family was celebrating 'small'. When the brother came for the winter *slava* to Dragan and Ana's house, the centre for celebrating a *slava* because it was where their mother lived, the mother symbolically gave him half of the *slava* cake. From that point on his nuclear family's celebrations could happen separately, and out of synch with the rest of the family's.

'At the next *slava* at our house, when the priest came round to say the blessing and Dragan's mother recited the names of everyone in the family, including Dragan's brother, the priest said that blessing Dragan's brother and his children would cost extra now because they counted as a different family.' I ventured a small smile and Ana offered an even smaller one back. It seemed to me a great medieval story of clerical wiles, but I wasn't confident that Ana saw it the same way.

Sitting in Kosovo with Ana, who teaches local Serbian children in Serbian, using a Serbian curriculum in a school funded by the Belgrade government, it might have been tempting to make a political point after this story. About what happens when bits of a cake break off, parts of the whole secede. It always ends up costing more. I thought about my hives and what happened when the new queen was born and half the colony felt they had to take off to the nearest branch. I bit into my baklava and savoured it, with my mouth shut.

21.
Rite of passage

New Albanian vocabulary: *bukë e bletëve* (hive fondant, literally 'bread for bees')

My first, and only, direct contact with Kosovars before that day we'd landed at Pristina airport was with a refugee family who had arrived from Kosovo at my London school. The children were beautiful, motivated, bright, and passionate about their homeland. The eldest, aged ten at the time, told me that when she left school she wanted to train to do a job that would enable her to go back to Kosovo and help her people. At the age of twenty she is now at university in London and close to being able to fulfill that ambition. When her brother, Leart, heard that I was moving to live in Kosovo he said 'you'll like it – it's a proper country, with proper seasons.' Of course, Kosovo wasn't a proper country – it was a UN protectorate, or a province of Serbia, depending on your point of view – but the seasons are certainly properly distinguished from one another: a battle between the Mediterranean and the Siberian, with hot summers and cold winters.

I'd found some evidence to back up Leart's claim on the Kosovo statistics office website, one of the first routes for me to understand Kosovo. The Statistics Office offered such nuggets of information as land use (agriculture: 53%, forest: 41%, urban: 1%) and the percentage of homes with central heating (7%). But even more chilling, it told me that January's average temperature in Kosovo was 2.5 degrees. This year it had been even colder than that and the bees hadn't had the chance for a 'cleansing flight' – a trip out of the hive to evacuate their bowels. My book tells me that the temperature needs to be 14 degrees before they will leave.

Meanwhile, they had been bundled in a compact ball inside the hive all winter, fanning their wings to ventilate the space. The temperature of a beehive is the same as the human body and the bees work as a team to maintain this temperature. They take it in turns to be on

the outside of the ball where it is colder. When they are getting very cold they circulate into the centre of the ball where the accumulated body heat of thousands of bees warms them until it is time again for them to take their turn at the extremity, exposed to the winter. I imagine this being rather like a huge tremulous human heart circulating its life-force and pulsing instinctively, despite the cold, in the hope of spring.

Adem had called to say that because of the cold, the bees needed food. He explained to me about the special bee food available in the shops as a slab of fondant. It is mainly sugar but includes some vitamins and medication to strengthen the bees against disease.

'The bees need you to bring some this weekend.'

This is the payback for having harvested my honey during the summer. If I had let the honeycomb alone then the bees would now be surviving on the food they had painstakingly gathered and refined during the warmer days. That, of course, is why they had gone to all that trouble. Naturally, when we harvested we had left them some honey to keep them going, and in a warmer winter perhaps what we left would have been enough. But at this point, without me adding more energy to the hives in the form of the fondant, my bees would die before the weather turned warm enough for flowers to bloom and for the colony to find and use new nectar.

Through Facebook I've 'met' backyard beekeepers from around the world. One of my virtual friends (who felt a lot less virtual after I posted her a plastic pot of my honey, and she was able to email me from Seattle with comments on its flavour) would never use fondant sugar supplements – she tells me she just limits the honey she harvests from the hives. Taken to extremes, this seems to turn the bees into little more than pets – creatures you look after but from whom you take nothing except their company. A beehive is, of course, the ultimate garden accessory, offering beautiful sounds and scents, movement and intriguing close-up insights into an awe-inspiring world, as well as the practical benefits of pollination. But if I was honest, and especially since the garden in question wasn't even my own garden, it was the honey I was after. So I went and bought the fondant.

Adem and I robed up in our protective veils and approached the hives. We lifted the lid off the box and as we puffed smoke at the

alarmed bees, we placed the fondant slab over the top of the frames of honeycomb. I felt rather like I was icing an exquisite cake.

It's possible to make your own fondant, one of my books tells me. And the recipe, without those added vitamins and medication, sounds tempting.

Ingredients:
1 part liquid honey to two parts icing sugar

Method
Add the sugar very slowly to the honey so that it forms a paste.

As we walked away from the newly candied hive, I felt a fluttering on my chest. It continued, and developed into a tickle. Doing some would-be decorous investigations with my hand up my protective suit, I discovered two bees wandering the skin over my ribs. I tried to brush them carefully away, and succeeded in putting off one of them from any more investigations of my underwear. The other was more intrepid, and by the time it had got caught beneath the underwire of my bra, it had been scared into a misguided attempt to defend the rest of its colony, and had stung me. The sting gets ripped out of the belly of the bee, so it would have died in the process, at just about the moment that I was saying 'ow!'

The Greek myth is that the ability to sting was given by Zeus to the bee in gratitude for having been nourished with honey as a child, but that when a bee then stung Zeus himself, the god decreed that the creatures should die whenever they used their sting. I could sympathise with the old god. Yes, I owed these bees who had provided for my baklava and yoghurt and teatime toast, but did I really deserve this?

I had never been stung by a bee before, so I waited with some anxiety to discover whether I was among the percentage of the population who go into anaphylactic shock from a sting.

I am not. There was an intense burning sensation on my skin though, right near my heart. The poet in me wondered if this was what true love was like, the bee like some dark blundering Cupid.

Xhezide was less bothered by any of that, and when she saw what had happened, she shooed me into the house and then the back room, away from the curious gaze of Lavdim. With the beekeeper suit rucked up, she hurried with tweezers to pull out the sting. A bee's sting can continue pumping venom for up to a minute, so seconds saved now would reduce the time my skin would need to heal. She was swift and accurate. She held up in her tweezers a sting that looked like a tiny gramophone needle.

Then she brought vinegar to ease the pain on the puncture. She wouldn't let me go out again. I smiled bravely. 'I don't think it's likely that I'll be stung twice in one day.' But Xhezide insisted. I learned later that she was right to have protected me – with their keen sense of smell the rest of the hive would have known immediately from the traces on my clothes that I had been stung, and from that they would have assumed that I was an enemy, and would have attacked again.

So I stayed away from the rest of the colony, but I thought of them, as I carried the tiny throb of pain around with me, close to my chest, for the rest of that day. It was a badge of pride – the vegetarian bee-keeper's equivalent of being bloodied with the fox tail after a hunt.

Xhezide looked after me attentively for the rest of our visit with a mixture of embarrassment and culpability, as if one of the children had misbehaved. We were sat down for glasses of her home-made plum squash – cool and tart and very refreshing. In my mind it will always be associated with the unnecessary death of one of my bees, an apiarist's coming of age.

22.
Plum *kompot*, and the soup that saved Xhezide's life

New Albanian vocabulary: *papuçe* (slippers)

The bee-sting had subsided but I still had the mark to show where it had been, and the associated memory of the taste of plum squash, when Xhezide rang me a few days later. None of my friends in Kosovo ever seemed to have enough credit on their phone to be able to pay for calls; when people rang off straight away you called them back. Among some of my friends elaborate systems had developed for these missed calls: two in a row meant 'see you at the bar', three in a row meant 'see you at the café'. But it seemed Xhezide just wanted a chat, and as ever she asked when we would next be coming to visit.

'Oh yes, we will come over soon,' I promised, going through in my mind the commitments that we had over the next few days. Because of the driving our trips could only be made when not only I but also Rob was free, and I often felt with Xhezide and Adem that I just couldn't meet their expectations of friendship – in terms of quantity if not quality.

'I'm really looking forward to it,' I said, trying to make up in enthusiasm what I was lacking in distance. 'I keep thinking about that lovely plum squash. Would you show me how to make it, when I next come?' She seemed interested in the idea. I had been Adem's pupil till now – maybe she was pleased to have a turn at tutelage.

I had a missed call notification on my phone again a few days later – it was her, so I called straight back.

'When are you coming to visit?' she asked. I repeated myself with added fluster, explaining that I couldn't be sure, that we were still waiting to find a time when Rob was free. 'Well, what about me and Mirlinda coming to you?' she suggested.

Was this what the little Cupid bee had brought me? It was cer-

tainly a new kind of relationship. This would be the first time that Xhezide and I would be alone without any men – neither Rob nor Adem – as chaperone. Under these new circumstances, I would lose my position as honorary man for the purposes of conversation, food portions and social rhythms. Instead, Xhezide would be in the sacred position of guest, with me running in and out of my kitchen to serve her.

The reciprocal visit would fit with her holding of the upper hand in language, for example – it was always me who was fumbling and approximating my way to communication. And she is older than me – not only in the perhaps hundreds of years which divide her experience on a smallholding in the least developed country in Europe from my British university education and the information and options I have as a result. She is ten years older than me, and that counts for a lot in Kosovo.

What's more, as she taught me how to make the plum squash, we would be based in the kitchen. The kitchen is not my natural element. I love food and I am fascinated by eating and cooking new things; the dining table may be my natural element, or the sofa, curled up with a recipe book. I am willing to spend large amounts of time trying out or improving recipes or foods that add to my repertoire but I do not do this on a regular basis. I have no children, and I have an independent, competent, liberal partner who cooks for himself or for us both, or will have a bowl of cornflakes for supper without complaint. The daily grind of washing up, the endless chopping of uninteresting vegetables, the monitoring of the processes of putrefaction in my fridge... these are things which I am lucky that my lifestyle and income free me from. My cleaner comes twice a week, my supermarket sells me more semi-prepared food than it should, my partner helps – and as a result, I have no feeling of the kitchen as my domain, as it is for so many women across the world. Instead, I probably have a residual sense of guilt and inadequacy attached to this space – a place where I could, should do more, spend more time, be less lazy, maybe even more feminine?

I knew from what I had seen as I had sat watching (from my man's position on the couch) Xhezide move around her sink and stove, that she is competent in ways that I am not; that she is spotlessly clean and particular where I am spattered and make-do; that she has the speed that comes with practice where I am clumsy.

This cooking lesson was going to change our relationship in so many healthy ways.

'If you have sugar and a big cooking pot, Elizabeth, I will just bring the plums,' she said.

On the day we'd set I woke early and went immediately down to the kitchen. I was learning to live like Xhezide.

I started scrubbing. I wanted the work surfaces to be gleaming, last night's washing up (OK, and the dishes from the night before that) done and put away: I wanted a tasty meal prepared in advance. At least for those few hours of bullying my kitchen into shape, I wanted to be Xhezide.

To reinforce all the middle-class guilt I had already about the state of my kitchen, and my competency in it, my cleaner turned up just before Xhezide arrived. Miradija normally came on a day between Sunday and Friday, at a time to suit her, so there was no reason why she shouldn't have arrived at this moment, but it added an extra layer to the complex dynamics of my kitchen. She was bemused to see me working at the sink, but pitched in. I still didn't feel the space was ready for scrutiny by the time Xhezide and her daughter arrived but I was able to give a great and genuine smile to greet them.

Xhezide had brought a plastic bottle she had filled with milk for me – she had milked the cow that morning. Doing the maths, I realised that this meant that as I was putting on my deodorant and preparing for my novelty stint of housework, Xhezide must already have been dressed, and squatting against the animal's flank getting the milk to bring for me. I had not yet learned to live like her.

She had brought some of her homemade cheese too – the sour white slabs that I found difficult to eat because their smell is so close to milk that has turned. We put the cheese on a dish and its intense stink filled my kitchen. It was going to be an intimate exchange, this working alongside Xhezide in preparing food – learning from her, making my house smell like hers.

She was an easy collaborator though, bearing with my strange ways (the fact that I wanted to weigh everything, write things down; 'it's in my head,' she said, laughing. I haven't yet discovered whether Xhezide is literate). Out of one of her bags she tumbled a gelid lump of bruise-coloured flesh. I was reminded of kidneys, and worried that maybe this

was another contribution she had brought from her animals for me to put in my fridge. It started to drip on the work surface.

'And what is this?' I asked.

It was the plums.

Working together in the kitchen turned out to be the perfect way to talk to each other. Other women have presumably known this for centuries, but I felt like I was only just being initiated into a female ritual. As things steamed and bubbled around us, we mopped fluids together, tested the softness of the food I was cooking for lunch, stewed and sweated. Like a visit together to a Turkish bath, it brought frankness.

She started talking about the war. I had heard something of the family's narrative before: with Adem, we had heard about the damage to the house, about the tree – he had pointed to one we could see in the distance from where we had sat eating lunch together outside one day – which still bears the bullet marks from when their neighbour was tied up and shot.

But I was now learning about the women's war. 'In slippers,' she said, gesturing at her feet. When paramilitaries arrived at their door the family had been forced out of their house with only the clothes they had on and had spent three days camping in the mountains before moving to a village where they had family connections and believed they would be safer. Adem had told Rob and me about this with his little shrug, as if to say in the face of ethnic cleansing, 'well, what can you do?' He hadn't mentioned the slippers.

Miradija joined in the discussion. Standing hands on hips, with the pot lid rattling over the plum *kompot*, she only added to the sense of a community of women freed to talk. Despite her work in my house every week we had never spoken like this before. She wanted to talk about the washing arrangements when you are hiding out in the mountains, evading an army you believe is going to kill you. Many people had left home on their tractors, she explained, and so the women could get undressed behind the trailer of the tractor, and have a quick wash without any men seeing.

I had heard similar stories of strategy in the war before, but they had focused on offensives and movements to take control of this or that mountain pass; no-one had ever told me before how the Albanian

Xhezide

refugees or internally displaced persons kept both their dignity and their bodies clean.

Xhezide talked about the sleeping arrangements too – in the house where they finally found shelter with relatives, they were sleeping 24 to a room. And she told me about her soup: 'they loved my soup, and I made sure I got up early every morning to make it for everyone. I knew that we wouldn't all be able to stay in that packed room forever, but I thought that my soup might earn us a place among the lucky ones.'

'It was a terrible time,' agreed Miradija. They recited the stories of the things that happened in their country – of the old people, the disabled, the helpless who were killed and beaten. 'Even women,' they said. 'They killed them, injured them…' The third thing they did was not said, not even in our newly liberated conversation. Like these two women, the majority of the Albanian women raped by Serbian police or paramilitary gangs in Kosovo have not spoken out loud the words that tell what was done to them. The consensus is that there is too much risk for the family's honour, the family's future – so the needs of the individual women, or their children, are sacrificed.

I asked about Adem's bees. What happened to them while the family was away?

'Oh no, Adem didn't keep bees before the war.' But Xhezide told me about how he started, finding a swarm in a tree trunk. 'He chopped down the tree, either side of where the bees had built the hive, and covered the ends with blankets. Then he decanted them.'

With the memory of my sting still fresh in my mind – and still visible on my chest in the shower that morning – I didn't believe the simplicity of the word 'decanted' did justice to the procedure involved. This story was as understated as the narrative of their experience during the war. There was nothing I could say to it. I stood quietly, listening.

Xhezide's family came back to their home after the NATO bombardment and the withdrawal of the Serbian troops.

'Serbs had stayed there, had burned part of it and looted the rest when they left. Most of my trousseau had gone – the tablecloths and mats and baby clothes and all the other needlework.' I knew that the stack of needlework in an Albanian trousseau was supposed to be everything the bride needs for the rest of her life. At the bottom of the trunk she brings with her to her husband's house is a shroud.

'I found some tablecloths left behind but they were torn and stained. The soldiers had used them to clean their guns.'

The plums were still bubbling away on the stove but the meal I'd been preparing was ready for us to eat so we sat down to an early lunch. In this new configuration around my dining table, and with Miradija now gone to her other job, young Mirlinda took a bigger role in the conversation. She had helped Rob with the literary competition he was organizing. He had needed fliers distributed around the city in the places that young people hang out, so we had asked her (and Adem) whether she would accept a small sum of money in exchange for handing them out in a list of locations we'd identified. She was now interested in what response we'd had from the competition, and seemed genuinely pleased for us – for herself as part of our team – that we had had a response that was ten times greater than our target.

I asked whether she herself had submitted anything – when she had come to the house to collect the fliers she had showed me a fragment of love poetry she had written which I had thought really powerful. When I'd asked her then whether it was written for someone in particular she had told me about a boy she'd met, but about whom she hadn't told her parents – and I wished I hadn't asked.

Her mother took this chance to talk about Mirlinda's poetry writing.

'She's always doing it. She hides it and all the poems she writes are about love. But she's too young to be writing about things like that.' Mirlinda gave me a conspiratorial glance and I wished again that I didn't know about the boyfriend.

We finished our lunch, and went to check on the cooling plum juice, which smelt deliciously fragrant. Then we went out into the garden and Xhezide admired my few flowers that were out. 'I can't plant bulbs on my land,' she explained, 'because the cow eats them.'

It was time for her to go but she asked if she could help with the washing up. I was already embarrassed by the way she had washed as we went, cleaning and replacing all the utensils we used for the plum *kompot*.

'No, no,' I insisted, 'you're an honoured guest' – and she was finally persuaded. We gave each other close hugs at the gate, and then she set off back to the cow and the kitchen that smelt a little like mine now.

The next day, she telephoned. I rang her back. We didn't really have anything to say to each other, but it was nice to talk, in the way that the morning after a good night out you have the instinct to call up the people you were drinking with and exchange memories of how it went, build the narrative of the events together. Or perhaps check that the bonds forged in one context still endure in another. Xhezide pretended she hadn't told me how to prepare fresh plums for freezing. I thanked her, as if I hadn't already written it down. We said what a great day we had had together. I asked whether she'd yet had time to plant the bulbs I'd given her in a pot. We said our goodbyes. Just before I rang off she asked 'and was it really alright, about the washing up? I've been worried – I really wanted to stay and help you.' It seemed it was as hard for Xhezide to learn about living like me, as it was for me to learn about living like her.

Xhezide's plum squash (*kompot*)

Take just over a kilo of frozen plums (with the stones taken out in autumn before freezing).
Put them in a large cooking pot and add approximately enough water to all but cover the plums.
Simmer for about 45 minutes.
Top up the water that has evaporated at this point, and continue simmering.
After a further 15 minutes, add 100g sugar (or more, to taste).
After a further 15 minutes, remove from the heat.
Strain and bottle the juice – serve chilled.
The remaining plums can be used to make the 'pistil' style jam.
For a more intense flavour, simmer for longer and/ or do not add extra water during the cooking.

23.
Hazelnuts in honey for a ladies' night

New Albanian vocabulary: *rrëmojcë* (toothpick)

As the date of my second birthday in Kosovo approached, friends asked 'what are you going to do to celebrate this year?'

Rob's contract for his work in Kosovo had initially been for one year with Prime Minister Çeku, but now he had secured a year's extension, even with a new Prime Minister voted in after the elections (Çeku had pledged that if independence had not come by the time of the election he wouldn't stand again. Bizarrely – for any politician, especially one in Kosovo – he had honoured that pledge. He had been succeeded by another man with good KLA credentials, but a very different personal style; Hashim Thaçi, wartime codename: The Snake). When the news of the extension had come through we had had animated discussions about what more we could do with this new opportunity, our second wind. But the extension brought challenges too; when you think you're only going to be in a place for a year, there's a temptation to use up all your ideas on a metaphorical and literal party splurge. I'd done that in the museum the previous November.

After a lot of thinking, my idea for celebrating my second Kosovan birthday was to hold a party in another one of Kosovo's little-known sites. Older than the Ethnological Museum – by at least 250 million years – the Gadime caves are a short drive outside Pristina. They hold stalactites, stalagmites, columns, rare star-shaped crystal formations, and combinations of these which, as you are shown during the guided tour of the caves, have grown in the form of the map of Kosovo, Scanderbeg's eagle, Scanderbeg's beard – or other parts of Scanderbeg's anatomy which are pointed out only to the men in the tour group. When we had visited earlier in the year, Rob had been laughing in a rather wearied way for much of our walk round the caves in the company of the over-imaginative, over-confiding elderly man guiding us.

That visit had been in the summer, but we were assured that the caves have a constant year-round temperature of 16°C. What had been refreshing coolness in August would be a welcome way to warm up on a Kosovan winter evening. The only logistical challenge was the distance of the caves from Pristina. A number of my guests didn't have cars, or would be wanting to drink during the evening, so I had to organise transport. One idea led to another, and I succumbed once again to the temptation to splurge all your party ideas in one evening – and booked not just a minibus but also a limo for the night.

The plan was that Rob and I would drive to the caves during the afternoon and set everything up. I would then return by taxi to Pristina, put on a party frock, and get into the limousine with nine suitably glamorous girlfriends to drink Baileys and eat chocolates during the ride to the caves. At university a friend of mine spent much of her time designing activities that she believed no-one else in the world could be doing at the same moment as her – living her life as a kind of googlewhack. I wondered whether drinking Baileys in a Kosovan limousine on the way to a party in a cave would count.

Whether it did or not, in the end I myself never qualified. Despite my carefully planned itinerary, Pristina's famous fog rolled in and took over. Most significantly, this risked my most important party guest – Rob – being able to get to the party at all. He had been in Vienna with the Prime Minister taking part in independence negotiations. Arriving at the airport to take the flight that would bring him home for bedtime the night before my birthday, he was told that no flights were landing at Pristina.

The first I knew of it was a call from the Ambassador while I was mulling wine ready for the party the next day.

'You're not to worry, but Rob is going to be a bit late back. He's not even sure he can get as far as Belgrade. But the Prime Minister knows it's your birthday tomorrow – they're doing everything they can to get Rob home in time.'

I finished mulling and put myself to bed, thinking that I mustn't make a fuss, but wishing that I could wake up next to Rob on the morning of my birthday.

I was woken many hours later. It was dark outside, but there was someone in the room. He smelt of diesel and cigarette smoke and fog.

An overnight bus from Belgrade had brought me the only birthday present I really wanted.

Rob was with me all the rest of the day. So was the fog. That afternoon in the bad weather all the necessary journeys to and from the caves – for me, the taxi, the caterers, a saxophonist – took longer than planned or didn't happen at all. At six thirty I was still waiting for a taxi to take me back to Pristina, as the dramatic fog swirled around the car park for the caves. If the taxi didn't come in two minutes...

It didn't come in two minutes, and I realised that I was stranded at the caves in the jumper and skirt I'd been wearing all day, with a bottle of Bailey's in my bag, while nine glamorous girlfriends were waiting for me in a limousine in Pristina. I phoned Alisa, my friend from the museum who was one of the women due to be there in the limo.

'Where are you, Elizabeth?'

'You'll have to set off without me' Or the chocolates, I realised. I put down the phone. And then I burst into tears. The daughter of the family who owns the caves, struggling with the last-minute repairs to the generator, saw that some social disaster had struck, and came over to comfort me. Mopping my nose, I asked if I could borrow a bathroom to put some make up on and somehow transform myself to party hostess.

She managed to find me not only a bathroom, but one in the house of a beautician friend of hers, who delighted in a *Grease*-style makeover of the smudged Englishwoman who had been deposited on her doorstep. I emerged from her house with bouffant hair, *two* colours of lipstick, and eye make-up I had to wipe off just a little bit.

As the caves filled with sixty people echoing along with a saxophone, I forgot my girly trauma. Almost everyone I'd invited had braved the fog and the directions to get to the party. There were more Kosovars than 'internationals', and for most people (both local and foreign) it was their first visit to the caves. The teacher in me enjoyed that. Only a few people hadn't been able to come – Adem, Xhezide and Mirlinda had politely said they couldn't make it, and I'd realised how much it would cost them to get from the village. Also absent were some of my friends who were abroad, and a friend who suffers from claustrophobia.

Even when the inevitable power cut came in the middle of the party, and we discovered that that generator never had been fixed, the

250 candles Rob had placed in every available rock crevice saved us from terrifying blackout. It was an unforgettable party.

But I felt that life still owed me some Baileys.

And so it was that a while later I organised a reprise version – and one which three of my friends who had been out of Kosovo for my birthday itself were able to attend. Many of the women who came had supported my honey habit in some way: Saskia, the German friend who had taken me to the Xhonaj folk festival and screeched to a halt so I could jump out en route and buy my first skep Alisa, the guide who had first encouraged me to return to the Ethnological Museum, Naxhije, who had been photographer in residence at the museum, and was now a friend who shared my croissant habit. The wife of Gazi, my Albanian teacher, came too, as well as the beautiful heroine of the *kulla,* Cindy. With us was my American friend known to my family as Coriander Sue because of her request whenever I went abroad for me to bring back the fresh herb you can't find in Kosovo, and so was a young Kosovan fashion designer I had got to know, and a politician I'd met through Rob's work, along with Mary, the British doctor working on women's health in Pristina and the villages beyond. We had no caves, and we had no limousine, but we made up for it at my house with drink, chocolate, very classy outfits – and honeyed snacks.

I worried that chocolate might not be sufficient to sustain ten ladies for a long night, and developed a menu of possibly limo-style snacks to keep us going. Along with the caviar on rye bread, the courgette korma petit fours, the salted popcorn with Nutella dip, and the Eton Mess in tiny Kosovan tea glasses, I brought out some of my honey. I soaked a packet of hazelnuts in the honey during the day, and provided cocktail sticks for serving.

We ate our way through all the honey, we chatted, and we played frivolous games. We played one game, too, that was not so frivolous – when conversation turned inevitably to Kosovo's independence, we ended up placing bets on what the date for a declaration by the government might be.

Late that night, a group of women tiptoed home on unsteady high heels with sticky chins – and crossed fingers, for at least one of the bets to come right.

Ingredients:
100g hazelnuts
enough honey to cover them

Method
Pour the honey over the hazelnuts and leave to soak overnight.
Serve with cocktail sticks.

24.
Advice on how to eat honey in the morning: independence for Kosovo

---

New Albanian vocabulary: *njohje* (recognition), *diell me dhëmbë* (sun with teeth)

Independence speculation was growing. On Friday 15 February, Rob came home from work with a posh envelope, lined with tissue paper like a box of chocolates. When I opened it I found a very precious gift – an invitation from the President of Kosovo, for us to attend the concert to celebrate Kosovan Independence. All the details of time and venue twirled in italics around the card. Only the 'date' section was left blank.

The information to complete that blank section had been missing for a very long time. Not only the month but even the year had been a matter for speculation ever since we had arrived in Kosovo. At the political briefing we were given by a British Office researcher on our first day, in June 2006, we had been told that 'final status' (the phrase sounded chilling) should be resolved by December that year. In December, it became clear that the New Year would pass without a decision, but the Kosovars were asked for patience.

In February 2007, Martti Ahtisaari, the UN Special Envoy to Kosovo, presented his 'package' of recommendations for the final status of Kosovo, which included, in its covering letter only, the word 'independence'. But neither independence, nor any other final status solution was agreed that month, nor in the weeks that passed. When Bush and Putin met at Camp David in early July 2007, experts predicted that Kosovo would be part of their discussion, and of the compromise they would reach.

But it wasn't. Instead, a new team was brought together – a new set of heads to bang against the brick wall of Belgrade, Pristina, and Russia's unfaltering stance on Kosovo's future. Russia had only grown more

powerful during the time I had been waiting for independence; the price of oil had gone up. The 'troika' of representatives of the EU, the US and Russia met with delegations from both Serbia and Kosovo over a period of four months. Rob went to Vienna in Çeku's entourage for some of these discussions, and came back pessimistic. The troika finally shared his view: there was no room for compromise, no common ground, and no way to keep the resolution of Kosovo's final status part of a UN process.

Elections in Kosovo and then elections in Serbia caused further delays. I felt I had waited long enough for this declaration of independence, which was now being spoken of, prepared for – but not yet confirmed officially – as 17 February 2008. I mentioned my impatience one day to the owner of the corner shop. His answer in Albanian translates to something like 'you think *you*'ve been waiting a long time?' He reminded me that he'd waited not just all his lifetime, but for lifetime after lifetime – generation after generation as his family had fought, waited, lobbied, endured, then fought some more for this day.

So there was a mixed sense in Kosovo as February wore on. When I asked one of my more passionately Albanian Kosovar friends what he was going to do to celebrate independence, he said, 'not much'. There were many people objecting to the terms (such as the positive discrimination for Serbs and the disproportionate weight of their votes in the Assembly) that Kosovo had accepted in order for their declaration of independence to be likely to be recognised by other countries; he said he felt it was all too little too late.

And, after all, the intention to declare independence still hadn't been announced. For reasons that were variously alleged to be conspiracy, cowardice, or cleverness, it was only a rumour that was identifying the big day as the 17th.

Many people still couldn't believe it was really going to happen.

On Saturday 16 February, Rob and I drove to Ana's village for a Serbian lesson. Ana was clearly terrified. We had always been careful not to discuss politics, and she still said nothing against the independence of Kosovo itself, but she did speak softly about her fears of the violence she thought might erupt against non-Albanian minorities from Kosovo Albanians cock-a-hoop that their centuries-old dream had been realised. Her shaky muttering answers to questions were a sobering reminder of

the implications of independence for some Kosovars. After the lesson, as we drove out of her little village inhabited only by Serbs, I wondered what the people we passed were thinking when they saw the British numberplates on our car. It was no secret that the British were carefully nudging Kosovo into independence from Serbia.

As we passed the café, people turned their heads to watch us go. They had probably done this every time we drove here, and they probably did it to every car that passed, but I was jittery now, catching Ana's nerves. I felt very conspicuous through the windows of our car, and I remembered the stories I'd heard of stones being thrown at vehicles with the wrong number plates in the wrong part of Kosovo. It seems a ridiculous gesture when I look back at it now, but with an uninformed instinct for self-defence I reached behind me and picked up my hat from the back seat. I put it on, pulling the brim down low over my eyes. Rob shifted his glance from the road.

'What are you doing?'

'I thought that my eyes might be protected from broken window glass this way.'

We drove on in silence and I wondered what went through Ana and Zorica's minds whenever they came to visit us in central Pristina.

Our journey from Ana's that day was taking us beyond Pristina. We were heading for a wonderful bookshop we had heard about in a corner of Kosovo that particularly needs wonderful concepts. The shop is in the centre of the southern (Albanian) half of the ethnically-divided-town-of-Mitrovica. The journalists' epithet has attached itself to the town almost as effectively as the stuttering spelling of it – *Mitrovicë/a* – which awkwardly mixes both the Albanian and Serbian endings, as is politically correct, given its awkwardly mixed population.

But once we'd joined the main road, the journey to Blackbird Books seemed less threatening. It was like watching a smile spread across a country. At first there was just the occasional car hooting its horn jubilantly the way we were used to hearing at Kosovan weddings (though of course this was really a divorce). The horns grew louder, more confident, more numerous as the miles and the minutes passed by. There were ever-increasing numbers of people in small groups, larger groups, small crowds, singing in the streets, cars flying flags, buildings flying flags, banners of congratulation and triumph all whipped by a winter wind.

The flags were mainly the black Albanian double-headed eagle on a red background – appropriate enough for the 92 per cent of the population who are Albanians, but sounding a slightly sour note to anyone hoping that this was a celebration of a sustainably multi-ethnic Kosovo. At that point, however, there was no other flag that could be identified as Kosovan. From a public competition in which my rather fine red, black and blue fountain was not accepted, a shortlist had been drawn up. But who is going to celebrate by flying a shortlist?

Nevertheless, it was not only eagles fluttering around Blackbird Books. Alongside the Albanian flag was the NATO emblem, there were stars with stripes as well as on the blue background of Europe, and a satisfying number of Union Jacks. One Pristina taxi company had all of its cabs flying a flag at each wing mirror – the Albanians' on the left and the United Kingdom's on the right. In all, there were probably more Union Jacks flying in one place than I'd seen since Charles and Diana's wedding. A poster series had been pasted up across the capital with the Union Jack and the positive if slightly bewildering slogan 'The association friends of USA, friends of President Clinton. THANK YOU We Albanians will not forget what have done for us the Britanic friend people and his aleats.' The poster was sponsored by a fuel company who said they sell 'ooil', and a language school who perhaps hadn't worked closely with their co-sponsors recently.

And there were more flags still going up. We saw people at the side of the road, worrying about how best to tuck theirs into car doors, and tableaux like the front garden where a man worked with his three-year-old son who solemnly held the hammer while his dad forced a flagpole into the freezing ground.

Some people were doing a roaring trade. Sellers of flags, of course. But also stalls with red and black wristbands, ashtrays, lighters, T-shirts. My favourite T-shirt had a picture of the unlovely Adem Jashari, a local thug turned nationalist hero when he held out for three days in his compound of family houses against the disproportionate fire power of the Yugoslav army. Photos of Jashari in other contexts leave me cold, but this one instead gave me goosebumps. The slogan said '*bac, u krye*'. '*Bac*' is a term of respect for an old man, for which we disrespectful English have no translation. 'Sir' is too formal; 'dad' too familiar. The rest of the slogan translates as 'job done'. It gave me goosebumps I suppose because

it was wonderful to think that the job might be done. Not that the Serbs were finally beaten (though that was one way of reading it), but that all that fighting and dying – which seemed by implication to be glorified whenever people hung a picture of Jashari in their office or home – really was over.

We discovered when we reached Mitrovica that Blackbird Books, by contrast, was not doing a roaring trade. There was a power cut and the door didn't open properly. When the guy inside had tugged at it to let us in I explained our reason for coming. Firstly, and most simply, we had heard that this was a place where young literary Mitrovica hangs out. And we wanted to reach young literary Mitrovica because of the literary competition Rob was organising, for which he wanted as wide a range of entries as possible. So we handed over a brick of leaflets about the competition, and explained our second interest in the Blackbirds. We had heard that the shop operated as a library, exchange, and market. Some of the second-hand books and DVDs were available to read on the sofas and chairs provided; some were available to swap (we had brought an English translation of some Albanian stories we had been given recently, but which we already owned a copy of. It turned out that the shop had one already too), and others to buy. I was tempted by *The Time Traveler's Wife* – the most wonderful book I had read in 2007, and one I would give as a present to anyone I really liked. But we were told that the person in charge today wasn't really 'authorised' to sell us anything. He was only standing in for someone who wouldn't be back for some hours, and the organiser of the shop was away in America, his home.

I was sad that the owner wasn't in – I had heard that he was a bee-keeper. But for now it was a cold February day, with all the relevant people away, and our money and our book swap being refused, so we decided we should leave, with our Albanian short stories still in our bag, throwing ourselves back into living the last chapter of the lengthy narrative of Kosovo's quest for independence.

But back in Pristina, there was still no news of anything definite for the next day, despite the adrenaline running high in everyone we spoke to. We dealt with it in our own ways; Rob went out with friends, into Pristina's hubbub to drink and talk (the same conversation over and over; would it be tomorrow? How would it be done? Might the cele-

brations get out of hand? Which countries would recognise Kosovo's independence once it was declared? Who would be first? How many EU states would recognise? Another *raki*?). I stayed at home, feeling tension tingle and tighten in every fibre of my body. I had no appetite, and no concentration. I would have been terrible company.

We woke the next morning with the same sense of uncertain jubilation around us. Making notes as I lay in bed at 10 am, I had a sense that I might end up looking like Michael Fish in 1987, gesturing benignly at his weather map. And what was there to say? So far, nothing had happened.

Except the black birds, perhaps like harbingers of historical significance. They perched on the roof overhanging our window; they tapped with their fearsome beaks on the satellite dish I could see from the bed. They came up close to the glass and looked cold – there were icicles suspended above them from the eaves, and each of their movements stirred up flurries of the powdery settled snow that swirled along with what was already falling in a light gusty wind.

There was only one fact of everything that I had read on the internet so far that day that, despite the ghost of Michael Fish, I trusted to turn out to be true, on this day when anything could happen. That was the online weather forecast that told me that we would have a high of –5 degrees, and a low of –11. So far, the day was what the Albanians call 'sun with teeth' – a stunning bright sunlight glittering on the snow-covered roofs that I could see across the street.

For the rest, who knew what would happen? There was the sense of being at the beginning of a slow crescendo though the only music I had heard since waking up was the solitary wail of a passing car playing a patriotic Albanian song. Since it passed, I'd heard nothing else. There had been three fireworks so far, set off at intervals of thirty minutes. You couldn't see the stars against the sky's brilliance: this was just pissing in the wind.

So perhaps it was more like the sense of taking your seats as the orchestra tunes up for what will eventually be the start of a crescendo. We had our invitation for the Kosovo Philharmonic's Independence Day celebration concert, and we were assuming that it would take place that evening. By then, I hoped, the music would be deafening.

And what does one do at the start of a day like this? Ordinary

things seemed banal; grand gestures not yet appropriate. It was, after all, only 10 am.

I put down the computer and looked through the pile next to my bed for a book. There was one that I had been meaning to finish since September 2006. I rejected the Albanian books, the thrillers, the parochial English paperbacks which all felt wrong for the moment. But picking up the Booker prizewinner that I somehow hadn't managed to get through right to the end, I sat and read *The Sea*, uninterrupted for an hour. This was a day for finishing off overdue business.

Later

By 1pm we had logged onto the internet and discovered that the Prime Minister of Kosovo had summoned the deputies to the Kosovan Assembly for an extraordinary 'extraordinary' session.

Things were moving forward. But there was still nothing to *do* yet. Even the most patriotic Kosovar would find it hard to celebrate the calling of a parliamentary session, however extraordinary.

We turned on the television, and channel-hopped between a variety of presenters all seeming to grapple with the same problem. Some channels had opted for traditional music accompanied by large ladies in traditional dress. Other channels were showing uncommentated cheap footage of the growing mob of flags in the main streets of Pristina. I skipped from one channel to the other (via the scantily clad Channel 39 that also goes for uncommentated cheap footage) and found the channel showing a previously prepared montage of 'the road to independence' including footage from the nineties, and the stages of the attempts at consensus in the recent round of talks. There were the civil resistance movement rallies of the 1990s, President Rugova, the intellectual with his bohemian scarf flicked over one shoulder, elected in illegal polls Serbia would not recognise; his declaration of independence in 1991 which no country recognised, and which therefore led to nothing but intensification of the Serb government's oppression. There was the grim footage of civilian massacres that had drawn the world's attention to Kosovo. Clinton, Blair, Milošević, Madeline Albright. The KLA's campaigns, with the young heroes' faces staring out from under camouflage caps sometimes recognisable as slick suited politicians I'd seen more recently. The Rambouillet agreement which was supposed to

bring Serb military personnel out of Kosovo and allow NATO
observers, Serbia's refusal to sign, the NATO bombardment which
lasted three months and left Belgrade and Serbian strategic installations
crippled, and caused tragic civilian casualties. And then the arrival of
the UN and NATO by ground into Kosovo, and the political process
that had lasted so unexpectedly long. Coming back to this montage as
I channel-hopped I was occasionally panicked by seeing international
or local politicians going apparently live to camera with statements such
as 'we do not think there will be independence this year.'

I was saved from the choppy television waves by a telephone call.
Valon from the Ethnological Museum was reiterating an invitation he
had issued airily when Rob had bumped into him the previous evening.
'My mother has prepared an Independence Day baklava; we are inviting you to share it.'

This was perfect. My fears about independence day had included
the worry that it would never happen, the worry that it would be
accompanied by inter-ethnic violence, proving right the cynics who
said that all the investments in peace-building over eight years had been
wasted effort – but also the fear that Rob and I might find ourselves at
home, grinning at each other in a rather sad lonely way. We had been
reticent of suggesting celebrating with Adem and Xhezide, or other
Kosovan friends, knowing that they would want to be with their families, and feeling that we hadn't earned the right to celebrate alongside
people who for generations had suffered and fought, and lost so much
in a cause we had just dabbled in on our international salaries for 18
months.

Equally, we hadn't wanted to celebrate without Kosovars, even with
the other international salaried dabblers we knew and liked in Pristina.
When people you love are celebrating you want to be celebrating with
them. What better way to watch the Declaration of Independence than
from one of the enormous extended sofas, built to accommodate the
enormous extended families, of a Kosovan front room.

We drove to the village of Hajvali outside Pristina and were greeted
by an enthusiastic Valon, beaming hospitality and national pride with his
every gesture and every garment. He was dressed in a tracksuit embla-
zoned with the England football logo, but on his head he wore the traditional Albanian *plis* hat, now normally only seen on old men, at folk

dance performances and on war memorials – the latter because of its iconic status as symbol of the Gheg Albanians. Today, everyone was proud to be an old Albanian.

Valon is serious and slow in his speech, which gives what he says the gravitas of ideas carefully considered. But his favourite phrase is '*jashtëzakonisht e mirë*' ('extraordinarily good'), and his sober pronouncement of enthusiasm for whatever is under discussion has inspired me in conversations with him about the museum, the people we've met together, the ideas we've sparked off each other.

But never, we agreed as we stood outside his house, had there been a day so *jashtëzakonisht e mirë* as today.

Brought inside his house, we were all introduced. 'I am the head of the family,' began Valon's father, and then went on to present in turn each of his family, including those who were absent, telling us their degree subjects and jobs. Three sons and a daughter were seated along the couch that ran around the edge of the room. A son-in-law and his daughter were also there, and we were shortly joined by a neighbour and his wife and son too.

The familiar rhythms of Albanian hospitality continued, and I felt increasingly delighted with the day and with our luck in being here – in Kosovo and in this home – and now. We were asked again how we were. We were asked how our health was, how our families were.

Drinks were offered generously. I accepted a juice; Rob a *raki*. Valon's father and his neighbour (though not Valon who doesn't drink, for religious reasons) discussed the traditional Kosovan *raki*, and Rob marveled politely at the Albanian habit of having a *raki* for breakfast.

The neighbour replied very seriously: 'the *raki* you have at breakfast should really be accompanied by a spoonful of honey.' My ears pricked up. He explained the science of the Albanian breakfast: 'the spoonful of honey should come first. This is enough to attract all the microbes that live in your gut. They swarm in to eat, and while they are busy, you down the *raki* which then kills them all off.'

It sounded like a terrifying start to the day, for all concerned.

And now Valon's father picked up the lecture, as Albanian hosts of a certain age are allowed to do. Moving on from advice about our health, familiar themes surfaced, surged, receded – the ancient history of his people, the superiority of his people (never asserted without sup-

porting evidence – in this case an international study which concluded that Albanians had the highest spatial intelligence in Europe), sparse and never indulgent narratives of the family's misfortunes in the 1990s under Milošević, and their experiences during the NATO campaign.

It is important to hear about the men of the family dismissed from work in the early 'nineties, just because they were Albanian. It is important to hear how Valon's father was called in repeatedly for questioning by the Yugoslav secret services, because of his political activities with the parallel Albanian government set up in opposition to Milošević. It is important to hear about the final time they came to question him during the first day of the NATO bombardment, when he chanced to be away from home. That night he took the children to someone whose name he still won't give me, near the family's old home in the mountains, and they hid out there until the end of the bombardment.

And as if as the continuation of his story, the television (that additional member of the Kosovan extended family, always present and often loud) was suddenly showing a picture of Prime Minister Thaçi entering the Assembly hall. The agenda of the day was read out; item number one was the declaration of the independence of Kosovo. Valon's father stopped talking.

It was really happening.

We sat in silence as the opening speeches were read. And then everyone realised that we should be videoing the big day. As the Prime Minister started on his Declaration, new machines were bidden to action in Valon's front room, the channel was changed, the signal wavered, the words of the Declaration became indistinguishable, were lost.

Valon skipped desperately across the bandwidth trying to find the channel again, and the room was one huge held breath. Eventually it was suggested that maybe we should just watch and leave the recording. 'There'll be a repeat tomorrow,' the neighbour said comfortingly, and we went back to the original channel, feeling calmer now – as if we were settling down to what promised to be a particularly good episode of *Eastenders*.

The episode was indeed *jashtëzakonisht e mirë*. The Prime Minister read the Declaration with dignity, and he mentioned all the right things:

Answering the call of the people to build a society that honours human dignity and affirms the pride and purpose of its citizens; committed to confront the painful legacy of the recent past in a spirit of reconciliation and forgiveness; dedicated to protecting, promoting and honoring the diversity of our people; reaffirming our wish to become fully integrated into the Euro-Atlantic family of democracies; observing that Kosovo is a special case arising from Yugoslavia's non-consensual breakup and is not a precedent for any other situation; recalling the years of strife and violence in Kosovo, that disturbed the conscience of all civilised people; grateful that in 1999 the world intervened, thereby removing Belgrade's governance over Kosovo and placing Kosovo under United Nations interim administration... honouring all the men and women who made great sacrifices to build a better future for Kosovo... we, the democratically-elected leaders of our people, hereby declare Kosovo to be an independent and sovereign state.

The deputies voted unanimously to adopt it (those who might have had dissenting voices – those whose names were later read out, and almost all of which ended 'vić' – had chosen not to come that day), and Valon's brother and sister and brother-in-law and father and niece and neighbours – and his two English guests with the odd accented Albanian – clapped and cheered and opened some sparkling wine and smiled at each other and still couldn't quite believe it.

Over the rest of the day we ate and drank to excess, with Valon's family, and then back in Pristina with multiple different groups of friends in bars and restaurants, the concert hall and people's homes, singing, dancing, hugging, luring and obliterating those microbes with exuberance, if without the attention to technical detail that Valon's neighbour had advised. Without a preceding spoonful of honey, Rob's final celebratory *raki* was, nevertheless, drunk early in the morning. So were we.

Eventually we climbed into bed, in the newest country in the world.

25.
Totally legal: a honey cake for Women's Day

New Albanian vocabulary: *tetë marsi* (8 March), *besheret* (scarecrow)

None of my fears about independence were realised – there were no inter-ethnic incidents and no casualties of the celebration. The posters that had appeared over town, urging people to 'celebrate with dignity for a propitious beginning' had clearly had some effect. So had the temperature – the extreme cold had dissuaded people from staying out in the numbers that might have caused trouble.

The feel-good wave of the independence celebrations continued for weeks. Every time you met someone for the first time after the Declaration, you wished one another 'happy independence'. I had the same conversation with my gardener, taxi driver, the headteacher of a school I was working with, all of them saying, 'it's up to us now to make a success of Kosovo. No excuses.' Everything seemed possible.

Weeks later I was still saying '*urime pavarësia*' to people when I realised that it was time to change my greeting – there was a new festival to congratulate people on.

I had never celebrated Women's Day before coming to Kosovo. This was partly something to do with a frustration with this kind of affirmative action, and the unoriginal quibble that if any days are to be celebrated as 'Women's Day's then there should be at least 178 of them in a year. It also had something to do with my experience of being a woman – brought up in a liberal family where I was given cars and footballs to play with as well as my dolls, was taken to science fairs and given the implicit and explicit message that there was nothing I couldn't achieve. Later, I'm not sure I even really noticed I was a girl, at my all-girls boarding school. And then I studied English literature at university, and went on to train as a teacher, and in doing so, while I was doing exactly what I wanted, my success in the field was unlikely to threaten any male hierarchies.

When I came to Kosovo and experienced my first Women's Day on 8 March, I was unprepared for the congratulations that came my way. Other women wished me a 'happy Women's Day'; at the school where I taught part-time, the (female) headteacher bought pot plants for all the women staff; one organisation I was working for left a piece of jewellery for me as a small gift on my desk in their office, and the courtous old (male) communist professor with whom I had a meeting later that day as part of the project I was working on with an international charity presented me with his hand and his felicitations. As I grumbled to Saskia, 'what are they congratulating me on? Having breasts?'

Saskia has lived in a number of socialist countries and has a different take on the day, as did the million or so women in the country where I was living. For most women in Kosovo, 8 March is the only day when they get presents. Despite the brave displays in some of Pristina's florists in the run-up to Valentine's Day, they didn't seem to have done much business the previous month. For the majority Muslim population, there's no hardcore celebration of Christmas either. The gifts at the Muslim celebration of *Bajram* (Eid) are given almost exclusively by adults to children. There is a tradition of 'Father Winter' (in his red and white coat with a sack of toys on his back, not a man I would be sure of being able to pick out in an identity parade with other old men who do the rounds in the UK at this time of year) but his responsibility is for presents brought for children – handed over at midnight on New Year's Eve.

But on 8 March all my Kosovan girlfriends seemed to get a present – mainly flowers – from husbands or boyfriends. And everyone was talking about doing something special for their mum. Lots of my friends got an unofficial afternoon off and went out for a meal together. Shpresa had told me that if they were lucky, their (male) boss would take them out to lunch.

In the days leading up to 8 March, the streets had budded with plastic. Artificial lilies and roses in the most unlikely colours were sold at improvised stalls. I saw children struggling home from school with over-sized drawings of implausible bouquets.

It was a lovely blooming, chiming well with the season. In our first year in Kosovo, I had been infected with the sense of imminent flowering, and during these days I had bought three small potted crocuses.

Placed at even intervals along a windowsill they were my own personal celebration of spring.

I returned home on 8 March that year to find that autumn had come rather early to my pots. Where the three had sat at the beginning of the day, now only the middle one was left. I could only assume that the others had been stolen – I imagined some boy shinnying over our fence with the image of his mother clear before him.

I was grateful for his restraint in only taking two – and in going about his petty theft so symmetrically. And that night as I lay in bed, I wondered about my unknown sister somewhere in Pristina, proudly displaying the gifts from her cheeky, daring little darling son; or the new bride feeling spoiled by her indulgent husband – the one with the thighs strong enough to clear railings in one bound – and little guessing at his dangerous thieving heart.

A year on, and I had slightly more sympathy for Kosovo's women and their brave little day of plastic floristry. I had now worked for Unicef on a project that had involved collating a frightening set of statistics. This is a hard place to have X chromosomes. If you are female in Kosovo, you are more likely to live in extreme poverty (28 per cent of females as opposed to 15 per cent of males; the World Bank notes that income poverty disproportionately affects female-headed households). As a cause and an effect of this poverty, you are more likely to be illiterate (nine per cent of women as opposed to three per cent of men).

As a woman or as a girl you are less likely to have access to the kind of information that enables you to make choices about your life and your health. A recent study found that 35 per cent of girls/women were not aware of sexually transmitted infections while for men/boys this figure is lower, though still worrying (26 per cent).

In the light of all this, it is unsurprising that you are less likely to be employed: Unicef had recorded that in the 15-24 age group unemployment was 74 per cent for women and 56 per cent for men. For those of us used to Western economic indicators, I'll repeat that statistic. Unemployment – not employment – levels stood at 74 per cent for women and 56 per cent for men. Participation in civil society is lower too; something like 12 per cent of females as opposed to 26 per cent of males are reported to be involved in political parties, fora, political organisations, youth centres, youth clubs or NGOs.

For me, there is one further statistic that I find most stunning, and most telling about the prevailing sense that it is somehow less important to care for the female members of the Kosovan population than its males: only 55 per cent of girls are fully immunised as opposed to 72 per cent of boys. I don't know how those kinds of decisions are made – a conscious choice that TB wouldn't matter so much because she's just a girl? An insistence on only the best for sons (and heirs) which ensures that every recommended procedure is followed to the letter while the girls' health care might just slip your mind?

It is a further piece of evidence to suggest that girls are not really wanted in Kosovo. You can see this, too, from the patterns of families' production of babies. Many have two, three or even in one case I met, *twelve* older daughters before the longed-for son arrives. I've never come across the opposite pattern. Superstition offers plenty of ways to end a line of girls – you can call your daughter by her mother's name, which will ensure that her next sibling is a boy, you can call her Shkurta ('short') as an imprecation that the line of girls may be thus. You can also give her such a foul name that the fates won't allow you to have another daughter. Anyone who officially names their daughter 'Scarecrow' or 'Ugly' doesn't deserve to have any children at all.

By my second year in Kosovo I had had experience of some of this, and had heard the stories from friends – Kosovan women, or foreigners like my friend Mary, working to bring healthcare to rural areas so that women can have check-ups or even contraception without having to ask their husband's permission first to leave their village. And so this year in a way I was pleased to see Kosovo's women clutching their pot plants on 8 March, and in a way I was all the more frustrated. In the context of women's education denied, limited access to healthcare, limited participation in political life, and disproportionately high unemployment, I was frustrated with a mentality among both men and women which thinks it is flattering to have one day a year when you are given a plastic rose and let off the washing up.

But it never hurts to be reminded to appreciate your friends – male or female. And in Kosovo I had learned new kinds of female friendship, and the cooking, conspiracy and creativity it could bring with it. So I could hear the smile in my voice when I discovered it was Saskia calling on the morning of 8 March. She was less upbeat.

'I'm not having a good day – I've just got back from holiday. I left the kids there with Wolfgang so I could get on with some work in Pristina. But now I'm back I've found our flat in chaos with the landlord in the middle of decorating.'

I don't know what I would have done in a similar situation in the UK, but I was aware of having new understandings of hospitality in this warm country that had extended us such a welcome. When we had chosen our house here I had specified that it must be one of the minority with a separate kitchen. I had been thinking of Foreign Office-style 'entertaining' I had imagined I would now need to do – some image of afternoon teas and politically astute table plans. Instead, Kosovo had taught me the real meaning of hospitality. I remembered with shame my grumpiness in London when friends based overseas had called to ask whether they could stay the night – *tomorrow* – while they were in town. Now I was learning what it was like in practice when, 'a home belongs to God and the guest.' It seemed the most meaningful way to mark Women's Day – of course I invited Saskia to supper and to stay the night with us.

Orange and walnut strudel

For dinner I wanted to cook something from my Albanian recipe book to show off, or at least include, some of my honey. The following recipe for 'strudel' (though it ended up doughy, not like anything that I would call a strudel) looked appropriate. I went through checking the vocabulary and was sure I understood everything, with the exception of one word in the title and the ingredients list – '*afion*'. Since I needed 500g of the stuff in the original recipe (the version below is modified in the light of my experience) and it was the title of the dessert, I guessed *afion* might be important. But it wasn't in either of my dictionaries. I sent Gazi an urgent text message asking for a translation, but I got no response.

Thankfully, reading on through the recipe I saw a suggestion for replacing the *afion* with ground walnuts so I made this version. The next day I finally received the reply from my teacher. He'd never heard of *afion* either but his much bigger dictionary defined it as 'opium poppy'. His message continued 'Are you making something illegal? If so, share a piece with me.' This is the walnut version, completely legal.

Ingredients
10g yeast
165 ml milk*
85g sugar
450g plain flour
1 egg plus 1 egg yolk
35g melted butter
35ml rum
the juice and rind of an orange
a pinch of salt
165g ground walnuts (or poppy seeds)
vanilla to taste
1 tbsp honey

Mix yeast with a little lukewarm milk and a pinch of sugar and flour. Leave in a warm place until the mixture starts to ferment.

Sift the flour and make a well in the centre.

Add the egg yolk, 35g of sugar, the butter, the rum, 80ml of milk, the orange juice and rind, and the salt.

Mix, adding the fermented yeast.

Place the resulting dough in a warm place for 25 minutes.

Meanwhile, warm the ground walnuts in 70ml milk.

Whisk the white of the egg until it is firm.

When the walnut mixture is cool, fold in the egg white and the yolk, the vanilla, and honey.

When the dough has had 25 minutes to prove, roll it to a thickness of 1cm on baking paper.

Spread the walnut mixture over the dough, leaving a 2cm margin at each edge.

Roll the dough like a Swiss roll and turn out on a greased baking sheet.

Leave for 10 minutes and then put in a 200 degree oven for 25 minutes.

Serves 6

★ Milk had been a problem for me in Kosovo, because I am so picky about the taste of UHT. With the electricity and thus refrigeration difficulties in Kosovo, it is rare to be able to buy anything else in the shops – and when I did buy some in unattractive bladder packs (small tough plastic bags where the milk lurches around in your hand as you pick it up, with an unsettling breast-like feel) it was curdled by the time I got it home. Then Shpresa, the farmer's daughter, said that it should be possible to get milk delivered to my door by a farmer. I mentioned it to Gazi who said that his cousin owned a café and used fresh milk there and that he would ask him to give my details to the farmer who supplied him.

And thus it was that I received a phone call one day when an unidentified male voice asked in Albanian: 'Is that Miss Elizabeth? Are you interested in milk?' Had the mafia come calling? This was clearly a coded question, and I didn't know the answer. While I cast about for a possible password, the caller identified himself as Shemi, a farmer who was offering to bring a two-litre bottle of his farm-fresh milk every week to my door for a euro.

The milk was delicious and in its floral notes I swore I could still taste the pasture Shemi's cows had munched on. The milk came in re-used fizzy drink bottles, and there was also one occasion when there was an unmistakable tang of Fanta, but once I'd pointed this out to Shemi the bottles seemed to come better washed.

26.
The honey for the General's porridge

New Albanian vocabulary: *gështenjë* (chestnut)

'This is the bee lady.'

I was being introduced at an official reception I attended with Rob. It seemed that I had gained a rather odd role as a honey ambassador among my friends. People asked me – a novice beekeeper and simple stickied honey-taster – for the truth about the story that honey from flowers local to the sufferer can cure a person's hayfever, whether I would recommend beekeeping for a young family, what I thought the causes were of the Colony Collapse Disorder reportedly wiping out the US and UK bee population... I had moved from unconscious incompetence, to the level of *conscious* incompetence. All I knew was that I couldn't answer these questions with any authority. I had been in the presence of honey, of bees, of a beekeeper, but I didn't yet feel I was confident to do anything with my knowledge.

I certainly felt tongue-tied in the presence of the British General who was now extending his hand. Even more so when I realised he wanted to ask me a honey-related question.

It turned out that this soft-spoken, urbane man of war likes to have honey on his porridge every morning, and that he prefers it to be chestnut honey. When the bees have gathered their nectar only from chestnut trees, the resulting honey has a darker, more treacly taste, with a hint of nuttiness which I could understand would go well with morning oatmeal.

'So do you know of anywhere in Kosovo where I could get hold of some?' He was touchingly interested in my answer. His Lieutenant-Colonel standing by was also looking at me with great attention. I realised it was in many people's interests for the General to have a comforting start to his day.

I said that I thought I knew a shop where chestnut honey was sold, and the Lieutenant-Colonel thanked me on the General's behalf. I

hoped I had soothed many mornings for them all. Perhaps by way of thanks, as we talked on about beekeeping, she asked whether I would be interested in contact with Abedin, a beekeeper she had heard about who had previously been in the Kosovo Protection Corps, the civil defence force largely made up of the demilitarised guerrillas of the KLA. Abedin is apparently now on a pension, resettled to a quiet life of stings rather than arrows. It sounded a compelling story – this former fighter now producing honey, like Samson's lion – and I hoped to be able to visit him, and see the reality of the transformation. She didn't know the details herself but she put me in contact with the Kosovan Colonel who could give me the beekeeper's phone number.

'Poverty doesn't shame those touched by it; poverty shames society,' read the sign tacked to the wall by Colonel Xhavit's desk. It was accompanied by many others, some in Albanian, some in English, taking in Cicero and Dreyfus, war and peace. Maybe it was just that my Albanian wasn't good enough, but none of the signs seemed to be of the 'you don't have to be mad to work here but…' variety. Hallmark Cards has thankfully not yet opened in Pristina.

As well as having impeccable guerrilla credentials, Colonel Xhavit is an international affairs Masters student, and he proudly told me that he has also been a truck driver – during his refugee years in Germany in the 'nineties. Now, however, he is a personnel officer and, as such, the person who was able to give me the telephone number of his former comrade, Abedin, the beekeeper.

There's no good reason why Colonel Xhavit could not have given me Abedin's number over the phone when I called him, but he had suggested that I should come to coffee in his office so I had dutifully gone, to spend a pleasant 45 minutes talking Hobbes and religious tolerance, urban planning and economics with this gentle soldier. All the same, I felt it was 45 minutes I could ill afford.

But that is ungenerous and ungrateful. I so often ended up feeling this way in Kosovo when people who have so little (Colonel Xhavit volunteered the information that he earns 300 euros a month) offered the only thing they have, which is their time and company. I, of course, have so much more when it comes to euros – but so much less when it comes to the time I am able (or perhaps willing?) to give to coffees and conversation. The difference between time and money as currency

is that when you give your money to someone you don't require simultaneous matched funding from them, but when you give them your time you are requiring at that moment exactly the same commitment from them.

So Colonel Xhavit gave me his time, and took mine too, and once I'd finished the drink he had also given me, and he had at last passed me Abedin's number, I made my escape. Walking down the road, I quickened my pace so I wasn't late for my next meeting, and I wondered about the time-poor in the world. Is their (my) poverty also something that should shame society or only the afflicted individuals? I had the uncomfortable sense that in the case of my own time poverty I really had no-one to blame or shame but myself.

So when I contacted Abedin I was determined to try a little harder to relish the time I spent with him. I explained that I'd had his number from the Colonel, and wondered whether I could come to visit him in his village near Mitrovica. 'You would honour us by doing so,' he assured me. I asked when would be suitable; 'this afternoon?' he suggested.

Before I answered his question I had to check what I was free to spend on him; not by looking in my wallet, but by looking in my diary. As I'd feared, it told me that I really couldn't make the three-hour round trip to see him that day. And like any pauper, like any Mr Micawber, hoping against experience that some income might just turn up, I leafed through the diary trying to work out when I could make the visit. The best I could do was in a week's time. Abedin was obviously surprised – perhaps disappointed – but he didn't make too big a deal of it (after all, one doesn't rub any kind of poverty in people's faces) and we set a time for me to go and see him then.

Inevitably, I was late. But I called Abedin en route to warn him. 'It's no problem,' he said. 'I'll be at the bus station to greet you when you arrive.' I didn't ask how I would recognise him – I had to hope that a British woman carrying a bag of beekeeper's protective clothing would make it easy enough for him to identify me amid the crowd of students and old women who shared my coach journey.

But as I looked through the window and scanned the people waiting in our bay at Mitrovica bus station, I wondered whether Abedin and I should have set up a better system for finding one another. There

was only a scattering of people there – a guy much younger than Abedin must be, an older man carrying a bunch of flowers presumably waiting for some loved family member back from their travels, a few women…

No-one new had appeared by the time I descended the steps of the coach, so I presumed Abedin was delayed. While I was getting out my phone to call him, the guy with the flowers approached me. 'Mrs Elizabeth?' he asked me, 'Welcome to Mitrovica.'

The bouquet was a foretaste of the beautiful garden he took me home to; but in fact there was nothing flowery about Abedin. He spent 33 years 'in boots' as he put it, and was keen to tell me about his experience as a professional soldier in the Yugoslav army, and then in the KLA.

But he was just as passionate about beekeeping – possibly more so than anyone I had met in Kosovo. He and his wife had planted a careful garden full of nectar-rich flowers; here were none of the flouncy cultivated flowers, the double-headed roses, chrysanthemums, dahlias, which are all show but little nectar and no pollen. The day I visited was such beautiful sunshine that we were able to sit in this bee-loud glade full of thyme, geranium, lupin, and enjoy it.

Abedin's wife, Valdeta, sat with us and told me about their family, her children at university in Pristina. She is a sensible woman with beautiful clear skin, working as a nurse, and obviously pleased by my compliment on her lovely garden. I told her that it was the closest thing to a traditional English country garden that I'd seen in Kosovo. I joked about how obsessed the English were about their gardens: 'in England if there's a garden only this big' – I sketched the table we sat at – 'there would be at least four little patches of flowers tak, tak, tak, tak' I gestured. She laughed back: 'But in Kosovo if there was a garden only this big there would be at least four little houses tak, tak, tak, tak…'

Luckily this rampant building virus hasn't yet reached Abedin and Valdeta's little village, unless you count the flourishing suburb by their house, inhabited only by bees. And in so many ways, this community of three million or so is superior to its human counterpart. Not only is its unemployment rate zero, but thanks to its benevolent dictator, Abedin, its design is harmonious but varied, like the best garden suburbs. In place of the blockish hives mirroring each other in rows like a Le

Corbusier dream, Abedin has experimented with different styles of hives. 'I plan to have a museum here to show different approaches to beekeeping through the ages.' He had a skep, and a hollow tree trunk also used as a hive. A friend had given him a beautiful Slovenian model, which Abedin had cleaned and repaired. It opens like a spice cupboard.

Abedin clearly loves working in wood, making things as efficient as possible, as beautiful as possible. He has modified the traditional hive design to allow for better ventilation, a real problem for bees during the winter when they may be inside for months at a time, building up potentially lethal carbon dioxide in the hive. And since bees need a nearby source of water as much as they need nearby flowers, he has designed his own water-drip where water falls softly from a controlled tap down a sloped board where the name of his bee farm, also the name of his son, is elaborately carved, 'Loriku'.

We walked around his tiny estate, for him to point out for me the innovations he has implemented. I suggested that I should get my protective suit, but he was blasé about such things and assured me that I would be OK, speaking like the owners of vicious dogs do to nervous guests.

As we walked, Abedin showed me the scaled-down hives that he uses for manufacturing queens for sale. He also explained his system for maximising the harvest of the bees. The hives are grouped and numbered in threes, and during the early summer he takes one of every group of three down to Deçan where the flowers open earlier.

I wondered how this is done, thinking about cats and the way they have to be oriented when they move to a new house. Don't the bees lose their way when they go out from the hive in its new position?

Apparently bees can tell when the hive's surroundings have changed and this will trigger them to redraw their mental map. The only time this doesn't work is if the hive is moved less than a few miles. It's not enough for the bee to think to redraw the map, but the old map will be useless for finding the way home. Under these conditions, bees will get lost and die looking.

And how can he be sure that he has taken all the bees from one colony with their queen – surely some must be out foraging at the point where their hive is removed?

'That is why only one from each group of three is taken away – the

bees belonging to that hive who happen to be away from the colony when it is removed will return to where their hive should be. They'll smell what's called the 'queen scent', of one of the neighbouring hives' queens, and won't think twice about following the scent and starting working for her.' Little traitors.

Suddenly I felt a tickle on my neck. Without my protective suit I was nervous. I put up a hand to try to brush it away, but the bee that had landed there was investigating me further and did not want to be brushed off.

'Did you put perfume on this morning?' Abedin asked with an accusatory edge to his voice. But I hadn't – I felt insulted that he thought me such a rookie beekeeper as that, because I knew from all my books that you shouldn't even wear deodorant when you are tending your hives as it's likely to arouse the attention of bees who are attuned to smells.

With one swift movement, Abedin snatched at my neck. 'There,' he said, and held up his finger and thumb. He was holding the bee's sting, plucked from its belly, and now well clear of my neck. This was a beekeeper with not just military, but ninja training. The limits of my own skill had never been more evident than in the presence of real bee-keeping expertise. I realised what a very long way I had to go.

We sat down to the lunch that Valdeta had been preparing for us: a salad fresh from the soil, with lettuce and spring onion and a perfect vinaigrette. But Abedin the enthusiast had saved something to show me, and once we were all at the table, he produced it – a diseased bee larva, a little gelid lump with the telltale brown mark of a varroa mite on it. I hadn't ever seen a varroa infestation up close, but this is a beekeeper's biggest nightmare. Impossible to eradicate, and capable of wiping out a whole hive, the varroa mite, related to the tick, attaches itself to the bee and sucks at their vital 'haemolymph' fluid until the bee dies.

'For a honeybee having one of these mites attached to it would be like you or I having a monkey clinging to you.' A blood-sucking monkey. I shivered. Abedin jabbed at the larva with his fingernail and told me about these revolting creatures. The mite creates a feeding site on the larva that her offspring can eat from as they develop. Then she lays an egg that develops into a male. Five more female eggs are laid after that. Abedin was tactful as he described how the mites breed, but

the book *A World without Bees* I read afterwards described the Jacobean drama of what happens next. When the mites emerge from their eggs they 'begin an incestuous affair on a mound of their mother's faeces, as the brother mates with his sisters, starting with the eldest.'

'Put it away,' Valdeta told him in her best nurse's voice. Of course, she was quite right, and we meekly submitted and settled down to her really delicious lunch.

That weekend I went to buy a pot of chestnut honey which I sent to the General's office with greetings from The Bee Lady. He and his staff had done me an enormous favour, leading me to such a wealth of bee expertise, and I wished him many happy breakfasts.

27.
On the trail of the 'primitives'

New Albanian vocabulary: *sera* (greenhouses)

Everyone in Kosovo knows the difference between theory and practice. The paper version of the country's systems is often unrecognisable from the comfortable chaos of life on the ground. But the paper version makes for interesting reading, and in March I was copied in on a series of slightly nervous group emails from friends in Kosovo alerting one another to new traffic regulations.

For example, from that date onwards, you were required to have your headlights on while driving, whatever time of day or night, and a new scale of fines had been introduced, bringing the price of infringement of even relatively minor regulations to an on-the-spot payment of what would be a few days' wage for someone like Colonel Xhavit, and an impossible amount for a smallholder like Adem largely outside the cash economy. Enough to get people checking their seatbelts and keeping their mobile phones in their pockets for the first few weeks, at least.

One friend sent round a link to the Kosovo Assembly website where you could find the full text of the law. I thought I might check whether there were any even nastier catches in the small print so I had a brief scroll through the many many pages of the legislation in its English version provided on the website. The first thing that became obvious was the charming – and sometimes unhelpful – translation. I sensed that the translator was perhaps a frustrated poet or thesaurus-compiler. For example, throughout the text, the adjective used to describe illuminated headlights was 'aglow'. It painted an idyllic picture of the rural roads of Kosovo, softly lit by their law-abiding drivers. It also revealed that there were indeed some extra rules to be aware of; for example, mud on your wheels would cost you an immediate fine, in an extension of the Albanian fetish about cleanliness which has led to the phenomenon of their near-monopoly on car washes, not only in

Kosovo but in the countries which host the Albanian diaspora. If you use a car wash in a major urban area in the UK, try saying *'faleminderit'* next time you're thanking them, and see what reaction you get...

The Assembly website made available a whole library of legal documentation to me and was another reminder of living in the newest country in the world. Sometimes in Kosovo I felt that I was getting a glimpse of what working life for Thomas Jefferson might have been like in the 1770s. Along with all the excitement about Kosovo's new flag and new anthem, a new country has to have new laws. Not that this had come as a surprise to anyone – people like Vedat had been working since 1999 on laws to be promulgated by the United Nations Secretary General's Special Representative for Kosovo. Kosovo now had sovereignty but there was still a long list of laws it needed to develop; the website announced that the country now had a law on blood transfusion and blood products, a law on personal names, a law on organic farming, a law on noise protection, a law on apiculture...

A law on apiculture! I clicked on that.

I learned that enshrined in Kosovan law is the principle that apiculture is 'an important sector of the country's agriculture, a source of natural high nutritive, dietary and medical value products'. The law also explained that there should be an annual register taken of beekeepers and the number of hives they have.

It made me wonder about numbers. How many beekeepers were there in Kosovo then? And how would that compare to the UK? Still at my computer, two clicks took me to the British Beekeeping Association and from there to an automated form where I had to enter a verification code (do the BBKA really get overloaded with malicious spam through their automated form?) and type my question about the number of beekeepers and hives in the UK. Within 24 hours I had received a reply from Letitia of the BBKA, telling me that they have 11 500 members on the register, and copied to the General Secretary in case he could give anything more specific. Two hours later he emailed me a link to the DEFRA website where I found what is known about Britain's beekeepers – that they are composed of 200-300 commercial beekeepers but, more importantly, 44 000 hobbyists with about 274 000 colonies who produce the bulk of the UK's honey. The numbers are approximate because registering is voluntary, but they

suggest an average of six hives per beekeeper in the UK. The total production in the UK is 6000 tonnes of honey.

I enjoyed the Kosovan version of information gathering rather more. I happened to see that a Kosovan friend of mine who had worked at the Ministry of Agriculture was online on MSN Messenger. So, despite the fact that she was in America at the time, I was able to send her a message asking who I should speak to at the Ministry. She sent back the mobile number of her colleague, Bajram, the Director of the Animal Production Department, and I called him to ask my question.

The Director's response to my question about how many bee-keepers there are in Kosovo wasn't the suspicion at being asked such a question by a foreigner (is someone checking up on me? Why?) that I'd feared.

'*Hajde*,' he suggested. 'We can have a coffee tomorrow and talk about it.' I thought about the BBKA's verification code to stop malicious spam.

When I arrived at his office I was introduced to his colleague who is responsible for the bee register in Kosovo. He seemed pleased to show me the results of his work which are a truly impressive and apparently comprehensive reflection of beekeeping in Kosovo (or at least in those parts of Kosovo to which a Ministry of Agriculture official would have access – Serbs did not accept the legitimacy of the Kosovan government so the bee-counters hadn't ventured to the Serbian-speaking bees north of the River Ibar).

Their data on the bee population of Kosovo, even given its significant geographical limitations, is strikingly more accurate and practical than the equivalent data available on the country's human population. Kosovo's last useful census was in 1981. This was followed by a census in 1991 but as that was boycotted by Albanians it is almost useless as a tool for determining population size. So you would have thought that it would have been pretty important for the international community to organise a census here as soon as possible after they arrived to administer Kosovo in 1999. At the very least it would have been useful to have a census at the time when it would have been expected in the normal cycles – i.e. 2001.

But the issue of the census has got bogged down in politics. There are some ethnic minorities in Kosovo who don't see their interests

being served by having their exact numbers known. So nobody does.

Nor does anyone know how large a population to plan schools for, to plan medical services for, how much sewage to expect to be accommodating, how much water, what the likely spending power of the population could be...

The best guesses for population information are based on primary school registration, but working out how large the Kosovan population is from looking at primary school enrollments is like trying to identify the number of bees from the number of pots of honey on sale in the shops. Bajram's colleagues had done a much better job.

Their findings tell us that there are 6453 beekeepers in Kosovo – as a proportion of the population this is four or five times the level of beekeeping in the UK. The beekeepers have an average of eleven hives so it is also a hobby carried on more intensively here than in the UK. And I was thrilled to think that of the 1774 hives recorded on his list for the wider Pristina municipality, two were my little boxes at Adem's.

But production here was 708 tonnes in 2007, so on average these hives are half as productive as the UK's. Curious about why that might be, I started looking at the data on the type of hives that are used in each municipality. I had assumed that they would all be the Langstroth-Root, filing cabinet type that I have on Adem's farm. But seven per cent of them are the 'Dadant-Blatt' hives about which the only information I've had is that they 'open like a book' which has given me a great desire to hold one and learn to 'read' honey. And there are still four per cent of Kosovo's bee colonies housed in the wicker skeps, called here 'primitives', of the kind that I'd bought and seen stored in Adem's barn for emergencies.

I asked Bajram about this; how might I get to see a skep that's in use? Bajram paused. 'Would you and your husband like to come to my house tomorrow, and we could go and visit my neighbour, Rexhep, who has these hives?'

For all the swift click-throughs to data provided in the BBKA's online service, I don't think they can beat Kosovo.

The next morning, Saturday, Rob and I set off with Bajram's hand-drawn map. He had assured me that with the map we couldn't fail to find his house, but I was extremely uncertain. The map showed four landmarks – the word PRISHTINA, the name of the village before

which we were to turn off the main road from Pristina after 25 kilo-
metres, a set of three greenhouses, and a child's-style drawing of a
yellow house. Bajram had taken his highlighter from the pot on his desk
specially to colour this house in. Reviewing these landmarks, I had
taken his mobile number too, considering that we would have a better
chance of finding him with that.

We were approaching the village of Komoran, before which we
were supposed to turn, but only once we'd seen the three greenhouses.
Greenhouses may be rarer in Kosovo than in the UK, but even so I
couldn't see them being a useful distinguishing feature.

Suddenly three hove into view, and right by them was a turning. We
screeched round it and continued along the track for some way, looking
for the highlighter-yellow house.

'There it is!' And there was Bajram coming out with his son to
greet us. We pulled up, and after introductions and greetings, the two of
them got into the car, and directed us further along the road, as it dete-
riorated considerably. They explained that they were taking us to
Rexhep's house where we could see a primitive hive in use.

After twenty minutes of driving roads bordered by fields and the
occasional farm, we stopped.

The main reason for this was that we had just seen something
extraordinary in a field: a Serbian tank.

It was a rather old Serbian tank, and a very burnt one. Apparently it had a KLA grenade thrown into it during 1999; when I asked, the people who came out to look at us were coy about telling me whether there had been anyone inside it at the time.

'Why is it here?' I asked, rather naively. The answer to that question could go on a long time. But the man standing nearby who I'd asked answered me very simply, 'Once it was burned, the Serbs didn't want to come to take it away.'

'Didn't you want it gone?' He shrugged and smiled. He seemed rather proud of it.

This is the kind of sight I'd expected to come across all over Kosovo – a war-scarred country with military hardware rotting in its fields. But despite the casual references to armed conflict I had got used to in Kosovo's urban landscape: the sign that said 'discharge your weapon here' on the way into the post office, schools I'd visited that were named after heroes fallen in the 1990s Albanian liberation campaign, the photographs of the missing hung up outside the government building which I saw whenever I went to meet Rob at work, this was the first time I'd seen anything as blunt as this as a wartime souvenir.

When we arrived at Rexhep's house, he was bemused but hospitable. He took us round his hives, which were stacked up on the slope near his house. I got out my protective clothing and he sneered a little in the most polite way. He himself was walking round in casual black clothes – the colour I had been told bees are most likely to attack; his jumper was made of wool, apparently a material which also incites bees to sting. He offered to open up a hive, and from behind my mesh hood I accepted happily. But I couldn't see his smoker – the tool that with Adem I'd learned was so invaluable to beekeepers for calming the bees enough to be able to study what's going on inside their hive. As he got out a pack of Marlboro, I discovered that Rexhep's was the open-necked, cowboy approach to beekeeping. Lighting up, he puffed some of the cigarette smoke out over the bees. A bit of fag ash dropped into the honey cells at the same time, but he wasn't bothered. The smoke seemed to work, and nothing flew out on the attack as we looked at the bees busy inside the hive.

Thinking about the burnt-out tank near his house, I was interested in knowing what happened to the hives during the war. 'What hap-

pened to them during the war?' echoed Rexhep ironically. 'Some Serb soldiers just got a lot of honey.'

He and the family had left their home and fled to Turkey. His wife had been heavily pregnant at the time, and gave birth while they were away. His silent nine-year-old daughter was standing watching us from a distance, and he explained that the name they gave her was the Turkish for 'refugee'. It's a hell of a start in life.

I didn't like to seem rude to either him or to Bajram who had so kindly arranged for us to come here, but in our tour of the bee farm I hadn't seen any skeps around; all the hives were the box type. I asked tentatively, 'and are all your hives Langstroth-Root?' He answered that he did have some skeps but they weren't in use this year. With Bajram standing next to me, I tried not to look disappointed.

Perhaps Rexhep felt he had let someone down; he took me over to see the skep that had been used last year. Turning it upside down you could see the remains of honeycomb.

'Where did you get the "primitive" from?' I asked.

'I made it myself,' he answered as if it was obvious. I took a freshly respectful look at the work that had gone into the weaving – one strong stick spliced and then each of the splinters used to structure the conical shape with other withies woven as a weft around the whole structure. Then it had been plastered with what looked like mud, or cow dung.

I loved this object – I loved its shape and efficiency and history. Evidently Rexhep sensed this and he offered the skep to me. Then I felt awkward that my cupidity or envy had been so obvious. He insisted, I said again how lovely it was, but how I wouldn't want to take it when he could use it. In the end I offered some money, hoping that this wasn't offensive. Rexhep refused once politely but on the second attempt at giving it to him he accepted, and I picked up my large, shitty, wicker bee trophy with a grin.

He continued showing us around his land, a typical Kosovan small-holding with some chickens, vegetables, a cow and calf, and a *hambar* (another traditional form that I have grown to love in Kosovo – a distinctive wooden construction built particularly for storing corn cobs). His was old and I asked to take a photograph of it. It was propped against the boundary fence to his property, and across the fence the neighbours stood staring at me. Fair enough.

A *hambar* for storing corncobs, a long thin shed seen on every Kosovan
smallholding

We were offered drinks and some intense spoonfuls of honey, and then we started our farewells. Rexhep was clearly uncomfortable about something, and I wondered whether it was the lack of a working skep – or maybe it was the money I'd given him. I thanked him again for the handmade hive and explained how precious it was to me. 'Thank you – for your time and your hospitality.'

But he was darting off, into the shed where the hens laid. He brought out three warm white eggs. A present for us. We were extremely grateful.

We thanked him for everything again – for his time and his hospitality.

Still Rexhep seemed uncomfortable. He darted away once more, and this time came out of the shed with a chicken. To my horror I realised he was offering it to us and I panicked – we wouldn't know what to do with a chicken. We had nowhere for it to run, and my vegetarian principles wouldn't allow me to let it die of anything other than old age. And how the hell would we get it home? And how to explain any of this without seeming prissy, ungrateful, foreign city-types?

I tried to explain about not having anywhere for it to live, until Rexhep offered to break its neck there and then. Hastily, I moved on to explaining about vegetarianism but then ran out of any vocabulary to do so. Reverting to the only theme I seemed to be able to master in this unfolding social disaster, and wondering how we and the chicken could get out of this alive, I thanked Rexhep again for the eggs and made movements towards the gate. To my relief, Bajram stepped in at this point. He would take the chicken, he quietly assured me, and I could keep my eggs. Some twine was found to wrap the chicken's legs, and as a party we thanked Rexhep again – for his time and his hospitality, for his extraordinary generosity. Everyone relaxed a little bit (even, perhaps, the chicken) and we made our way out to the car.

The chicken was placed in the back of the 4x4 and we all set off along the bumpy track to Bajram's house. This is what the Landrover sitting in our city carport must dream of, bouncing along challenging roads with livestock in the back. What an adventure for all of us – even, perhaps, the chicken.

I was overwhelmed by what I had received from and through Bajram. And I thought of the poor, efficient staff at the BBKA who

didn't have the chance to work like this.

Bajram was enjoying himself too, I think. After all, he had got a free chicken out of the day. And just as Rob and I were doing some slightly bizarre tourism among the farms of western Kosovo, he was taking the opportunity for some cultural exchange. He was a nice, respectful man, and seemed almost out of his depth on this one. But I liked him even more for trying. He cleared his throat. 'Elizabeth? I have heard of vegetarianism of course, but can you tell me a bit more about it. About its rules?'

I dread this question, even when it's asked by people who I think might have the cultural context to understand my answer. And I don't have a clear answer. My vegetarianism is composed of squeamishness, habit, concern for health, something about humanity which I can't articulate properly because I'm not an animal lover, and some sound environmental science about methane and trophic levels and the number of calories it takes to produce a kilo of beef compared to the number of calories it takes to produce a kilo of cabbage. And I didn't think Bajram was going to understand any of it, certainly not in my Albanian translation.

But I gave it a go. I explained that I am not a Hindu, I explained that I do eat fish, that I don't eat chicken, that I do eat eggs and I do wear leather. He didn't understand. But I had increased respect for him for trying. I didn't think I'd even scratched the surface of the reality of rural life in Kosovo either, but I hoped people might give me credit for effort.

28.
Honey fudge in the KLA heartlands

New Albanian vocabulary: *gjallë* (alive)

Since my visit to Rexhep's house had still not given me sight of a 'primitive' hive in operation, I wondered how I might find another chance. I felt I was working backwards in my beekeeping apprenticeship, becoming familiar with the Langstroth hives without understanding the extent to which they were modifications of the bees' natural environment. I just couldn't understand what the architecture of a bee colony would look like without Adem's neat frames of wax starter sheets – the Ikea model of flat-packed interior design. I imagined the 'primitive' hives as heads that could buzz with ideas like bees. The ones I had bought and kept at home as decoration were empty-headed, vacant. But perhaps if I could see inside one of these composite brains, I could understand the fundamentals about bees and beekeeping.

From Bajram's register of Kosovo's beekeepers it had looked like my best chance to see a skep was in the municipality of Skënderaj. I was going to have to enter what has been described as 'the rural rebellious region of Drenica'. This region, with Skënderaj its main town, has always been the poorest part of Kosovo, previously the poorest part of Yugoslavia, and now has a disproportionately young population, even by Kosovan standards – the average age is twenty-one. Great ingredients for rebellions.

From a walking group we belonged to, I knew an Englishman, Bob, who had held the unenviable post of UN Municipal Administrator of Skënderaj in the time before these UNMIK positions had been returned to local people. By chance I bumped into Bob in a Pristina street and when I explained my quest he said that he knew a bee expert in his former municipality. Apparently, if Avdyl himself didn't keep bees in skeps then he would be sure to know someone who did. With a phone call it was arranged that I would hitch a lift in Bob's car one day

when he was visiting the municipality on business; while he was having his meetings, I could visit the homes of Avdyl and his bees.

The journey down to Skënderaj with Bob was an education. As he and I drove through the villages which formed the furthest boundary of the municipality, he started to parse the landscape for me. Whether it is with Adem listening to his hives, or a masseuse telling me what she reads in the knotted grammar of the muscles of my back, or a teacher engaging her class, I love being in the presence of people exercising their expertise. And just as Adem will point to a cell that looks just like all the others to me, and tut about problems to come, or a masseuse will notice the way I have been storing tensions that even I'm not aware of in my right shoulder blade, Bob was reading the villages, the small businesses, the new greenhouses, the state of the roads that formed part of his manor. He told me which car workshop was owned by the mayor's cousin, which piece of land was lying fallow as a result of political interference in the plans for building, showed me which houses and factories and roads were due to which international aid agencies.

Soon we passed the road which leads to Prekaz, the deepest I had penetrated into Drenica before now. Prekaz is the home of Drenica's most famous son – and grandson, daughter, nephew, niece… It was the home of the whole Jashari family until the day that 51 of them were killed by Serbian forces. The story of their death occupies a special place in the history of Kosovo's Albanians. It was Adem Jashari's face on the 'bac u krye' t-shirts that had been worn to celebrate independence.

Hunting for bee skeps is not a common reason for visiting Drenica. If ever there had been a bucolic idyll in these rolling valleys, it was thoroughly shattered in March 1998. By then Serb police had already come to Prekaz twice to arrest Adem Jashari, wanted by them for his contribution to the formation and arming of the KLA. On both occasions, Jashari had resisted their attempts to enter his family compound, meeting fire with fire. When the Serb police withdrew, Jashari had declared his village a 'Serb-free zone'.

I had read the vivid account of what happened next in the book that Shpresa's boyfriend had told me to buy on our first meeting. In *Be Not Afraid, for You Have Sons in America*, Stacy Sullivan narrates the forming, arming and activity of the KLA. Her book has all the pace of a thriller novel, with the chilling edge of the events having really hap-

pened. It describes what took place in Prekaz on 5 March 1998, when the Serb police returned for a third time, this time fully prepared for confrontation with Jashari. They sealed off fifteen villages in the region and moved into Prekaz with tanks, helicopters and artillery. Surrounding the Jashari compound, they asked Jashari to surrender, and when he refused they attacked. The Jashari family – men, women and children – held out against the attack for two days but were ultimately unable to match the Serbian force. When the Serbs moved into the compound, they found the only survivor there, Adem's eleven-year-old niece, hiding in a kitchen cupboard. They forced her to identify the bodies of the rest of her family. Later reports on the corpses showed that some had their eyes poked out, and one was decapitated.

These killings were not the largest massacre committed against Albanians by Serb forces during the dark days of 1998. But they were to be the most significant. This is as much a result of what happened after the Jashari deaths as the events which caused them. The remaining villagers of Prekaz demanded that a team of international forensic experts should be given access to the Jashari bodies before they were buried. Foreign diplomats supported the call for forensic workers from abroad to be granted visas to attend the bodies, but Milošević refused. Stacy Sullivan's book had drawn powerful images of how the Serb police had meanwhile gone to the barn where the bodies lay, loaded them into trucks, driven them to a hillside and bulldozed earth over the top of them. In the face of this further insult by the Serbian regime, the Albanians of Prekaz went to this burial site the next day with rakes and shovels, and retrieved the bodies for proper burial. Tens of thousands of Albanians from across Kosovo attended the funeral. Sullivan narrates how immediately afterwards US diplomats met with Milošević and threatened to use 'every appropriate tool we have in our command' to stop Serb aggression if paramilitary forces were not withdrawn from Kosovo. Two days later, Tony Blair called an emergency meeting of the UK, France, Germany, Italy, Russia and the US which recommended to the UN security council a comprehensive arms embargo against Yugoslavia and the denial of visas for senior officials.

The death of Adem Jashari and his family was therefore a turning point in international attitudes to Kosovo and the Albanians, and started NATO thinking on the route that would lead almost exactly one year

later to its bombing campaign which forced Serbian withdrawal from Kosovo. Despite the voices of human rights activists questioning Adem Jashari's right to take his non-combatant women and children with him to his hero's death (he was apparently asked by the Serbs with loud-hailers to send the women and children out before they began their attack), the sense of bravery and nationalism embodied in the story of his family's resistance has maintained it as a powerful shorthand for what Kosovo Albanians suffered and of how and why they ultimately triumphed. Prime Minister Çeku had only two pictures on the wall of his office: that of the fourteenth-century Albanian hero against the Ottomans, Scanderbeg, and the other showing Scanderbeg's twentieth-century counterpart against the Serbs, Jashari.

So my previous visits to this area had been coloured with blood, not honey. I had visited Prekaz three times; indeed, it is the most visited site in Kosovo, a statistic that made me sad when I saw what the site offers to the visitor. The Jashari houses have been left as they were in the immediate aftermath of the attack – burned and gutted, splattered with shot marks. If the 1389 Battle of Kosovo is the Serbs' repeatedly picked scab, then Prekaz is the Albanians'. The first two visits I made there were in daylight, but most recently I had attended the annual 'night of the fires'. This is held on the anniversary of the final attack on Prekaz and is a mixture of pilgrimage and party – the spirit of Glastonbury in the fourteenth and the twenty-first century simultaneously. With an evangelical message, 'He is still alive!', proclaimed on enormous banners, the temporary stage mobbed by a crowd of tens of thousands hosts scantily-clad stars, political figures and traditional dancing.

When I went there for the March celebrations in 2007, Rob had already arrived in the government party, and with a bit of text-message echo-location, I negotiated my way to him through the crowds and the mud and the sunflower-seed sellers (I am sure that British youth would be in better shape if our rock concerts and festivals were fuelled by sunflower-seeds rather than doughnuts and hamburgers). The government party had front row seats, and space was found for me squeezed next to Rob. So while young Kosovo gyrated behind us, we genteelly tapped our feet in time to the various acts rolling across the stage. A few places along from Rob in the front row sat an older man with an enormous grey handlebar moustache. A really astonishing moustache – bushy, but

tapering to impressive points out beyond his cheeks. Occasionally the camera-happy concert-goers would dive under the barrier, avoiding the police supposedly separating the VIPs on seats from the groundlings, and take snaps of the performers, and then sneak a quick picture of the moustache. A couple even dragged their children with them and had them pose with the moustache.

I mused on how direct and tactless Kosovars can be, and how tolerant Mr Moustache was of people focusing on his facial hair. After a few more people had come up and snapped the man, Rob turned to me and asked whether I would like to be introduced to his photogenic neighbour. I declined, whispering that I didn't want to be as rude as everyone else. And then Rob explained who Mr Moustache actually was: Rifat Jashari, the brother of Adem, and only surviving member of that generation of Jasharis, having been living out of Kosovo at the time of the attack on Prekaz. No wonder people wanted to take his photo.

I was an ignorant, foreign fool.

I was, nevertheless, introduced to Rifat, and beneath the wail of the loudspeakers and the singing I muttered something to him. I can't remember what I said, and I don't really know what I could have said. What is the appropriate way to address a man famous now mainly because the rest of his family were murdered, while he was out of the country. I don't know what the days – or the nights – must be like for Rifat Jashari.

I was grateful that on this trip, Bob and I could ignore the turn-off to Prekaz and its legacy of blood, and follow the signs taking us to Skënderaj – and bees. Though it was impossible to ignore this area's past; if you were only looking at the roadsigns, you could still be forgiven for thinking that this KLA heartland was still the 'Serb-free zone' that Adem Jashari had dubbed it, even though there are, in fact, Serb villages dotted around the area. The official convention (and legal requirement) in Kosovo is for road signs to be in both languages. The unofficial convention, as I'd seen from my very first day, is for the second (Serbian) of the names to be regularly spray-painted out. This occurs even when the name of the settlement is, as is sometimes the case, the same in both languages. I once commented to a friend in the British Embassy that in these cases the government could save on materials and just print the name once. 'Then each community,' I said, 'could assume that the gov-

ernment was privileging only their name for the settlement on the road sign.' The diplomat corrected me: 'No, then each community would assume that it was their language that had been missed off.'

As expected, most of the signs on the way into Drenica advertised 'Skënderaj' with a black smudge in place of the Serbian version of the placename, 'Srbica'. However, as we passed Prekaz, the sign announced proudly 'Skënderaj/Skënderaj'. Perhaps there is still no place for a Serb in Drenica.

We followed the patriotic signs to arrive at my rendez-vous with Avdyl and his families – both human and insect. Despite the conflict-scarred setting where I met him, in the brief time that I spent with Avdyl that day, he seemed to embody all the best elements of my experiences in Kosovo. He is gleefully multi-talented, coming from a family of beekeepers going back generations, and being proud chairman of the local beekeeping association, he nevertheless trained in business and textiles, and then worked in a Socially-Owned Enterprise textile factory until the 1990s. Then, like most Kosovo Albanians in SOEs, he was dismissed from his job.

During the war his family suffered: a father, brother, and uncle all killed. 'In front of their children,' he added with no further explanation. He himself fought in the KLA. He has children of his own now – a coy, chubby three-year-old girl, a more serious five-year-old son, and two others who were at school when I visited. It was clear that he adores them, taking an almost embarrassing time to show me a pile of paintings that his son had done which genuinely showed precocious talent, but which were nevertheless mainly daubs of colour.

'Working before the war in an industry which was mainly women was important preparation for one of the jobs I've had since the conflict,' Avdyl told me. 'I trained as a psycho-social counsellor, and then I became a part-time beekeeping trainer for the international Women for Women programme.' The programme offers women training and resources for small start-up businesses.

'From the beekeeping I spotted a gap in the market for beehives – the modern Langstroth-Root wooden boxes. I taught myself a bit of carpentry, enough to set up a small workshop in my garage producing hives.'

Before I was allowed to see his working hives, let alone a working

skep, we went to see the empty boxes, stacked up to the roof; a minia-ture Manhattan ready for insect inhabitants. He said he is the only Kosovan producer in this quantity. 'I hate waste,' he explained. 'If you just have flowers, they look nice for a while, and then they die. But if you have bees, then they take the nectar from the flowers, and you have honey which you can eat and you can sell. The flowers aren't wasted.'

Did he know that the Rev. Langstroth had had a similar passion for maximising resources? His prototype was apparently an adaptation of a champagne crate. Avdyl smiled appreciatively. 'I hate waste,' he repeated. 'And while I was making my hives this year, I started think-ing about the offcuts of wood and what I could do with them.' He showed the little blocks to me and I tried to explain the game of Jenga, the tower made of wooden pieces of almost exactly these dimensions, which competitors remove one by one until the tower falls down. I mentioned how popular it is in London, where my friends will sit together of an evening, carefully demolishing a tower in this way. He didn't seem to be impressed with this as either a money-spinner or a leisure activity for Londoners.

When he heard that some of my work in Kosovo was with kinder-gartens, however, he asked saw an opportunity immediately: 'do you think they might be interested in buying a sack of the offcut blocks? It's untreated wood – no varnish or chemicals. You can chew it' – he mod-elled for me – 'and have no ill-effects.' He spilled a handful of the little blocks into my hands, and another handful in front of his son. The child immediately started thoughtfully laying them out. It was pure Montessori.

I was rapidly warming to Avdyl, the former counsellor, textile engi-neer, freedom fighter, now trainer, carpenter, entrepreneur, devoted father and beekeeper. Perhaps this is the apotheosis of the rural rebel-lious spirit of Drenica – all of that energy channelled into creative rather than destructive activity.

But before I had the chance to see the traditional beehives, Avdyl was keen to show me his skills in another area – hospitality. Another thing I love about Kosovo.

We went into his house and I was seated while Avdyl got out bee-keeping magazines, certificates, newspaper cuttings, to show me. I didn't like to ask again to see the skeps but I was wondering whether this

would be a repeat of my experience with Rexhep. Given his attitude to waste, and his enterprise manufacturing Langstroth hives, it seemed unlikely that Avdyl was really going to have one of the old, inefficient 'primitives' in use.

Avdyl's wife appeared, silently bearing a tray of drinks and food for me. I said hello, asked her how she was, complimented her on the gorgeous children I'd met outside, and she answered politely, but with some embarrassment. Looking back on the situation now, I try to find the equivalent of her discomfort for a similar situation in London. It was rather as if someone took you out to a restaurant, where, instead of talking to them, you tried to engage the waiter in small talk. She was our waitress. Or servant. This is one of the things I love less about Kosovo.

The tray she had brought in offered me not only tea but the ubiquitous Fanta. A nation whose tastebuds and habits seem sophisticated when it comes to the appreciation of honey appear to be completely blind to the true foulness of Fanta. They even call it 'juice', as if there is somewhere a Fanta tree, budding little bubbles of orange carbon dioxide, where luminous fruit bursts open hyperactively from the branches.

From the tray I was also offered a fine glass of what looked like sludge – or fudge. It had a small spoon in it and when I helped myself, I discovered it was crystallised honey. Avdyl chatted away as I savoured it: did I know that honey crystallises naturally in the cold but that, conversely, jars can be brought back to liquidity by warming them in a pan of water on the stove?

I tried to match him fact for fact. I had read that it takes the lifetime of twelve bees to make a teaspoon of honey. Lovely as it was for me, I wondered whether it had been worth it for them. Not to be outdone, Avdyl got out a magazine cutting and started painstakingly reading out loud about the properties of honey. He told me how excellent it is because of its high energy content. I looked sadly at my spreading stomach. One kilogram of honey – he put in front of me a kilo jar of his own honey as a visual aid and present – has the same calorific value as three kilograms of bread, 1.8 kg meat, 2.1 kg fish, 780g cheese, 5.5 kg milk, 50 eggs, 1.2 kg walnuts, 30 bananas or 40 oranges. I tried to imagine eating any of these quantities of food, and failed. I felt slightly sick.

The article Avdyl was reading also compared the average per capita consumption of honey in different countries. In Kosovo it is apparently only 200g per person a year. Looking at the empty glass in front of me I realised I had been doing extraordinarily well at raising that figure. In the UK we apparently eat 300g of honey per person per year – still way below the world average of 1000g per person per year.

Avdyl asked his wife to bring in more honey – I was told I should have some in my camomile tea. He was quite right, it tasted great, and I thus added another few grammes to my daily intake. I was feeling slightly dizzied by the high levels of blood sugar and statistics.

And I wanted to see a skep. But Avdyl really wanted to go on talking. He was bursting – buzzing – with schemes. He told me about the programme he had run for Serb and Albanian beekeepers, together, in 2004 (two thousand and *four*, he emphasised, reminding me of the inter-ethnic violence which marred that March). 'Imagine, there were Serbs and Albanians sitting in a room together learning about bee-keeping. It was great. But then the funding was withdrawn.'

'Why?' I asked, but he didn't know. There may be more to it, or it may just have been a classic international aid agency cock-up. The fact that he didn't know reinforced his sense that the strange, willful, unpredictable international gods might be willing to donate again. He had no idea of their criteria. I said that I would like to help – perhaps we could sit down together and write a proposal. I said I would speak to Bob about it.

'There are other things that are needed, too – reforesting of the area, to increase pollen to increase honey production. And systems for beekeepers to be able to work together, pooling their produce for joint analysis and marketing.' He talked about micro-credit schemes. I believed he was right about all of them, and I checked that he had my phone number so we could keep in touch and take some of this further. He stored the number in his phone and as he did so, asked me my name again. 'Isabel?'

No, I repeated (this was perhaps the third time). I tried to connect it for him – the same as the Queen of England? I am constantly amazed at the lack of recognition of the Queen's name in situations like this when I am abroad. Gritting my teeth, I tried my other famous namesake, which has achieved nods and smiles when I have introduced

myself in countries from Syria to Ghana, Indian villages to Mexico City: 'Elizabeth Taylor?' No, Avdyl hadn't heard of her either.

'I'll just put you in my phone as Anglia [England]' he said. Then I really did feel like the Queen.

At last he suggested we went out and looked at the beehives. I held my breath. The majority of Avdyl's hives were of the wooden type, which he had, of course, made himself. But off to one side was something that might have been a very short wizard. It wore a sheet of metal (Avdyl uses the discarded plates from newspaper printing. I shouldn't have been surprised – he hates waste) curved into a conical hat, and little winged creatures blew in and out of its small mouth like breathing. It was perhaps what would result if two L Frank Baum characters got themselves mixed up.

Avdyl went over to the strange form and lifted its metal hat off. And I finally got a chance to see a working skep.

The skep had been woven from withies – Avdyl again – and then plastered with mud to cover the holes in the weave. Studying it I could understand the exterior architecture of the skep but I still couldn't imagine how the bees made their honeycomb within it. Luckily Avdyl, ever the beekeeping trainer, had one they had made earlier. In a corner of the field where the hives stood, there was an old skep, with some of its empty honeycomb still inside it. To my surprise, the honeycomb was in slabbed layers, perhaps two centimetres thick, running vertically down the skep. The space between them is just enough for a bee to pass. Seeing this, the sense of the Langstroth Root hive design was obvious. If the bees like building in straight lines, then giving them a square space to do it in is most efficient for everyone. The Gotham City of Avdyl's garage was nothing to what the bees themselves were building in his garden.

So this is where it began. This is what bees did before beekeepers interfered and harnessed the honey-making process for their own sticky ends. It felt like something profound that I'd learned today – a glimpse of the structures that develop in the absence of exploitative superior forces. I was still thinking about Adem Jashari.

But it was time for me to go, and I thanked Avdyl profusely and genuinely for his kindness. I tried to thank his wife, too, but that just embarrassed everyone further.

As I left I said again how much I was going to enjoy the honey Avdyl had given me. I was running low on my stores, having resolved to substitute honey for sugar in all the baking I did, as a way of supporting local economy, cutting down on food miles. It was very kind of him, I said. 'No,' he said. 'That's marketing.' I got the sense that the untiring Avdyl didn't see this as an ending – that he saw in me the beginning of a beekeeping project. I felt the same about all the things I'd learned from him.

29.
The real bee queens

New Albanian vocabulary: *mësit* (matchmaker)

As I tended to my own hive, and felt the growth of my knowledge, skills and my identity as a beekeeper, I kept thinking about the other women going through the same apprenticeship, on the Women for Women programme where Avdyl ran beekeeping training. I shared with him a sense of frustration at waste, and I had a new perspective on the possibilities for the half of Kosovo's rural population who have unused skills and potential beyond the home.

I did some research and discovered that Women for Women is based in the US, and offers women in post-conflict countries around the world a year of weekly or fortnightly training in fields including human rights, women's health, parenting and small business management. At the end of the year the women who have taken part in the training are given the raw materials to set themselves up in a business. Perhaps a sewing machine, seeds and tools for market gardening, a loom, or – naturally – bees. Funding for this life-changing programme comes from sponsors in the developed world who are twinned with a 'sister' in a very different country. The monthly sum given by sponsors is split, with some supporting the programme in general, and a certain amount going directly to their 'sister' as cash. I talked to the head of the Women for Women office in Kosovo and, like Avdyl, I was impressed by the programme and its approach, and I signed up to become a sponsor.

In particular, of course, I loved the idea of bees changing people's lives, and I asked whether I would be able to visit some of the women in Kosovo who, as a result of the project, are now beginner beekeepers like me. The organisation arranged to take me to meet the bee queens, in the company of my friend Saskia.

I had some misgivings when we arrived at the home of one of the Women for Women 'graduates'. Despite being accompanied by our Women for Women chaperone, it was clear that our arrival was a com-

plete surprise to them. We entered the one-room kitchen and living area, with foam mattresses laid around the edge, and were ushered to sit down cross-legged, and offered coffee – *Turkish* coffee, our host assured us, assuring us that we were honoured guests, not to be fobbed off with Nescafe. Of all the countries in the former Ottoman Empire, where its coffee has left its strong stain on drinking and social habits, Kosovo is significant for its honesty in attributing provenance. In Sarajevo I had been offered Bosnian coffee, in Edessa, Greek coffee, but in Kosovo they knew where coffee really came from.

I saw that in a corner of the room, next to the stove, there was a crib with something strapped into it. I politely asked how old the baby was and was told, by the rather tired looking woman stood next to the crib, that her son was three days old. She had come home from hospital yesterday.

What were we doing, barging into a home which clearly had higher priorities at the moment? I suggested to our Women for Women

host that we should leave, but *he* assured me it was OK. And the coffee had just started to boil. I was torn between not wanting to disrespect the family's hospitality, and wanting to acknowledge this young woman's exhaustion. What I ended up doing probably made everything worse: I moved myself off the mattress where I had been sitting near the head of the house, to sit next to the crib and the new mother. I realised afterwards that it probably suggested disrespect to him, and only wearied her with my attempts at chatter and solidarity.

I admired the crib, which was a traditional design, made from wood that is often recycled, so that you see babies cradled on the slats from fruit crates that had held snuggled nectarines or apricots a few months previously. In the cribs I'd seen for sale at the market the painted trade names for the fruiterers had still been visible on the underside, in the same gaudy colours with which the date would be daubed on the sides, a record of when the peachy contents were produced. There was the traditional pole along the top of the cradle, with a cloth hanging over it like you might put over a parrot's cage. Inside, the baby was wrapped up in tight swaddling like a bunch of flowers.

While we were all sitting drinking our coffee, I did some maths, and calculated that the new baby Alban shared a birthday with the new baby of my London friend, Kate, whose son had been introduced to us by email the previous day. Little Jamie had been born on the other side of Europe but, like Alban, he had an older sister (the perhaps three-year-old Albina sat looking serious at the side of her brother's cot) and a mother who seemed to adore him. I wondered at what stage their fates might start to diverge, barring the obvious point that the head of Kate's household would certainly not be allowing a party of foreigners into the house today to be entertained while they talked about bee-keeping.

But it became clear fairly soon that it was not only us, along with Alban, who were making demands on the new mother. Where Kate might right now be lying looking slightly drained but quietly elated in a pretty nightie with flowers all around, her 'sister' in Kosovo was carrying out the usual household chores. There was another woman in the room (the two were the wives of the brothers of the house) helping to serve coffee, but when Saskia asked their father-in-law about buying a pot of honey, it was the new mother who was sent outside to the honey

store to get it.

I had read about the tradition that women must be made to work immediately after they give birth in order to exorcise the evil spirits of childbirth which otherwise make them unclean. I love the guys who come up with these superstitions. Edith Durham, the British lady-traveller-turned-anthropologist who visited Kosovo in the early years of the twentieth century, had noted that a woman was expected to fetch wood and water three days after childbirth. Perhaps being sent out for a pot of honey was getting off lightly. But it was sad to think that in this respect a hundred years had changed nothing for Kosovo's women.

I continued trying to make conversation with the girls, and when it palled one of them got out a little album of photographs to help us along. They included a holiday snap of her other sister-in-law – the last woman that had married into this family, whom I hadn't met. I was interested to see that she had her head covered with a scarf. It is rare, but not extraordinary to see this level of Muslim observance in Kosovo, and I asked about it.

'It's for people to choose,' the girls said easily.

'*People* or *husbands*?' I asked.

'Yeah, husbands,' they conceded. And that was the end of that conversation.

Reminders of that dynamic were everywhere; I was intrigued to see that one of the photos in the album showed a bride wearing a red scarf over her face. I had been told at the Ethnological Museum that this had been the traditional dress for Kosovan brides, but I didn't know that it was still worn anywhere. The scarf was made of simple cotton, not the translucent tulle of what I would think of as a bridal veil. With this over her face, the bride had no chance to see where she was going when she was collected from her house by the bridegroom's party who took her back to his home. The theory was that if she couldn't see where she was going then she couldn't find her way back to her parents if she didn't like her new life.

I was called back to the main conversation by the Women for Women trainer. The principal beneficiary of the Women for Women programme in this house had been our host's wife who, it turned out, was away from home today. So I discussed beekeeping and honey-eating with the men. Like so many people I spoke to in Kosovo, this family said

that they didn't use their honey in cooking, but simply ate it on its own, by the spoonful. Before I saw people doing it in Kosovo, this would have seemed unthinkably indulgent – like spooning Nutella from the jar. This family told me that they eat their spoonfuls of honey with milk; a truly Biblical sense of indulgence.

Without the Women for Women 'graduate' being at home, I sensed, and rather hoped, that our visit was coming to an end. Then Alban's mother could get back to resting or caring for him (and probably her father-in-law), and we could move on to the other home we'd been told we'd be visiting, where perhaps they would be prepared for our arrival. I looked around me, at this warm little family centre, with its alien rituals and obligations. In the opposite corner of the room from where baby Alban was swaddled and rocked beside the wood stove, there was an electric cooker where our coffees had gurgled on the hob. I glanced at it and looked back again, in shock. There was a woman's face staring at me through the oven door.

I looked again. It was, of course, not a real woman. It was a life-sized photograph of a model's face with her hair streaming out behind her, applied as some kind of transfer to the glass door of the oven. It was just decoration. And as you got close to it, you would presumably get the whiff of baking. Welcome to the life of women in Kosovo.

We did at last move on, to a house where the bees were cared for by two other young women, Shqipja and Lendita. Despite my hopes, they apparently hadn't been warned that we were coming either, but they were charmingly hospitable all the same, moving in what I recognised now as the Kosovan hostess scoop, sweeping away with swift movements all the things that had been out on the table before our arrival, and making space for fizzy drinks for us. One sat at the table with us ('How are you? How is your family? Your health? Are you well?') while the other disappeared, reappeared with the tray of drinks. When she'd transferred them from tray to table she walked backwards respectfully to stand near the wall, awaiting our next need of her. The routine seemed elegant, civilised to me, but I have a militantly modern Kosovan friend who refuses to have a tray in her house at all because of what it represents to her of this ritual and its oppressively unchallengeable rhythms and roles.

Once we were all seated, Lendita and Shqipja talked happily about

the Women for Women course and all the things they'd learned from it. We had so little in common, but the one bond of beekeeping was a good start. I had seen Saskia in action like this before – her two children offer her a way to engage with any woman who has children, just through the mediation of her kids, whether they are present or not. Comparing the ages, feeding habits, health, sleeping of children; these things are a connection for mothers everywhere. I had no children, but I did have my bees. How many kilos had my hives produced this year, Shqipja and Lendita asked? I wanted to know if they'd had any trouble with varroa. Did I use glucose syrup? Had I been frightened when I'd started beekeeping? Shqipja said she'd been terrified. But she had never actually been stung. Had I? In these limited social situations, that little community of mine on Adem's farm was a great substitute for a family.

When I asked the girls about business they said that they didn't have enough honey or access to enough markets to be selling it; instead they ate it themselves.

'So why are you so enthusiastic about the programme, then? What benefits has it brought, if it hasn't left you with a sustainable business?'

'Just to meet with other women in the village,' their faces lit up as they talked about it. In rural Kosovo traditions keep women well out of public life, and Women for Women had challenged that, not only with its talk of human rights and business plans, but by the very act of getting the participants together. So the women had wanted to continue meeting. Shqipja told me that the municipality had made a room available to them for weekly meetings that she organises herself.

'How many women come?' Maybe this was one of those schemes that was all talk.

'About a hundred come in all, and usually fifty turn up each week.' As agents of emancipation these bees had done a wonderful job. I congratulated Shqipja and said that if there were ways to help her group of women I'd like to try to be of use. We exchanged email addresses and I took some photos of her and Lendita and promised to send them soon.

A week later, I contacted Shqipja and Lendita by email to send the photos. They are on MSN Messenger and so after that, when they had electricity and time, and I also had electricity and time we managed some typed conversations online. For me this was easier than speaking

to each other, as their Drenica accent is the Glaswegian of Kosovo, and in our spoken conversations there were moments when I lost the sense of the discussion completely. Electronically, we had time and space bars to help us. A hesitant relationship built up: I asked about their bees and they asked about my strange life in faraway Pristina. One evening I was on television, running a charity art auction; the next day I got a message from Shqipja congratulating me: 'When we saw it was U, we watched the whole show. U were great.'

On MSN one day Shqipja mentioned that at the most recent meeting of the women's group, the women had put together the plans for an 'excursion' they wanted to go on. It was madly ambitious – they wanted to take in Prekaz (the Adem Jashari massacre/ battle site), a park where you can see fish which supply the attached restaurant, the Rugova gorge and Pristina. 'But we have no money to pay for the bus for the day.'

Well, I had said I would like to help her village group, so I offered to pay for the bus, on the condition that I could go with them. This caveat was partly fuelled by suspicion, wondering where 200 euros might end up if left unattended. I couldn't believe that this group of 50–100 village women with an idea for setting off for a day trip round their whole country was really going to materialise. But I could also now understand, in a way that I wouldn't have done before meeting Shqipja and her sister, how getting two or three euros each from their husbands or fathers to fund the trip just wouldn't be possible.

They claimed that they would love to have me along, so we fixed a date and with some nervousness I caught a shared *kombi* minibus from Pristina to join the Skënderaj beekeeping women for a works outing, Kosovo style. My nervousness was in many forms – had my Albanian been good enough for the women to know that I would be paying for the bus, but not for anything else? Had it been clear enough that I would be paying for the bus but not organising hiring it? If they had hired it and it then fell over/broke down/killed us all, would they or their legatees hold me responsible? Morally, would I be responsible? Would it be a day full of the wearing form of organised jollity that as a boarding school survivor I rebel against? Would the women see my presence as a dampener? As a sign of my suspicion? As a patronising gesture? Would I get travel sick?

And then in the *kombi* on the way to join the group in Skënderaj I saw a new risk to my health and happiness. This small space was shared by ten passengers, squeezed onto each other's laps, up against hips, sharing unanticipatedly intimate moments on the bumps in the tarmac. And then someone called out from beyond my neighbour – I couldn't see quite where – 'is it OK if I smoke?'

My English soul cried out about laws concerning such things in public places, about my own little lungs. But I found myself inexplicably soothed by the poisoning humanity of the driver's reply – not 'it'd cost me my job, mate' but 'it's fine; would you like a cigarette?' It was then that I remembered that I was going to be spending a day with a large group of nicotine addicts in an enclosed space. I breathed deeply – and wished I hadn't.

At the end of the *kombi* route, Shqipja was waiting for me, the excursion bus-driver was waiting, and an excited gaggle of 25 women was on the bus already. I handed my money to the driver and hoped that my responsibilities were over for the day. I sat down and leaned back and started to count how many of my worries were still valid.

None, as it turned out. Shqipja was an excellent manager – of time, of people, of me. We did indeed get to Prekaz, the trout park, the Rugova gorge, and even had time to divert to Prizren before coming to Pristina. She conscientiously counted everyone on and off the bus at each stop, warned them about staying together, charmed the driver when he had to be asked to do a few extra favours for us, and was clearly a born leader. Bee metaphors naturally sprang to mind. I saw the power of the little (or not so little) group she had organised in her village and had a growing sense of respect for her. I just wished she had something else to do all day than watch her bees and kick her brother off MSN to send me messages.

Chatting with her and her neighbours, the main topic of conversation was marriage. Two of the girls were engaged and had proudly shown me their rings. I asked how they met their husbands-to-be, and after the briefest of pauses they explained that these were arranged marriages. A member of the family or of the village would have done the scouting for appropriate partners, and then the couple was allowed to meet.

I knew that this sometimes happened, but hadn't realised how

widespread it still is. I asked Shqipja whether she would use a match-maker and she said she wouldn't. She has four sisters married through matchmakers, and said she doesn't like any of their husbands so she didn't see it as a very reliable method. But another unmarried girl I asked said that she would. After all, she explained, if something goes wrong in the marriage and you've used a matchmaker then people will help you. If you've chosen the partner yourself and you have problems then you're on your own.

I was told that when the matchmaker goes to the potential groom's house to arrange the match, honey is smeared in his shoes, to ensure that his words will be sweet. When I was also told that he puts eggs in them to ensure the fertility of the relationship it sounded like a recipe for a rather nice dessert. But when I heard that his shoelaces have to be untied too, to ensure that there will be no knots in the matchmaking process, I decided it was more like a recipe for disaster. What good family would allow their son to be married to someone who is cham-pioned by a fool with his laces undone, and a squelching sound as he walks?

As it was a Saturday, we passed a number of wedding processions as our bus drove along the crazy roads of Kosovo, and at each one the beekeeper girls were set off squealing and squinting at the bride and the decorations. The music playing in the bus, too, was all about wed-dings. I'd never noticed until hearing it in this new context, but the traditional songs that are still the main thing you hear on Kosovan taxi drivers' cassette players, or on the radio, are largely about weddings. Not about love, but about marriage. And when they came on over the bus sound system, Shqipja and friends grinned, 'it's like a wedding', a 'kanax-heq' (the women-only day out of the three or so that make up a Kosovan wedding) and some of them got up and started dancing on the bus (time for a little more of Shqipja's charm on our driver). I realised that weddings were the only chance they got to dance.

Many of the women told me this was their first sight of their country's tourist spots. I kept quiet about the times I'd visited all of these sites in the two short years I'd been in Kosovo – how many trips I'd taken beyond my home, with or without my partner, free in our safe, affordable jeep, to follow our whims.

The older women – that day there were a few with us in their sev-

enties, including the mother of Shqipja and Lendita – seemed to be having a whale of a time too. Like so many older women in Kosovo, they were headscarved and large. It struck me that once the indulged phase of childhood is over here, old age might be the next best part of a Kosovan woman's life. There is a genuine respect for old age that translates into a care for older people even when they are in full health and energy. At that point, women seem to have less, if any, housework to do – if you have spent your middle years successfully then you have a household full of your sons' wives to do that – just like baby Alban's grandmother who was out when I'd visited, but whose household was being serviced by what families refer to as 'our brides'. You may still have children to look after, but, as much as any grandmother in the world, you can spoil them without regard for consequences. And when guests come, you have no obligation to talk to them or busy round them as the rest of the house does. You may sit and hear them out, get up and shuffle off to your room (as many women have disconcertingly done while I am in mid-conversational flow with the younger generations of their family) or speak your mind and know it will be listened to. With the limited requirements for exercise, you can grow fat, and no-one will mind. You can grow into your old age without hair dyes or gyms or any of the curses of the Western mutton dressing as lamb.

From listening to these older women you would think you were on a school trip. They oohed and aahed with the rest. When we got to the deep and dramatic Rugova Gorge, one turned to another and said 'we should have come *here* during the war' as if the Albanians' exodus to Macedonia had been an adventure chosen inadvisedly from a tourist brochure.

At lunch time we sat down in the Rugova Gorge and brought out our picnics. Some of the group hunted wild strawberries and Lendita shared the water she'd bottled from her well. This was my first chance to have a proper conversation with any of the group other than Shqipja and Lendita who had been sitting next to me on the bus. Others from the group now crowded round, seeming intrigued by me. I thought we would talk beekeeping, but they were interested in other things. One touched my nose stud and wanted to know whether it hurt. Another was near my feet, and started playing with my anklet like a child. I wished I had shaved my legs more recently. Since we were all looking

at my feet now, her friend spotted the scars on each foot 'did your shoes rub?' she asked, fingering the ragged blisters. It's intimacy that I'm just not used to with other women.

As ever, they wanted to know about my marriage, my lack of children. My answer to the procreation question varies according to context. Most of the time I try to be honest, explaining that I don't want children – want to be independent, have time with my 'husband', be able to travel and to work. There are enough children in the world, I don't need to produce any more. And I have a lovely nephew and niece and three god-daughters, I teach in a primary school – I have plenty of children I can enjoy spending time with. And it's 'different in England.'

All this usually cuts no ice with Kosovars. So sometimes I just say lamely 'not yet', which receives a pitying look because they know my time is running out, and they presume I am still hoping. There are still cases of bigamy here where a man takes another wife when his first has failed to produce a child, and in some cases, the older woman even chooses the younger on his behalf.

I haven't yet had the guts to act on the tip from a friend who has also chosen not to have children but who, in Kosovo, invents a family that she can refer to at awkward moments like this.

I decided that their attitude to someone who doesn't want children might be similar to the attitude towards a childless woman in the UK who doesn't want a job. Protesting that you wanted to be free to follow your own interests, have time with your husband; that there are enough people looking for work, and that you don't need to add to their competition – it would still be considered by many to be a waste of talent. British mainstream culture can't help it, and nor could the Kosovars when faced with a childless woman.

When I got off the bus, at the end of our intense, exhausting, oestrogen-rich beekeepers' holiday, all the women thanked me, shook my hand, kissed me. Two of the older ones gave me the best blessing they could think of: 'may God make you pregnant with a boy child tonight.' I thanked them politely, and of course couldn't stop myself from wishing Lendita and Shqipja luck that somehow soon we could find them a job…

30.
Honey ice-cream

New Albanian vocabulary: *pranverë* (spring)

Over the Easter weekend Rob and I took a short break from Kosovo, though not from honey. We drove down to Greece – a land that they say is impossible to leave, because your feet get stuck in the country's honey. Certainly we indulged ourselves, breakfasting by the sea on yoghurt drizzled with thyme-scented honey, walking along sunlit pavements eating sticky pastries, picking at honey cake and paperbacks on our flowery balcony. We also treated ourselves to ice-cream. Of course, Kosovo has ice-cream but it doesn't have much electricity. With that in mind, it always feels like Pristina Roulette to choose a tub in the supermarket; under which lid will the salmonella bacteria be hiding? The chances of having had constant refrigeration from the factory where the ice-cream is made, in the van in which it is transported, to the wholesalers where it is stored, and the shop where it is offered for sale, are slim.

So should we be, now that we have cut out regular Häagen Dazs from our diet. But of course you find ways to compensate – one of which was glutting ourselves when we left Kosovo's borders. On a recent trip to Italy Rob and I had managed 24 scoops of ice-cream in 48 hours. I hadn't thought of Greece as being a destination dripping with ice-cream in quite the same way, but a small café in the Plaka, under the spotlit Acropolis, changed my mind. Not only did they offer rice ice-cream which I had previously seen in only a few Italian gelaterias, but you could have baklava ice-cream, which I had never heard of before. The ice-cream was vanilla with a gentle swirl of honey, studded with nuggets of golden filo pastry with their clumps of chopped nuts. I had one scoop after supper on Easter Sunday, and then we got up early on Easter Monday and before catching the train back home we found time for another scoop for breakfast.

Despite the sticky treats we were leaving behind us, I wasn't sorry to get back to Kosovo. I always get a thrill at the border, and a growing

sense of homecoming as it approaches. When flying back, the first clue that you are on your way to Pristina is the crescendo of Albanian words you snatch out of the hubbub of the airport crowd. Usually the first word I hear is '*hajde*', the generic Balkan 'come on', 'let's go', 'this way'. All very useful airport vocabulary. The next phrase I hear is usually '*ama dorën*' ('hold my hand'), and with this brusque Albanian wooing, I know I am back.

My first chance to speak Albanian myself doesn't usually come till we have crossed the border, when with the formalities of passport control I feel my Albanian muscles flexing once more. I love speaking the language again, and I can't think of a rational way to explain or describe this. It's like trying to explain why you enjoy kissing someone. In part it's because of who they are; and partly it's just the feel of it on your mouth.

The day after we got back from Greece we invited some people to supper. On my honey high from our holiday, I decided to make my ice-cream recipe to eat with pieces of cut comb.

I don't have an ice-cream machine, but I do have a brilliant recipe that doesn't require a machine. I inherited the recipe from my mother who in turn learned it from her accomplished expat friend, Trish. Trish has lived in a number of hot and interesting countries where buying ice-cream wouldn't even have the fun of Pristina Roulette – because it would be a dead cert that you would find the salmonella bacteria.

Ingredients
4 eggs
85g sugar
570ml double cream
1 pot of honey

Whip the eggs and the sugar together until they are white. (This doesn't mean whipping just the egg whites until they lose their transparency, but whipping the whole egg until it's white. Don't even bother trying if you don't have an electric whisk. The air which is added to the

eggs by doing this extensive whipping is the key factor in being able to have fluffy ice-cream without an ice-cream maker.)

Whip the cream until stiff.

To determine the flavour of the ice-cream, add a pot of whatever is appropriate: chocolate spread, fruit jam – or of course honey. Alcohol can be added at this point too – I have made a delicious raspberry and sweet Muscat dessert wine ice-cream, for example. I've also combined butterscotch chips with the honey very successfully.

Combine the ingredients, folding carefully to keep in as much air as possible.

Freeze overnight (I always find this a rather strange direction as it suggests that you would be eating the ice-cream for breakfast. After our indulgence in Athens, I can recommend this, but I didn't think that other people would share my odd eating habits).

One of our guests was Dardane, a Kosovar working internationally as a consultant for the World Health Organisation as well as having been the Kosovan Prime Minister's adviser on health. She is the perfect target for a recently-established group called Brain Gain Kosova which aimed to lure back to the homeland all the educated, skilled members of the diaspora currently using their expertise in the service of other countries. When the Homeland Calling fund was set up to gather funds for the KLA in the late 'nineties, it was an enormous success; everyone seemed more sceptical about this new attempt. It seems that Kosovars might have been more willing to give money to arm their soldiers than to skill up their newly independent government.

Certainly Dardane – young, beautiful, talented – talked about her frustrations at working in Kosovo. The job she had accepted here is at a fraction of the salary that she was offered elsewhere (recent consultancies had been in Fiji, Copenhagen, Kazakhstan), and she still felt that she had not been able to contribute appropriately. 'I feel so frustrated that I go round the world helping other governments to improve their health services, and I've not been able to do things for my own country. You realise what that Kosovan expression means – 'one bloom doesn't make a spring'. There's not much you can do when it's just you against the system.' The reasons she gave for the inability to bring full-blown

spring to Kosovo include party loyalties that stop the best people getting the job because old party ties have more power. She also talked about being female and young; according to her, Kosovo's problem is its fifty-year-old men.

Rob asked her what she would change about Kosovo if she could change one thing. She said she'd like to see a willingness to employ women in leadership, decision-making roles.

So I asked Rob what his one thing would be; he answered, 'corruption. There's a sense amongst the big fish that corruption is an accepted part of life in Kosovo, and that they are therefore untouchable. And the little fish, because they know (or believe they know) what their bosses are up to, think that no-one will go after people committing crimes that are so much smaller. There needs to be a high-profile case where someone apparently untouchable is taken down.'

I think that people would just assume that whoever has been caught had simply not paid off or brought in the right people. They'll change their protection mechanisms, but not their corrupt behaviour.

I wondered myself about Rob's question, and decided what my own answer would be. I told Dardane, 'but at the point when the flower opens up its petals, it doesn't know whether it is going to be a lone bloom or part of an enormous spring display.' That's what I'd like to see – a belief, in every part of life in Kosovo, that your actions can affect the whole, and that no spring display is possible without that attitude. But in Kosovo there are too many people who don't want to take the risk that Dardane took, because they worry that they will find themselves a lone bloom. It feeds into the issue that Rob highlighted: people believe that they might as well make a bit (a lot) of money on a government tender, because everyone else is doing it, and their probity won't change anything. In the face of the chronic water shortages, when Kosovo's lakes were at their lowest recorded level, I had a conversation with the museum guides who lamented the terrible situation – *as they hosed down their paving stones*. They didn't believe that their own small water-saving measures could do anything to improve the enormous problem facing their country. There is the same problem with the widespread non-payment of electricity bills ('Why should I pay? Nobody else does.'), which leads to the lack of investment in the electricity system – which leads of course to power cuts – and inedible ice-cream.

31.
Unorthodox Easters

New Serbian vocabulary: *peršin* (parsley), *vosak* (wax)

This, from a recipe book I bought in Pristina called *The Kosovan Kitchen,* is called 'Honey cream'. It tastes delicious though to be honest I am not sure whether it really sets off the honey which is one of its ingredients, as much as the raspberries.

Ingredients
375g raspberries
375g cream cheese
1.5 tbsp lemon juice
1.5 tbsp vanilla sugar
6 tbsp honey

Wash and drain the raspberries. Mash half of them with a fork and keep to one side. Combine the other half of the raspberries with the other ingredients, and spoon into tall glasses. Top with the mashed raspberries.
　　Serves 6.

The Orthodox calendar runs twelve days later than the Julian, so as soon as we had finished celebrating our Easter we could start looking forward to another one. And as soon as we had finished one honey recipe, we could start looking forward to another one of those too. We invited Dardan, our fellow beekeeper, to come round to eat our honey cream at dinner with his new wife, Ana. The focus of our conversation together was, for once, not honey-gathering but honeymoons; we wanted to hear from him and Ana about their first three weeks of married life.

'Well, Ana has just experienced her first challenge of living in her new home in Pristina,' Dardan spoke for her. Ana's family home is many miles, and a border away, in Albania; the challenge stemmed from the fact that theirs is a mixed marriage – while Dardan comes from an

Albanian Muslim family, she is an Albanian Orthodox Christian. There are hardly any Albanian Orthodox Christians in Kosovo, despite the significant numbers in Ana's native Albania, and the Kosovo Serbs who are *Serbian* Orthodox Christians. There is a significant minority of Kosovo Albanian *Catholics*, but because Orthodox Easter and Catholic Easter differ not only in date, but also in traditions, for all practical purposes Ana was alone among the Albanian population of Kosovo as she tried to prepare to celebrate Easter with her traditional egg dyeing. Ana said, 'I don't feel like an outsider here at all, but this time of year is tricky' – none of the shops in ethnically-Albanian Kosovo knew what she needed.

She described the trip that she and Dardan had therefore made to the town of Gračanica, at fifteen minutes drive away, the nearest Serb community to Pristina, and the nearest place that would be preparing for Easter as Ana was trying to. Dardan pulled a face when he described the journey. It's not a place they would naturally go, and certainly not somewhere they would normally feel comfortable. It's a mono-ethnic Serbian town whose numbers were swollen after the war by Serbs from Pristina and other areas nearby, clustering for safety round the medieval Serbian Orthodox monastery in its centre. The shops in Gračanica take Serbian dinars as payment; the car numberplates are registered according to Belgrade's conventions, not the Kosovan government's, and Cyrillic lettering makes the shop signs incomprehensible to most young Kosovo Albanians.

Nevertheless, Ana and Dardan had gone shopping there, using their broken Serbian to ask for help in buying the egg dye from Ana's fellow believers.

I hadn't realised until this conversation how significant this egg-dyeing process is for the celebration of Orthodox Easter, but when I arrived for my weekly lesson at the home of another Ana, our Serbian teacher, I found her supervising her teenage daughters in the dyeing of about a hundred eggs.

'How so many eggs?' I asked haltingly. The family only has a couple of chickens so someone was on overdrive. Poking at a saucepan which bubbled and bobbed with eggs, Ana said that you need enough to be able to offer an egg to any visitor you have or friend you see over the period of the festivities. And what do you do with the multi-coloured

clutch you collect from your own friends? I presumed that re-gifting was not an option. She told me about a game that sounded a bit like conkers – you bash your egg against someone else's and the one to break first loses.

But it would be terrible to do any damage to the beautiful eggs that she had decorated so far, heaped in a large bowl of fertility on the table. They were golden, green, yellow, red, purple, orange, blue, some with designs and fine leaf motifs somehow picked out in negative against the colour. With pride, Ana explained that although the purple, orange and blue came from commercial dyes, the others were the result of natural colouring. She gestured to the pile of onion skins, spinach, marigold flowers on the kitchen counter.

Some of the eggs had simply been boiled with the colorant until they took on their jewel hues. But I was shown, on the hob, a saucepan bubbling with a variation on this basic dyeing method; here an egg and a single parsley leaf had been put inside the toe of a pair of tights before being boiled up with onion skins in what could have been an exotic soup or witchy ritual. I'm told that Nigella makes *bouquet garni* in her old popsocks so this is perhaps the Balkan equivalent. However, at the end of the lesson I was shown the finished product. Ana had laid an exquisite egg, showing the outline of the parsley leaf in white where the dye had been unable to reach it, and the rest of the egg golden as an onion dome.

The other designs had apparently been 'painted' on the eggs with melted beeswax. Once the wax had dried, the eggs had been soaked in the dye, and when they were removed from the liquid, the wax had been gently scraped off to reveal the pattern in white beneath.

But I was told that the most important eggs were the plain red ones. They seemed to me the most pagan, the most blatantly symbolic of fertility, but another Serbian friend assured me that their significance is because they're the colour of Christ's blood. If I'd managed to translate her correctly, Ana said that the colour comes from boiling with cinnamon, but I was puzzled by this – the only time I have known cinnamon to be red is in the case of Tic-Tac sweets. Surely eggs boiled with cinnamon would come out brown? Or am I wrong, and those Tic-Tacs have been carefully simmered with spices to give them that carmine colour?

During that lesson Ana wouldn't give me an egg because hers hadn't yet been blessed, but, arriving to drive me home, Zorica handed me a red one from those she had decorated and already taken to the priest.

'You have to keep a red egg from Easter in your kitchen cupboard and then you can be sure of prosperity to the house for the coming year,' she explained. I told her that I knew this already – we had been given a red egg last year when we visited an Orthodox home in Macedonia at Easter time.

'Ah, in that case...' Zorica was concerned to explain the correct procedure for disposing of the previous year's egg and replacing it with this year's, with no interruption of the good luck they bring. I thought of the pause for breath in the calls of 'The king is dead; long live the king' – those frightening spaces on thresholds, where the potential for change, for mayhem peek through.

On Easter Sunday I should throw the previous year's egg into running water; only then would I be able to put this year's egg in my kitchen cupboard. The running water posed a challenge as Pristina is famously 'the city without a river'. Even more problematically, I was due to be competing in the Pristina half-marathon on Orthodox Easter Sunday and wasn't sure that I would be able to manage a trip out of Pristina to do this thing properly. But who would turn down the chance for prosperity for a year? The Macedonian egg had ushered in the year when I got my own bee suit, my own bee skeps, and finally seen what they would look like in use, and first harvested my own honey. I had made precious friendships, worked on unforgettable projects at the Ethnological Museum, and the *kulla*, even passed my basic Serbian exam. I had started writing this book. The Slavic good luck egg had actually heralded the year that offered Kosovo independence; I wanted more years like this!

I was reminded that the route of the half-marathon would take us past one small stream. If I could take the old egg with me and throw it strategically as I passed (which, after all, would sadly not be at great speed) then I could come home from the race to greet the beginning of a prosperous year.

Of course, there was a significant drag on my otherwise aerodynamic physique as a result of the egg bumping around in my bumbag,

but as it turned out, throwing it provided a nice diversion at kilometre 16 when things were starting to hurt a little. When I got back home, smug and sweaty after my 21-kilometre haul, I went straight to the kitchen to inaugurate the new year appropriately.

The next week I was working with a Serbian colleague so I told him about my egg experiences.

'And what did you do with the red egg on Good Friday?'

On Good Friday? My efforts had all been focused on Easter Sunday.

'Ummm, nothing.' Oh no, had I got it wrong?

Sure enough, he told me that on Good (or, in Serbian, 'Big') Friday, the woman in charge of the house – his mother, for example – boils up the red eggs at dawn and with the first one that is ready she goes into each room touching the sleeping family members on their faces with the hot egg for good luck. It sounds to me like the kind of thing you'd be offered as an expensive spa treatment, and I couldn't believe that I didn't take my opportunity for this. But Ana hadn't mentioned it...

I had been reading *Black Lamb, Grey Falcon,* the account by Rebecca West, the mad and extraordinary British traveller to Kosovo in the 1930s, and remembered her bafflement in the face of a similar range of customs. *Koliko sela, toliko običaja,* she was told – 'there are as many customs as there are villages.' It didn't seem likely that I would master all, if any of them. But there was one more to try in the season of egg-dyeing.

That year, Orthodox Easter was only ten days away from the day celebrated in Kosovo as St George's Day. In the Balkans, St George's Day carries none of the slightly fey connotations with their National Front edge that I had got used to in England – no morris dancing pig-roast on the green – but is a day celebrated by Christians and Muslims alike, with origins which seem all to be connected with fertility and new life, similar to some of the vestiges seen in May Day in the UK. One of the rituals is to collect nettles and flowers and then sprinkle them in the water for an early-morning bath that brings good luck, health and strength for the coming year. And Ana told me that in the bath water that morning I should also put the red egg which cousin Zorica had given me.

On the dawn of St George's Day, I sat feeling rather like one of her

eggs myself, warming (and no doubt staining) nicely in my bath of nettles and flowers, along with the potent red egg rolling around my toes. It seemed like I was tempting fate if I really didn't want to get pregnant; you could almost smell the hormones in the air.

Ana and Dardan clearly knew what they were doing with those eggs they dyed so painstakingly. Shortly after our honey cream meal together, shortly after Orthodox Easter and St George's Day, they sent us an ultrasound picture of the baby they were expecting later that year.

32.
Honey for healing wounds

New Albanian vocabulary: *me dhunue* (to rape)

Ana and Dardan's excited message about their baby was a welcome relief to an inbox which was filling up with email about victims of domestic violence and trafficking. I had started doing some consultancy for an organisation that worked with women's shelters and I was learning that not all homes were so happily honeyed. One of the shelters I was working with had a beekeeping project running, and so on a day in early summer I caught the bus to a meeting place in the town of Gjakova where Sakibe, the director of the Safe House women's shelter, would wait to accompany me to the unmarked building some miles away.

Once in her car, I was soon lost on a convoluted route through Gjakova's suburbs. I wasn't sure whether Sakibe was doing this on purpose, but I knew that the shelter's location was kept secret; there was certainly no way I could find my way back here. It was an ironic echo of the scarf placed over the bride's face that I'd seen in photographs on my Women for Women visit.

We were driving through a gracious residential area – wide streets and houses each set in a little piece of garden. It was very different from Pristina's chaos of concrete and disregard for planning regulations, but Sakibe was negotiating the grid pattern of streets with frequent switches left and right, like some chess master. Finally she pointed out the building up ahead that was our destination. As we approached the shelter, we saw a man standing in the garden. She stiffened and suggested quickly that I should go in alone while she found out why he was there.

So I saw myself into her office and sat reading the posters on its walls.

The rules about anger:
Don't hurt other people

Don't hurt yourself
Don't destroy the things you have
Talk about it

The women who live in this house know all about anger, I guessed.

Sakibe had told me that there are about fourteen of them there at any one time. 'They come for a minimum of six, a maximum of eighteen months, and while they're here they have free medical services, psycho-social support, computer classes, English classes. They do all kinds of work, including beekeeping, to raise money for the shelter.' Most importantly, as the organisation's name assures them, they have a Safe House. In Albanian the word for *house* and the word for *home* are not differentiated and the atmosphere in the shelter could probably even be called homely. Rugs on the floors, non-institutional furniture, the smell of coffee, the sound of children's voices. I had only been to one women's shelter before, where I worked briefly as a volunteer in the UK in the 1990s. The shelter in Gjakova compared favourably from what I saw of it. It was clean and purposeful and upbeat.

As is Sakibe. She came back from her discussion with the lurking male.

'He was only wanting a job.'

It is this desire for work, for an income, that led so many of the women under Sakibe's care to where they are now. Research done for the project I was working on found that eighty per cent of victims of trafficking in Kosovo were lured by their traffickers with false promises of work. It is easy to see this as a consequence of dangerous naivety, but the research also showed that in almost half the cases, the trafficker was well known to the victim. So although we may comfort ourselves with ensuring that our daughters wouldn't get into cars with strange men, in some cases prevention of human trafficking would be better served by warnings against getting into cars with uncles, brothers-in-law, your friend's boyfriend... or indeed your best friend herself; many traffickers are women.

It seemed unbelievable that such things could be done within the family, when I had seen such repeated and powerful evidence of the priority put on the family unit in Kosovo. But I knew that in traditional Kosovan families, the head of the family has absolute power – for

good and for bad. I remembered the *Kanun*'s description of woman as a 'sack to be well used'; I could see that if something unspeakable was done to one member of a family by another, all the mechanisms that ensure safety and solidarity against strangers would become collusion.

Having once been an established transit point for trafficked women, Kosovo had recently become a source country. Women and girls from Kosovan villages are trafficked internally and to the brothels of Western countries. The reports I had seen in my work had made harrowing reading: 'my father's friends came to our house and offered me a job in a fast food restaurant but the agreement was that they would take me and follow me back home every day. The very first day the owner tied me up, closed my eyes and raped me. The next day he forced me to sleep with people...This continued regularly and he eventually sold me to five people who raped me and later on six brothers abused me sexually.'

For those who remain in Kosovo, their customers include shameful numbers of men from Kosovo's international community – all those UN bachelors or NATO squaddies, NGO employees far from their wives. One report interviewed men in Kosovo who have used the services of prostitutes, to identify the level of understanding they had about the possible histories of the women whose sexual services they were paying for. One strategy for tackling human trafficking works on the premise that if appropriately informed, clients of sex workers can be a powerful means for rescuing or at least alerting the police to the presence of victims of trafficking in brothels. Despite what it said on the wall of Sakibe's office, I felt anger rising in me, and a distinct desire to punch someone as I read some of the testimony from these men.

'I am concerned about trafficking because it is widespread and there are many victims. On the other hand, I think these kinds of services should exist because we have fun. I am somewhat concerned about my close relatives, particularly if they get involved and become victims.'

You vicious, smug bastard.

Sakibe told me that once women have escaped the company of men like this and have settled in the shelter, as far as possible attempts are made to find work for them. Beekeeping is an obvious choice – the area is known for its beekeeping and this municipality has the second highest number of hives in all Kosovo. Ten of them belong to Safe House.

Sakibe got out a small plastic pot to show me. It contained the nightcream made at the shelter from hive products, including propolis. Propolis is the dark brown, faintly unpleasant-looking sticky material that bees use as a multi-purpose disinfective coating in the hive. It is gathered from the shiny protective substance that covers buds and the shoots of young plants. Adem had pointed out to me how it was used for plugging gaps when they appeared in the honeycomb. Equally, if any intruder – for example, a mouse or beetle – appears in the hive, when the bees have stung it to death they will cover the corpse in propolis to disinfect it and prevent unhygienic putrefaction.

'We mix the propolis and wax together with Vaseline and almond oil,' said Sakibe, and allowed me to stick a finger into the rich, sweet-smelling nightcream. Of course I bought some, liking the idea of slathering myself like a queen bee every evening before bed.

Then Sakibe got out another pot that she explained was a cream with a different balance of ingredients, used for spots and blemishes. I hadn't encountered the word for 'spot' in Albanian before, and Sakibe and I had an uncomfortable moment while she tried to mime a skin complaint, before finally abandoning tact in the interests of linguistic accuracy, and pointing to my chin. I bought some of this cream for 'puçerra' too, with the curious image in my head of anointing the little pustule every night like some exotic flower waiting to bloom. Or, of course, like a little dead beetle perched on my face, kept from doing any more damage...

The money from the sale of the creams goes for some of the extras that make the shelter so attractive – Sakibe told me that those rugs on the floor, as well as the office computer and the women's television, were all paid for out of the funds raised by the bees' hard work. I had heard about the healing properties of honey; about the forest fires in Australia where koala bears suffering terrible burns had been treated with manuka honey applied direct to the skin. The more I heard here, the more I thought of this building as a hive of healing activity.

But Sakibe wasn't done. 'As well as the honey and skincare products, the women also produce handicrafts.' I made noises of polite interest and Sakibe called in some young women to show me their work. The girls' faces were lifeless and it seemed they could hardly bring themselves to answer my questions; they certainly didn't look me in

the eye. I had the strong impression that these were women who had not had a good deal from strangers in the past. And I felt instinctively that our common experience of beekeeping was not enough to bridge the gap between their experience and mine. No amount of chummy questions about glucose syrup was going to make the connection that had been managed with Shqipja and Lendita. I didn't try. But I did like to think about these fragile women at their work with the hives, wearing the veils that would enable them to look out at a small world of little dangers, and feel invincible, inviolable in the face of them. If anything was going to offer a sense of possibility for women to take control of their lives, then the microcosm of the hive where the queen rules over a healthy community in which everyone has a role, might just do it. From their faces, I could see it was a tall order.

However, none of their bitterness or suspicion had been communicated in the exquisite work they showed me. I got the same sense I'd had before when Kosovan women had shown me their needlework. It seems that these genteel handcrafts, all lace mats and embroidered towels and frilly aprons, are a kind of dreamworld, the careful stitching of an escape route. I have sat under corrugated iron roofs, or in homes that smell of farm animals, and now at the shelter with women who have been so terribly betrayed and hurt, and yet on all these occasions, it seems that all the spare energy these women have had has gone into magicking these puffs of fine living or fine dining out of the hard grind of real life.

Women start stitching well before they're married, producing crochet, embroidery, woven work, and the 'oia' I'd seen at the Ethnological Museum that I still can't describe with an English word. In Kosovo girls seem to pick up these skills like children in bookish homes pick up reading. By adolescence they are preparing the little woven coasters, the sets of three mats (always in sets of three) that go on shelves and tables, the mats that go on television sets, the tablecloths and traycloths that are used when serving guests with drinks and sweetmeats. And so, at the end of a day spent sweating with heavy kitchenwork or on the smallholding, the young women of Kosovo sit preparing beautification for their homes of the future, for the potential grooms they can impress with the nimbleness of their fine fingers, for the husbands they will have who will love or flatter them. And one by one

these fine lamina of aspirations are piled up to fill large cases kept on top of wardrobes (a bottom drawer would be too small for a Kosovar's trousseau). They sit there like a dream narrative.

I suppose that there is no better place for fantasies to be spun than in this Safe House. And the women who Sakibe had called in showed me theirs for sale. To be honest, I don't really like little lace mats around my home. And I didn't have space for any more – as a result of the generosity of the women I had met during my time in Kosovo, I had been given more than I could ever possibly display or appreciate. But I wanted to tread lightly around the work they'd dreamed up, so I asked to buy one small flowered traycloth.

The other work they did at the shelter was something I'd not seen for sale before, though I had seen the finished product when I had been invited to the wedding of Elmaze's brother. On that hot day in rural Kosovo I had turned up to the family's smallholding to find incongruous tableaux of gorgeous finery against the backdrop of haystacks and chickens. I'd seen a honey ritual, too – the bride invited into her new home, with the groom's family, dipping her fingers into a saucer of honey with which she then anointed the lintel to show the sweetness she was bringing to the house.

The bride, and the wives of the groom's brothers were all dressed in trousers of extravagant swathes of fine white tulle. Over their fine white blouses cuffed in lacy *oia* they wore elaborate waistcoats embroidered in intricate patterns of silver thread. Later I had some frank conversations with Elmaze where I heard the extraordinary prices of these wedding outfits – even more, of course, when the silver or gold thread is made from real metal.

The women at Safe House had started production of these waistcoats and they showed me not only the intricate finished product, but also a half-finished model in which you could still see the cardboard base cut into the required shapes. It seemed appropriate that it was in this women's shelter that I was offered an insight into the mechanics of marriage, of what goes on beneath the glitzy embroidery.

Sakibe told me that the shelter gave one of these waistcoats to Nicole Kidman when she visited Gjakova in her role of Goodwill Ambassador for the United Nations Development Fund for Women last year. I had pointed out to me the photograph sellotaped on the wall

Traditional dancing troupe wearing embroidered *jelek* waistcoats

which showed Sakibe with her arm round Ms Kidman. I remembered reading about her visit, a low-key trip in which she focused on Gjakova as the city hardest hit in Kosovo by atrocities during the war. So many men were rounded up in the streets and killed, or targeted in other ways by Serb forces, that there is now a large number of Gjakovar families who have a female head of household. A great strike for feminism, at an immeasurable cost.

I clearly couldn't rival a Hollywood star, but Sakibe was keen to thank me, too, for my visit. To increase the market for their honey, the shelter had been distributing recipes for dishes with honey as an ingredient. Sakibe gave me a photocopy of a recipe for *kurore* ('crown') to take away with me. I told her that I would include it in my book, and that I would do what I could to spread the message about the shelter's needs. And then I left her to get on with her work, her beekeeping, her nurturing of damaged women, her production of soothing ointment.

Kurore

Ingredients
3 eggs
sunflower oil
2 tablespoons of brandy
the grated rind of 1 lemon
approx 300g plain flour
50g dried fruit
100g ground almonds
500g honey

Beat the eggs with 2 tablespoons of oil, the brandy and the grated lemon rind. Add as much flour as is necessary to produce a soft mass. Divide this repeatedly into half and half again until you have 32 pieces.

Flour your hands and roll the pieces of dough between your palms to make them into small balls. Fry them lightly in oil and drain on kitchen paper.

Cut the dried fruit into small pieces and mix in a saucepan with the almonds and honey. (A tip for transferring honey easily from the jar

is to coat your spoon in oil first.) Warm on the hob until the mixture binds together.

Add the fried balls to the honey mixture, turning so that the balls are covered in honey. Leave for approximately 10 minutes and then transfer to a well-greased round baking tray, placing the balls round the edge and leaving a space in the middle. Leave to cool before serving.

Makes 32 pieces.

33.
The bees and the *gurabies*

New Albanian vocabulary: *grabitje* (robbing)

No-one in Kosovo quite understood this book. I told people that I was writing about bees and beekeeping, about honey and the people who'd led me to it, but it was losing something in translation. Despite my protests to the contrary, people saw it as a technical book about bee-keeping, even though they knew that I had first seen a hive up close less than 18 months before. I suppose this isn't so surprising given that the international missions which ran this country were mainly staffed by people who first saw Kosovo up close less than 18 months previously. If you treat these people as experts, then perhaps you'd accept a begin-ner lecturing you on how to mind your own beeswax too. I'm not just being snide – there really is a sense that any given member of the inter-national community is likely to know better about any given subject than their Kosovan counterpart. It's most frightening when this view is articulated by Kosovars themselves.

So people thought that I was writing a 'how to' manual for this arcane and complex art and science of beekeeping; and unreservedly they seemed to want to help me get it written. Valon, *jashtëzakonisht i mirë* Ethnological Museum guide and friend, had been suggesting for a while that I should come and speak to his neighbour who was a bee-keeper of some thirty years experience. So we finally fixed a time, and I turned up at Valon's village, soon to become a Pristina suburb as new building infilled the precious few green spaces between the two.

Muharrem, whom we visited down the road from Valon, shares his name with the Bektashi Muslim month of fasting (similar to Ramadan for other branches of Islam). When we arrived at his house we were shown into the garden where he sat in the shade of a spreading tree, with a younger beekeeper taking advice from him. The ascetic con-nection made by his name was reinforced when he reminded us that one of the most famous of his beekeeper brethren was Gandhi. I took

my place near the other beekeeper, and listened to Muharrem talking.

He was a natural lecturer – and did not welcome interruptions. He had heard that I was writing a book about beekeeping and told me what should go in it. He started with a history of beekeeping, taking in India and the ancient Egyptians (who apparently kept a species of bee that doesn't sting); he talked about different hive designs, sending his daughter off to bring out as visual aid a 'primitive' hive he was given by a beekeeper in Turkey. From this he explained about the 'Dadant-Blatt' hives I've never seen, and the modern Langstroth-Root versions that his bees are in, like mine. All the time he was gesturing with his packet of cigarettes – first it was Asia, and around it he mapped the world and the spread of beekeeping. Then it was the frames of the Langstroth-Root hive. As he outlined his personal method for organis-ing the frames within the hive, he used it again, explaining that the bees fill their honeycomb from right to left 'like Arabic'.

I tried to stop him to explain what kind of book it was that I was writing, but he just put up a hand. I wondered what it would have been like to have attempted interrupting Gandhi.

Luckily a natural break in the conversation came when his daugh-ter came out from the house with some little scone-like cakes. She told us they are '*gurabie*' which I presumed was a direct translation of 'rock cakes' given that the word '*gur*' is Albanian for stone. My etymology turned out to be wrong, but the idea was right, and the 'rock cakes' were tasty.

While Muharrem had his mouth full, I sneaked in a hurried expla-nation of my book. I wouldn't presume to write a technical book on beekeeping; only been a beekeeper for 18 months; interested in learn-ing more about the story of beekeeping in Kosovo now and in the past.

I think he was pleased by this, and he relaxed into the story of his own bees. He used to have more than a hundred hives, but at the time of my visit was down to something less than forty. During the war in 1999 he and his family left as refugees for Turkey (where he introduced his personal system for organising the frames in a hive to people he met there, and was given the 'primitive' he had shown us earlier, in thanks). When he came back he had only nine hives left. I asked why that was: were they ransacked by Serb forces like Rexhep's, or stolen, or did they die from neglect?

He explained about his neighbour's son who was being attacked by Serb forces in the house next door. The boy ran away from them, escaping into Muharrem's garden where he tried hiding between the hives. A helicopter overhead – Muharrem's cigarette packet came into action again as visual aid, though my imagination was working quite well anyway – saw him, and started firing, wounding him, as well as damaging some of the hives. In his panic and pain the boy thrashed out and knocked over several more, leaving the honey accessible to the bees from others of Muharrem's colonies.

In a situation like this, bees have a short-term strategy for success which is disastrous in the long term: if other bees' honey is left exposed, they will abandon the regulated harmony of their own hive for a 'robbing' spree when they will gorge themselves on the free honey – until it runs out. Their own hive will by this time have been neglected past redemption and they die. This is what happened in Muharrem's garden when hives were abandoned for bees to raid the spilling honey, and he lost the majority of his colonies.

It was a powerful, poignant story to hear on this sunny day, sitting quietly under the tree by Muharrem's hives, and it seemed like the story of the Kosovo campaign in miniature – the damage, the injury, the looting and economic devastation.

But Muharrem wasn't depressed. He was telling me now how much he loves his bees, how he takes his coffee down to the hives every morning and sits there sipping it and watching them going about their business. I was jealous. I have never yet found a way to explain to Adem that I would like to pursue my beekeeping apprenticeship like this occasionally. I wondered whether Adem ever even does this himself. Does he sit watching my bees swirling round those from his own hives on their endless mission for flowers and sweetness? I would love to think so.

It's an image of peaceful cohabitation. I had no idea of Muharrem's politics, and from his implacable hand in the face of my attempted interruptions earlier I could imagine he could be a fierce defender of the way he thought things should be. But maybe his Gandhism might extend to an acceptance, a promotion, of the idea that with 'an eye for an eye, the whole world ends up blind.' Maybe. After all, it's a sunny day in a beautiful garden.

His daughter reappeared from the house. Following my praise of her *gurabie* she had written out the recipe for me. For me, the cakes will always have the memory of the garden where a boy tried to shelter from gunfire among the beehives; and where homes and families then built themselves up again, so you can now sit there in the mornings with a coffee and feel at peace.

Gurabie

To make 15-20

Ingredients
70ml oil
1 egg
140g sugar
1 teaspoon bicarbonate of soda
70ml yoghurt*
500g plain flour

Preheat oven to 220 degrees. Mix ingredients together to make a stiff dough (the instructions I was given here say that it should be 'thick as dough for making *pite* (see p.109. Test your earlobe again). Form the dough into balls of 5-8cm diameter and coat with egg yolk. Bake for 15 minutes until golden.

---

* I had wondered at the repeated use of yoghurt in Kosovan baking where milk would be used in English recipes. I had assumed it was related to the difficulty of keeping milk fresh, making a virtue of necessity. It was only one day when I wanted to make a basic cake recipe from the UK and wasn't able to find baking powder in the shops that I realised why yoghurt is so important. The gas which makes cakes rise is produced by the combination of acid and alkali; both these are present in baking powder (or self-raising flour) but another way to achieve the same raising agent is to combine alkaline bicarbonate of soda with yoghurt's acidity.

34.
Russian honey dessert with Moroccan tea and an Albanian *mangall*

New Albanian vocabulary: *filxhan* (dainty coffee cup, espresso size)

My folder of recipes copied down from beekeepers and their colleagues and daughters was growing nicely plump, and so was I, from trying so many. I was learning about the techniques for making these recipes, and for serving them, learning how to substitute honey for sugar – adding a pinch of bicarbonate of soda to counteract honey's slight acidity, slightly reducing the amount called for in the recipe, to allow for honey's greater sweetness, and adjusting for its (approximately twenty per cent greater) liquid content. My appetite was growing for entertaining Kosovo-style, and I decided that it was time to expand our entertaining hardware so that we could offer our guests the honey from our hives in appropriate settings.

In Kosovo, stylish entertaining means coffee. People say that the coffee served in Kosovo is the best outside of Italy; there is certainly enough fuss made of it. I knew that making coffee for your guests was traditionally men's work in Kosovo. So while the women of the house would have struggled in the heat of the kitchen, hefting sacks of food bought in quantities to feed extended families (even now in Kosovo the average household size is seven – no vegetables are sold here in measurements less than a kilo, and the supermarkets carry what I would call 'catering' size packs of flour and rice), the men would have practised the fine art – in the Balkans almost a science – of coffee-making.

I'd seen at the Ethnological Museum how in a culture where it was not considered suitable for a man either to abandon his guests in the room where visitors are received, or for him to enter the kitchen (i.e. women's) quarters, the practical consequence of the host's coffee-making was the often beautiful piece of furniture called a *mangall*. It is a decorative brazier, with a removable metal bowl that can be filled with

The *xhezve* for making Turkish coffee

hot coals outside the house, and then brought in to be used as the heat source for boiling up the coffee grounds in the traditional *xhezve*. Around the edge of the bowl to hold the coals is a brim wide enough to hold the attractive little coffee cups.

Sadly I had only seen these *mangall*s in museums. Don't go thinking this is because the modern male Kosovar is now comfortable in the kitchen – it has more to do with the advent of electricity. But the *mangall* struck me as both useful and elegant, and I wondered how I could get such an accessory for our own sitting room. I made enquiries of my colleagues at the museum and was met with polite indulgence mixed with bemusement.

'You can't buy *mangall*s any more in Kosovo. And, er, why do you want one?' I gestured at the bronze dome, the ornamented handles.

'Don't you think it's beautiful?'

'Well, yes, but would it go in your sitting room?' I had not taken account of the fact that this was a country where if you could afford it you would buy your sitting room as one piece: wraparound sofa, huge matching cabinets, all still smelling of plastic and varnish, and the foreign

factory where they were produced.

Yes, it would go in our sitting room! The room was already a strange mixture of John Lewis imported fabric, things we'd had made by a local carpenter, and a leather sofa and chairs we had haggled for having found them abandoned in a field of chickens on a journey out of Pristina in our first few weeks in Kosovo. My friends' scepticism only made me more determined to find us a *mangall,* so Rob and I planned a weekend in Albania. Rob would go walking, exploring the Shala valley, on the other side of the Accursed Mountains from Kosovo; I would go shopping.

The trip would be a fun tourist opportunity, but there was something more fundamental than that. Because of Kosovo's close relationship with Albania, and the aspirations of some Kosovo Albanians to unite politically with their older brother, I was beginning to feel that I couldn't move much further in understanding Kosovo without meeting the family across the border.

It made me sad to think that this was the sibling who had done so much better at preserving the family silver. Kosovo was empty of its own antiques – the result of historical poverty (*mangalls* of the style I was looking for would always have been a rare luxury item) and pillage: the European Agency for Reconstruction estimates reckon nearly fifty per cent of Kosovo's houses were, like Adem and Xhezide's, burned during the conflict from 1998 to 1999; far more were abandoned when their owners fled during that period. These were just the last in a series of attacks on the property of Kosovo's inhabitants over hundreds of years.

The town of Kruja, where Scanderbeg had his castle in northern Albania, has known pillage of a different kind, and was – I was assured – stuffed full of antique shops which in turn would be stuffed with *mangalls.* Villagers from the surrounding area come to Kruja with their grandmothers' hand-woven aprons, the hand-embroidered belts used for swaddling babies, the *kilims* from rooms that are being upgraded with Ikea design rugs – and when they've fitted the central heating and bought the cafetiere, they also bring in their *mangalls.*

When I reached the cobbled streets of Kruja, an old town sitting high on an escarpment, and started visiting the tens of shops huddled there, I saw it was true that there was an enormous choice of braziers in Kruja. It was lucky that I had planned Operation Mangall as a two-

day campaign.

Scanderbeg himself couldn't have been more careful in his tactics. I arrived late one afternoon and spent almost four hours going into every shop asking about *mangalls* and prices and taking photographs of the options. Some were ancient to the point of shabbiness, and I could imagine the Kosovars' faces if I came home bearing any of those as booty from my trip. Others were made of copper shined pink as fingernails – they would not have looked out of place in one of the plastic all-in-one rooms of the Kosovan elite. But they would certainly not fit in with a leather sofa that had had to have the legacy of chickens wiped off it before we could use it.

While making the decision I comforted myself with buying other smaller handcrafts: some old rugs, some jewellery, a carved wooden block that the shopkeeper told me was used to mark your bread when you took it to the village oven, but from the dye that seeped out onto the dough I first tried it out on, seems more likely to have been a textile printing block. Yuk. I tried on traditional waistcoats, ornate necklaces and embroidered blouses. I haggled as best I could, as the shopkeepers looked on in some bemusement. They could tell from my accent that I wasn't from round here, and when I used '*kqyrë*' instead of '*pa*' for 'looking' at their wares, when I said '*tash*' instead of '*tani*' to tell them I didn't want to buy *now*, they could tell that my Albanian had been raised in Kosovo. But somehow it didn't fit together for them. Sometimes I wondered whether it fitted together for me either.

Finally I decided that our humble sitting room couldn't quite carry off the *mangall* with the elaborate dome crested with an eagle, and I settled for the *mangall* with more than a passing resemblance to the one at the Ethnological Museum. Was it this that I had been trying to recreate in this long quest across a mountain range, across a border? I realised that I had a long way to go before my chicken-shit sofa and Oxford Street curtains could attain the elegance of the museum's *oda,* but for cosy evenings, attentive hosting and good times with friends my new acquisition seemed to bode well.

It was wrapped up in sacks and then bundled, with me, into a minibus taxi to take me on to the town of Shkodra where Rob was waiting to drive us back to Pristina, exchanging our traveller tales. I had my antiques; he had stayed the night with the family of a man he had got

talking to in one of the villages on his walking route. The man's elderly mother had offered to wash Rob's feet to welcome him to their home. If I hadn't been so pleased with my *mangall* I might have felt outdone.

With all the effort that had gone into buying this large lump of old metal, I was keen to use it as soon as possible. We organised an evening meal including honey dessert for our American friends, 'Coriander' Sue and her husband, Mike. Sue's appreciation of my honey had recently led to her visiting the bees with us and watching the harvest of more honey. I had enjoyed the visit – she had asked the same kind of questions I had a year before. This time, I had been able to answer them myself. I had begun to accept what the limitations of my beekeeping skill and scope were always going to be, at least while my hives were on Adem's farm, but I could also now see my growing competence in my work with the bees. There's nothing like explaining something to someone else to make you aware of what you've learned. I was going through the parallel process in my relationship with Kosovo – we had had a stream of house guests from the UK over the summer and I had surprised us all in being able to talk authoritatively about this place, despite the complicated identity of resident foreigner I knew I had here. When outsiders appear, you feel you belong more than ever before.

I had planned that we would sit outside and use the *mangall* for warmth after the sun had gone down. But when Sue and Mike arrived they announced that they had brought with them their set for making mint tea, bought during their time living at the other end of the former Ottoman Empire, in Morocco. It was a perfect companion to the *mangall*, and at the end of our meal we sat on the terrace with Mike presiding over water boiled on the brazier and flavoured with his homegrown mint. We all knew that the rules had got a bit muddled when it was the guest who made the drinks, but once women are allowed out of the kitchen and into the conversation, you've already unleashed all kinds of chaos on Ottoman structures. We drank happily.

Before that, we had indulged ourselves in a honey recipe I had seen in an Albanian cookery magazine that had started circulating that month. The dish calls itself 'Russian dessert', which was a bold bit of marketing for the time, given that Russia was obstructing recognition of Kosovan independence. The country's natural cultural and religious ties with the Slavic Serbs mean that Russians – and maybe even Russian

desserts – are viewed with suspicion or worse by most Albanians. However, with our Moroccan mint tea and our imported *mangall*, the Brits and Americans sitting on a terrace in Kosovo were prepared to welcome new international ideas to our dinner. Anyway, apart from the thirty millilitres of sour cream, the recipe didn't seem very Russian to me. As I had discovered, it takes more than a dab of a country's national foodstuff to make you one of them.

'Russian dessert' (though since this ends up as something like a loaf, I felt afterwards that this would really be best served at a tea rather than as a dessert for a meal. My friend, Martha tried the recipe and suggested that it made a very successful pudding served with fruit and cream)

Ingredients
170g butter
4 eggs
200g sugar
2 tbsp sour cream
2 tbsp honey
130g ground hazelnuts
80g plain flour
1 sachet yeast
juice of half a lemon
130g icing sugar
1 tbsp water

Preheat oven to 200 degrees.
Beat the butter until it is soft. Break the eggs into the bowl and combine with sugar, sour cream, honey, hazelnuts, flour and yeast.
Grease and line a loaf tin and pour in the mixture. Bake in the oven for 45 minutes.
While it is cooking, put the lemon juice in a bowl with the icing sugar. Add a tablespoonful of water and mix until combined.
When the loaf is baked, cover the surface with the icing using a knife. Slice and serve.

35.
Something old, something new, something borrowed; the politics of the hive

New Albanian vocabulary: *gaz lotësjellës* (tear gas)

Bees have been used as a metaphor for political systems from the first time some sticky-fingered analyst took a look inside a hive. I'd recently read Bee Wilson's book *The Hive*, which devotes a whole chapter to the way that bees have been seen in political terms: as republics (Virgil's *Georgics*) or as socialist paradise (for Maeterlinck the hive was where 'private life was eroded in a sacrifice of the individual to the common interest').

I'm not really interested in politics, but I'm glad someone else is. In Kosovo, there is one grass-roots political movement in particular whose passion had impressed me, and I was to discover a new respect for their beekeeping too.

One of the first words my sister learned to read was the word 'Hoover', as she followed my mother around the house, with the distinctive font on the vacuum cleaner just at eye level for a three-year-old. In the same way, one of the first words I learned in Albanian was the word '*vetëvendosje*' ('self-determination'), sprayed in even red and black letters wherever you look in Pristina.

Vetëvendosje is probably the most efficient organization in Kosovo – a movement of mainly young Albanian activists fighting for full independence and sovereignty for Kosovo, and thus the withdrawal of UN and international missions. They protest with a creativity and vibrancy that is unusual in Kosovan public life, and they lobby with an articulate voice of opposition lacking elsewhere in Kosovo's political life.

As well as managing to daub almost literally every public building in Kosovo with their red and black 'no negotiation; self-determination' slogan (formed with stencils that maintain a brand consistency that

many multi-national companies would be proud of), Vetëvendosje activists have developed a range of attention-grabbing stunts and campaigns. On the ubiquitous white 4x4s which roamed Pristina labeled with 'UN' in big letters on their doors, Vetëvendosje added an 'F' and a 'D' to spell out *'fund'* (Albanian for 'end'), making each official vehicle driven by UN personnel a mobile advert for the idea that the internationals' time was up.

When in early 2007 the UN envoy Marti Ahtisaari published his 'package' of recommendations for the future of Kosovo, falling far short of recommending the unconditional independence which Vetëvendosje considers Kosovars to have won for themselves in 1999, the organisation launched another campaign. Every skip in town was graffitied with the words 'Ahtisaari package' – and thus every litter-conscious citizen who threw their rubbish away was made complicit in the view that Ahtisaari's package contained only garbage.

The organisation has done more, and far more controversially. There is a ruthlessness to their mass actions that gives them an uncomfortable edge. In the demonstration in May 2008 that railed at the UN but also the Kosovan government for their weakness in the face of the Serbian local elections being held illegally in Kosovo, and their undemocratic acceptance of a new constitution without proper debate, Vetëvendosje activists sprayed sewage water at the Assembly, government and UN buildings. When they didn't move away after Vetëvendosje's warning, police officers standing on guard were caught by the spray too.

In Vetëvendosje demonstrations on Albanian flag day – my birthday – in 2006, activists broke windows in the government, UN and Assembly buildings, with thrown bottles containing red paint. So when the organisation announced another demonstration in February 2007, the police stepped up their level of preparedness. The British Office issued warnings asking British citizens in Kosovo to stay at home. I did as I was told; my friend Alex didn't take any notice. She is a British woman who came out to Kosovo to interview some of the Vetëvendosje activists as part of her PhD in non-violent resistance movements. She stayed, and stayed, and is now a leading figure in Vetëvendosje, writing their weekly newsletters and helping to organise their campaigns.

What exactly happened on 10 February 2007 is still a matter of legal debate. The protest certainly began peacefully. When the protestors neared the government building they discovered that the police had blocked the road to prevent them accessing it. UNMIK police and Kosovo Police Service officers were lined up facing the oncoming demonstration. The protestors started removing the barricades and linked arms trying to push through the police cordon, some throwing the wooden staves on which their slogans were mounted. To disperse the crowd, the police responded with pepper spray, then tear gas, and then with rubber bullets.

As they ran from the crowd, two Vetëvendosje activists were pursued by a Romanian contingent of police, posted here as part of the international effort to support Kosovo. The activists were shot at close range with plastic bullets later found to be of an outlawed type.

Sitting at home in the centre of the city that day all we could hear were the sounds of police sirens. Later the phone rang. Rob was being asked to accompany the Prime Minister to visit the injured activists in hospital.

I was in bed when he came back late, and quiet. He didn't want to talk about it.

'It was just a hospital. The two guys were young; they looked terrible.' He turned the light off and we lay there in silence.

When we woke up the next morning we heard the news that the two men had died. Eighty-four other protestors had been injured, three seriously – one lost an eye.

The leader of Vetëvendosje, Albin Kurti, was arrested on the charges of calling for resistance with force, participating and leading a crowd which committed a criminal offence (the offence being the intention to throw 351 glass bottles filled with red paint at the vehicles and buildings of Kosovo institutions) and participating in a group obstructing official persons performing official duties. He was moved from prison to house arrest, without charge. When his case did come to trial, court procedures were farcically irregular. Kurti wasn't allowed to address the court, reportedly being told to 'shut up' by the international presiding judge. Amnesty International and the Helsinki Foundation, among other human rights organisations, took up Kurti's cause.

And all this took place under the auspices of the United Nations

and international judges, imported to Kosovo at great expense to show a new country how policing, how justice should be done.

Alex and I talk about this and other stuff when we meet. We naturally have much in common – she, too, has learned Albanian with Gazi, it was with her that I ran the half marathon, and limped through training for it – though I disagree profoundly with some, but not all, of her and Vetëvendosje's conclusions. However, I really appreciate their existence. Alex tells me that in political science there's a recognised challenge for all movements agitating for change, because the presumed benefit they bring will be a benefit for all society, not just their members or those who take to the streets. Which means that there is no reason for any one individual to take to the streets, as long as he knows that his neighbour will do so.

During one of our conversations it turns out that Alex is scared of bees. I check, 'but you like eating honey?' Oh yes. 'Well, if you want honey, someone has to get close to bees.'

'Yes,' she answers, 'but someone else.'

For the political metaphors of the hive, Virgil and Maeterlinck rest their case.

Alex offered to take me to visit a Vetëvendosje supporter, political activist and former KLA fighter who now keeps bees. The trip was the perfect combination of our interests, off to hear an expert's take on both bees and organised resistance movements. Halil lives in an idyllic spot high up in the hills above the town of Suhareka, some hours from Pristina. According to the statistics I had been given when I visited the Ministry, this municipality is the area with the highest number of beekeepers in all of Kosovo; as we drove through this blazing hot day, amid fields spattered with poppies and blue flowers I don't know the name of, and looked out across the area's lush hillsides, I could see why.

We continued driving up and up, and arrived at Halil's house. Greeted by him and his family we were immediately ushered to a deliciously shaded table in his garden. Chickens and children clucked around us, and I could hear the hum of the hives.

He has a lot of hives, and most of them three or more 'storeys' high. Nectar gathering here must be rich – looking out over the drowsy fields and woodlands with not another house in sight, I could imagine that this is a bee paradise. Halil wanted to show me the hives close up so, while

Alex and the others sat talking politics, I set off with Halil and his young daughter, who was wearing her own small bee suit, to see inside the hives.

We walked down the aisles of hives, looking in on occasional colonies where there were things of interest; Halil was fascinated by one hive where there was an unusually high number of drones being hatched. These are the males whose only task is to fertilise queen bees. They do no work (Bertie Wooster's gentleman's club took its name for a reason) but their life is really rather sad. They are harmless old chaps (they don't have a sting as this is a part of the egg-laying equipment possessed by their sisters who make up the majority of hive inhabitants) who hang around until the time seems right to them to go on a mating flight. They will look for a queen (usually not from their own hive) and couple with her in flight. As they pull away at the end of this giddying process, their genital organs are left inside the queen and ripped from their body. They die shortly afterwards. It doesn't sound like the queen stops to worry too much about the fate of her paramour – a queen will mate with up to twenty drones in one flight. We looked curiously at this *fin de siècle* hive where so many of the distinctive outsized drone larvae protruded from the honeycomb, capped with wax.

Once we had taken off the covers, and held frames up to the light, we could see that they were nearly ready for harvesting. They were dripping with pale lemon-coloured honey and as we lifted each one, we marveled at its weight. My mouth watered, and Halil told me that the honey should be ready to harvest in a week or so.

Suddenly, on a whim, Halil levered out another frame from the hive. He handed it to me and asked me to take it back to the table. We were going to get a chance to eat some now!

I had never eaten honey this fresh, even from my own hives because I had always centrifuged the frames before eating the honey. But in Halil's garden, once we were all sitting down with saucers in front of us, he simply took a knife to scrape the wax caps from the cells and then, in great sweeps, cut the honeycomb into enormous honey steaks and gave one to each of us.

The honey was really the best I'd ever tasted. It wasn't cloying, and was served to us at the temperature of the hive, which is pretty much the same as the core temperature of the human body. With its liquidity and warmth, I was almost unaware that I was actually eating

anything – just that my mouth was suffused with a sweet light fragrant treat.

And when the honey had gone, we were all still masticating on the wax, like a high-class chewing gum.

Once we were sat back down together to eat, Alex had her chance to hear Halil's politics and his stories of the resistance he was so active in during the 'eighties and 'nineties. He had been a comrade of the national hero Afrim Zhitia, and Alex asked about him. He had been in prison with Halil, and Halil became nostalgic and animated talking about their time there.

'That man was incredible. Honestly, sometimes you could believe that he might grow wings, and fly – it seemed that there was nothing he couldn't do.'

In Kosovo at that period, Albanian-language education had become scarce. Albanian-language schools were run as an illegal activity, in people's garages and basements, with minimal equipment. With this dearth of schools and universities open to them, intellectuals and the young had few legitimate structures where they could share their ideas, and little opportunity for work. The cream of Kosovo's Albanian youth instead put their energy into organised resistance. In some cases this was peaceful demonstration, and in others it was the militarisation that led to the formation of the KLA. Either way, the result for many activists was imprisonment.

Political prisoners were kept together and thus these prisons of the former Yugoslavia were stuffed with young thrusting Albanian men who were bursting with ideas and arguments. From what Halil says, the cells replaced universities in the education of these young men. Another activist I met through Alex who had also been in prison during this time told me that he learned his English in prison, with a book. Sometimes they weren't allowed books or television or other forms of entertainment: 'we would work out calculus on the flour sacks that lay around the room.'

Halil told us 'I wouldn't change my time in prison for anything – it was the biggest gift I ever had. The only problem was when it ended and we had to work out how to recreate it.'

Vetëvendosje seems to have reproduced that forum for many young people, in a way that the University of Prishtina, now open to Kosovo

Albanians as it wasn't for Halil, may not have done. In many ways, this could be seen as the fundamental challenge facing Kosovo today – how to channel the energy and ideas of its young men (the dominant group in a society where fifty per cent of the population are under 25) who have traditions for using that energy only in resistance to formal government structures. Halil himself now works as a teacher in the local school, high up in the hills. I wondered how it compares to doing calculus on flour sacks.

Moving from the beekeeper to the bees, I asked about the history of Halil's hives and he narrated it from the beginning. There's a superstition that I heard here for the first time that to set yourself up as a beekeeper you should go out into the woods and capture one wild colony, buy a second hive, and steal a third. It sounded rather like the rubric for being a British bride, without the requirement for the blue garter. It also made me realise that I wasn't yet even one third a proper beekeeper.

Halil assured us that he didn't start up like that either. Nevertheless, by the time the war started he had something like sixty hives. But when he and the family left their home, fleeing from Serbian forces, he knew that he was abandoning his hives.

'Sure enough, when we came back all the hives had gone. I found them later in the garden of a Serb who lived in the village,' he pointed it out to us at the bottom of the hill. Maybe, I suggested, the Serb was wanting to set up in beekeeping. He'd bought one hive, gone out and claimed another wild colony, and this was the final thing he needed.

Halil wasn't put off by the wholesale loss of his beehives, and began beekeeping again, building up his colonies although they are now less than pre-war numbers. Since the war he's had no more thefts from Serbs, he said, only from bears that have occasionally come down from the mountains and helped themselves to pawfuls of this excellent honey.

36.
Finely chopped cabbage and fine lines

New Albanian vocabulary: *turshi* (pickled vegetables)

Talking to all these other beekeepers was making me miss my own bees; it had been a few weeks since I'd seen them or Adem and Xhezide. Ironically, I had been too busy writing about other people's bees to be visiting my own. So we arranged to drive over to them on the next Sunday. When we arrived, we discovered that we were sharing the visit with a senior Kosovan judge who has a house in the village nearby. He goes there only at weekends, spending his working days in the capital, in a Kosovan approximation to Virgil's model lifestyle. My heart sank when we met because I knew that the hospitality which so often got in the way of my visits to the bees would only be increased this time when it was multiplied by one more guest.

Also visiting was Enes, Adem's nephew from next door. The last time we had met had been the previous summer when he was five. I doubted that he would remember me, but he did, even managing to greet me with my name.

'Have you started school now?' I asked.

'I'm registered,' he lisped proudly. So I asked him whether he could count, and with a bit of help we made it to 19. He was inordinately proud of himself, so while the grown ups chatted across the room, I suggested that Enes and I moved on to a bit of writing. He and I huddled in one corner of Adem's front room over some paper I tore from my notebook, and painstakingly made our way through his name, though with some reluctance over the S, possibly because I told him it was like a snake. He wanted to do more; with memories of my own efforts learning to write my overlong name, I suggested we tried *Adem*.

Meanwhile the judge was trying to tell us about the history of the region. I saw him look at me occasionally, with a schoolmaster's stern stare. He didn't seem impressed that I quite clearly enjoyed the six-year-old's learning more. There in the room were Yeats' two models of edu-

cation, perfectly elaborated – the judge's painstaking filling of a pail, and Enes and I enthusiastically lighting a fire.

Nevertheless, eventually Enes wriggled away with 'I'm tired,' carefully folding over and over his piece of paper covered in letters, and sticking it in his pocket. I started listening to the judge. He was holding forth on how outrageous it was that Adem had been sacked from his recently-acquired job working on the new road to Skopje. We hadn't even heard that Adem had lost his job – the last we knew was when Adem had come to visit us in Pristina one day without warning, and brought with him unexpected gifts: a pot plant and two lovely earthenware vases, carefully chosen for our sitting room. He'd told us then that he was working on the road – the first job he'd had beyond the farm in years – and we had realised that he must have spent much of his first pay cheque on our presents.

And now he had apparently been let go, with no reason, and no pay. The judge was furious on his behalf. He ranted about justice and how it should be blind. 'Any Hashim or Fatmir [the prime minister and the president] should know that they are going to get the same treatment as anyone else,' he said, and we of course agreed.

I had hoped we might have been able to visit the bees by now. The judge also kept bees and I thought perhaps he would understand, or even help with a pally lecture as we stood observing my hive. But it seemed we were stuck inside, and as a woman, as a guest of lower social status than the judge, I didn't feel I could do anything to get us moving. I tried to steer the conversation onto bee-related topics. Then the judge wanted to talk about the liquid for varroa treatment which is imported from Serbia. I gathered that there was a recurrence of a poisoning-the-wells story I'd had sent to me some months before in an email circular about imported foods from Serbia. Kosovo is still heavily dependent on Serbian manufacturing in a number of sectors, including food, where old Yugoslav trade patterns die hard. All the population over the age of nine were brought up as good little Yugoslavs on Serbian baked goods, and most cut their teeth on Plazma brand biscuits. However, according to the story in circulation, separate conveyor belts in the Serbian Plazma factories produce the goods destined for Kosovo. People who have eaten the biscuits in both Serbia and Kosovo claim that they taste noticeably different, and there are a series of unproven cases of poisoning which are

widely considered to be a result of Serb food-tampering. I just didn't believe it.

This time it was the Serb–produced varroa treatment exported to Kosovo that was being alleged to be poisonous.

'Do you believe that?' I asked the judge, the educated, self-consciously educated man.

'Oh yes. There have been cases – my neighbour treated his hives with some, and all of those bees are now dead.'

The way he phrased his reply reminded me that the death of bees is a serious business in Kosovo. When bees die in Albanian, they don't '*ngordhë*' like all other animals; instead they '*vdes*', a word otherwise only used for the demise of human beings. As for the theory surrounding these significant little deaths, like all conspiracy theories, there was of course no sane response I could make which wouldn't receive the answer 'that's just what they want you to think...'

Thankfully, Xhezide came in at this point with lunch. She had prepared a *pite* pie, with pickled cabbage that she had chopped using the food processor we'd bought her as a present some months ago. I was really pleased that she was using it: I had worried that with such sporadic electricity – the farm sometimes goes days together without power – it might be little more than a spare mixing bowl, with an irritating lump of machinery on top. But I had wanted so badly to give her a present that might really make life easier for her in some small way.

A previous present with aspirations to chic had been a cultural disaster; I had arrived one Saturday with a chichi little decorated tin with bath salts in it that I'd brought back from England for her. She had smiled and thanked me and I had thought nothing of it.

It had been months later that I had had a call from Mirlinda. 'You know that metal thing? What is the stuff inside it?' I didn't even know what she was referring to until she sounded out the word written on the side, 'l-a-v-e-n-d-e-r'. 'Is it to eat?'

'Oh no!' I explained. 'It's to put in your bath.'

'We don't have a bath,' she said rather sadly.

Of course they didn't. Although I didn't know exactly what the washing arrangements were – I had never seen the family's bathroom. The one time I had needed to use a toilet when we were visiting,

Xhezide had gently asked 'is it for a big need or a little need?' and then led me out to the wooden privy that stood next to the barn where the skeps hung.

So feeling that I had got something right with my food processor gift gave extra piquancy to the pickled cabbage.

Before anything else could be done after the meal, we had to have tea. I swiftly finished my cup, and Mirlinda approached with the teapot, offering more. I refused politely but she pressed me to take another cup. I refused again but she kept insisting. Finally I managed to assure her that I really didn't want any. Next to me, I saw the judge drain his own small teaglass and place the teaspoon, convex side up, over the top of it. Mirlinda silently took his cup away. Finally grasping the elegant little system, I belatedly tried to do the same without anyone noticing, but Xhezide doesn't miss much and started laughing.

When everyone's tea glass had a spoon balanced on it, and with Enes now knowing how to write his own and his uncle's name satis-factorily, I could see no other reason for us to delay. Perhaps I might check on my bees?

I suited up and went down to the hives with the smoker. Adem had found some of the special fungus that grows on trees, which he had told me made the best smoke to use with bees. These were great tough ringed bulges that smelt like the autumn of autumn as they burned.

Lifting up the hive lid I could hear the drone, and hear its tone change as the bees realised that someone was looking in on them. The smoke calmed them to the point where I was able to lift out the frames to check what was going on. Everything seemed in order, the cells filling up nicely and the bees busying back and forth with pollen visible in the little pouches on their legs. My reference book had told me that when a bee returns to the hive it will be carrying up to 75 per cent of its own weight; aeroplanes carry only 25 per cent of their weight.

Adem said that there wasn't anything more I should do for the moment, and he was standing waiting. It was time to go. Rob and I offered the judge a lift down to his house, and set off, following his directions, taking us past a memorial. As we approached he told us of the massacre that had been committed there by the Serbs on his grand-father's family. Fourteen of them had been killed, from children to old men. They were buried in a communal grave. I asked which year this

had been, assuming it was something from the 1999 atrocities, or maybe the previous year.

'1921,' he said. God, this history stretches back; and around.

Beyond the memorial, he directed us down the hill to the main road and as we approached I saw a police car stationed at the bottom. I had noticed before that the judge wasn't wearing his seatbelt, in contravention of the new and now zealously-policed law, and I alerted him now. 'Sir, put your seat belt on – the police will fine you.'

He was gung-ho about it, swatting away my insistence.

'Don't worry. They know me.'

Sure enough, we sailed past the checkpoint, with the judge's seatbelt flagrantly and illegally loose, and I wondered then what had become of the same law for Hashim, Fatmir and everyone. I don't think that the judge would have understood my point even had I articulated it. I don't think he would have seen any connection between the local police failing to impose on him the fines for contravention of the seatbelt law, and the need for an impartial judiciary. And I don't know how that connection can be made.

37.
The honey leaking away

New Albanian vocabulary: *shikime të shkurta* (glimpses)

Rob's contract finished at the end of May, and we were preparing ourselves for the possibility of his future work being based outside Kosovo. He applied for a range of jobs – continuing in Kosovo, going back to London, moving to Georgia... With no idea how our future was going to work out, I lived in a way that was perhaps the most Kosovan I had ever felt, unable to make any appointments or commitments more than a month ahead.

It's a good discipline, living and judging each day on its own merits. I learned a lot in those months in Kosovo, savouring each meeting with my favourite people, each of my favourite views of landscapes, all the food that I knew I might never taste again. I noticed new things in familiar relationships, familiar sites. Lying awake one night, I realised I was listening to cicadas. I had never before been aware that we had cicadas in our garden; maybe they had just moved in, to serenade our final weeks. The next night I heard them again and paid attention to their strange sound, thinking about all those little hairy legs frotting away. As I listened longer I realised that I was hearing the sound of an unbalanced clock ticking. This was what it sounded like when time went too fast.

I wondered whether this was what the twilight years of life would be like.

But maybe we would be here for years more. I was reluctant to give up on Kosovo even as it looked increasingly likely that the job Rob would be offered would be UK-based. Stubbornly, I threw myself into new projects, as if I was playing chicken with fate, daring it to run over my plans. I worked with a friend to develop a training programme for walking tour guides in Pristina, and launched a full recruitment and marketing programme to make the project a success: radio interviews, press releases, coffees with journalist friends.

A few weeks later Rob received the email that said that he was being offered an excellent post back in London. We knew what we were going to do if he was offered that job; he called them the next day and accepted. We had a month to prepare ourselves.

How do you prepare for such a huge change to your world? I remembered my strategy when we were moving out to Kosovo – minimal practical preparation beyond checking the website of the hotel we would be staying at on our first night; and instead how I used all my energy to enjoy being with the people I cared about – saying proper goodbyes. And this time, it wasn't just people I had to say farewell to of course; there were also the bees.

We went to visit Adem and Xhezide to tell them that we were going to have to leave Kosovo. 'Are you going this week?' they asked.

'No, in about three weeks.' They were unmoved. Three weeks is not a timescale you can worry about in Kosovo. Live for the day. Conversation picked up on previous, well-worn and more enjoyable themes.

I tried again, explaining that with all the things we had to do in preparation for moving back to England, it was possible that we wouldn't be able to come and see the bees again, though we hoped that the family would come to Pristina to a leaving party we were planning.

They weren't sure. 'It depends on whether we can get a lift with someone,' they explained, rather offhand.

'We were hoping that when we are back in England you can keep looking after my bees, and enjoying their honey yourselves.'

Whatever.

I was confused. I couldn't work out whether this implacability was a reflection of a lack of affection for us; or whether that as part of that strange, shifting international presence in Kosovo we had always been seen as only a temporary part of their lives. Where we thought we were building relationships to endure, viewed through a beekeeper's eyes perhaps we were just part of that unpredictable community of queens who come and go; thrive and swarm, produce and die off.

We didn't see Adem, Xhezide and Mirlinda again until the week we left. The leaving party we held was a wonderfully self-indulgent cel-ebration of our time in Kosovo, or – as the invitations put it – our reasons to return here. I had become very proud of the photographs I

had taken over the previous two years, and it had been while we were here that I had had the first external encouragement for my photography when a picture of mine was highly commended in a national competition. So we decided to put on an exhibition of celebratory photographs – *Thirty Glimpses of Kosovo* – and invited all our friends to the opening night.

It was an exciting evening which, like the cicadas, went too fast. The director of the National Gallery of Kosovo, whom I knew from the artists in residence project at the Ethnological Museum, agreed to host the exhibition at his gallery. More than eighty of our friends were able to come to the opening. Among them were Adem and his family.

In fact, they were there twice over. Among the traditional costumes, market scenes (the cheese barrels from that early shopping trip), curious sidelong looks at modern Pristina, communist architecture, a Serbian Orthodox monastery, Adem Jashari's shelled home in Prekaz, haystacks and houses, Xhezide and Mirlinda stood making *fli* and serving drinks. I had taken the photograph on one of our earliest visits to them, and I wanted to include it as one of the experiences that had meant so much to us while we'd been here. I'd spoken to them on the phone to check that they would be happy for me to include the photo in the exhibition, and – bemused – they had given their consent and had promised to be there.

They were the first to arrive, along with the National Gallery's official photographer. I stood at the drinks table we had set up, ready to serve Pimm's, and wondered whether I was equal to this social situation.

It felt odd, standing together with glasses in our hands and wearing our best clothes. But we talked our way through it. Adem told me that this year's honey was ready for harvesting, and I had to tell him that in the days left to us in Kosovo I didn't think I was going to be able to come over for the centrifuging and filtering that I had just got the hang of the previous year. I asked whether Xhezide and Mirlinda liked the photograph and they said they did; I offered to give it to them when the exhibition came down.

The gallery began to fill up. It was a great mixture of many of the people who had created our Kosovo for us. Shpresa, my first Kosovan friend, was there; Coriander Sue and Mike came along, the guides from the Ethnological Museum, friends from the British Embassy, artist

friends I had got to know when I worked on the charity art auction, colleagues from school, from the charity. Shqipja and Lendita, the sister beekeepers from Drenica also came, and I introduced them to Adem and Xhezide, hoping that there would be enough beekeeping in common to give them something to talk about. Before I could see whether I had been successful, I had to go and say hello to someone else.

I was standing talking to a group of American friends when I noticed Adem's family at a polite distance waiting for my conversation to end. Excusing myself, I turned to them and they explained that they were going; they said that the person who had given them a lift into Pristina had to return to the village. Even as I thanked them – *so* much – for everything they had done for me, I could see another guest arriving and I knew that I really didn't have long with them. I gave them all a brief hug, and they were gone. It was a sad, low-key leavetaking, with no honey in it.

The next day, Adem called. He told me for the second time that the honey was ready for harvesting. 'I'm sorry, Adem, but I can't come today. Today, the movers for our furniture are coming. Then tomorrow, the packers are coming to take the rest of our belongings away before we leave this house.' One by one, my ties with Kosovo were being dismantled, removed, undone. And Adem didn't seem to understand.

'No, no. You don't understand, Elizabeth,' he said. 'I am going to harvest it, and I want to bring it to you.'

It was yet another instance of his generosity. But unlike all the delicious meals, the easy hospitality, the knowledge transferred, the earthenware pottery… this time I really wasn't able to accept his offer. The United Kingdom takes a dim view of imported honey. Along with fish and meat it is considered a 'bio-product' and customs will not accept any with provenance outside the EU or other countries with strict regulations in place. Flying in from a country where smuggling across borders involves guns and young women sold into prostitution, the stern posters at British airports asking you to yield up your pots of honey seem rather over-cautious. But a law is a law, and with the recent widespread colony collapse in the British bee population from causes unknown, I didn't want to try dodging customs officers with my illegally sweet and sticky cargo.

So I tried to explain to Adem that I wouldn't be able to take the honey. But he wouldn't accept my protestations, and he asked if he could come the following morning to deliver it.

At 6.45 am the next day, the doorbell rang. I really wasn't ready for this.

I pulled on some clothes and went down to find Adem waiting outside with the friend who had driven him into the city. After saying hello, Adem went back to the car and came back with his arms around an enormous, weighty basket, inside which were jars and jars of honey. They were all shapes and sizes – the jeroboams I had seen before, along with jars that had held commercially-produced jam, *ajvar*, sauces. He handed the basket to me and went back to the car. He returned with a further cardboard box weighed down with more jars. Altogether there were twenty kilograms of honey.

I was overwhelmed. Just when I thought that I was stripping my Kosovan home, and my life in Kosovo; losing chairs, tables, possessions by the boxful, here my home was filling up with sweetness. At the same time, of course, I was wondering what the hell I could do with twenty kilograms of honey before my flight back to Gatwick.

But in the meantime I tried to be the perfect early morning hostess to Adem and his friend with the car. We had no furniture left to sit them on, but they politely professed themselves comfortable with the cushions on our wooden flooring that was all that remained. I found a spare plate and the watermelon that we had been given the previous day as a thank you by the family to whom we had given our unshippable items of furniture. We still had our kettle, so we sat down to an improvised breakfast together. I put out small glasses filled with the excellent honey that Adem had brought – this was just the beginning of what would be a sickening honey orgy if we were to eat it all in the next 24 hours.

Rob found a saucer for Adem's cigarette, and in the sleepiness of early morning we sat eating watermelon and talking about nothing in particular while Adem's smoke filled up our sitting room until it smelled just like his own. Occasionally he ran his hand over his face – all the way from the chin up over the forehead and then down the back of his head – and I realised that something was bothering him. It was bothering me, too.

'You will keep in contact, won't you?' he said, and we promised that we would.

'And we'll come back to visit Kosovo,' and we all nodded.

'And I'll look after the bees.'

Adem called Xhezide for her to say goodbye by telephone. She said she had heard me on the radio the day before when I'd been a studio guest talking about my walking tour guide training on the morning programme. She told me that she had burst into tears, thinking that it would be the last time she would hear my voice. We were all nearly crying now.

'You will keep in contact, won't you?'

'And we'll come back to visit Kosovo.'

'And I'll look after the bees.'

At each repetition of the formula, Adem rubbed his hand more furiously over his face and I felt closer to sobbing.

After he'd smoked another cigarette, Adem got up to go. I hugged him on the doorstep, and he rubbed away at his face, tears in his eyes. Rob escorted him in proper Albanian fashion to our front gate and they hugged too. We stood and waved them off, swallowing hard at the large lump in my throat that I guessed that even twenty kilograms of honey – particularly twenty kilograms of honey – wouldn't soothe away.

The last 24 hours were a ridiculous rush around Pristina with jars of honey in my bag – a small sad bee in reverse. This was my final chance to try the tricks I'd learned from Vedat's mother, from Xhezide as I'd left their houses – a sudden splurge of generosity in parting. I took one pot over to the small gym opposite us to thank the staff there who had helped not only with keeping me fit, but also generously lent us outdoor heaters for that first birthday party here at the Ethnological Museum, the day I'd been given the beehives. Despite it being our last evening in Kosovo, I insisted on going to my yoga class – more chicken with fate – and at the end of class I left a pot next to my teacher's mat at the front. I walked up to the corner shop which for two years had been a constant friendly source of chocolate and newspapers, and gave a pot to the owner who had put me in my place when I'd grumbled about how long I seemed to be waiting for Kosovo's independence. He seemed to be as much in denial as I was about us leaving. 'How long are you going away for?' I didn't know how to answer.

I sent an email round to friends advertising that they could come and collect as much honey as their arms and blood sugar levels could manage, and gave pots away to my favourite people: Saskia, with whom I'd celebrated Women's Day and visited Women for Women's bee-keepers. Naxhije, the Ethnological Museum photographer, came round with her husband, and so did Cindy, with whom I'd run the workshops at the *kulla*. I went to visit the offices of Cultural Heritage without Borders, the NGO that had funded the workshops I'd led at the *kulla*, and were now giving money to enable the Pristina walking tour guide training project. Along with the paperwork they'd asked me to hand in before I left town, I brought a pot of honey for the director and one for his finance manager. I took a taxi to the Journalism Institute who had given us rooms for free for the training, and left a pot of honey on the desk of the Director there to thank him, and gave another to Bryony, my colleague in the project. One pot went to our mercurial, generous, slightly mad landlord when we handed over the keys.

This was an intensification of a process that had been going on for several weeks. We had found families who said that they would like our furniture, had brought women we'd found begging in the streets to take their pick of the clothes and lamps and crockery we really couldn't

justify keeping, let alone transporting across Europe. The 'Safe House' shelter in Gjakova had inherited the drawers of unopened cosmetics and toiletries that I had collected, and the Vetëvendosje movement had said they could use one of the beehives for which I had leapt from the car on the way to the Xhonaj music festival. One of their activists had made it into a lampshade which hung over the courtyard of their head-quarters; I liked the idea of it illuminating their political discussions.

Along with my delicious honey, I had been sure that British Customs would also turn their noses up at the former hive that I had had in our garden. It was the used 'primitive' made by Rexhep, and given to me along with the chicken on our visit to his farm. With cow dung plastering the outsides and bits of honeycomb still clinging to the inside, the object would scream 'bio-product' to any customs officer.

On our final morning in Kosovo, we walked to meet the guides from the Ethnological Museum for coffee. I brought with me the hive and over a rather solemn *makiato* I handed it over to them. It was almost unbearably ashes-to-ashes.

When we'd finished our coffees, the guides had to get to work, and Rob and I went to see to our final suitcases, and our trip home.

And so the love story of my beekeeping adventures in Kosovo, like so many love stories, ended in the car on the way to the airport. Ramiz, Rob's friend, was driving us, and in the glove compartment of his car sat the last pot of honey we had had to dispose of. Handing it over hadn't marked the end of our relationship with Kosovo, of course, but surrendering the last jar of all that concentrated sunshine, flowers, hard work, was a difficult thing to do. But there was nothing for it; Rob and I sat squeezing one another's hands as we rushed through the outskirts of Pristina, nearly at the airport, as we drove on into the suburb of Fushë Kosovë, past the signpost with the Serbian name spraypainted out. For perhaps the last time we were journeying over the field of blackbirds, the field of my bees.

Glossary

Ajvar	Typical Balkan sweet pepper chutney. See p. 99 for recipe
Çardak	The elegant conservatory-like room extending from the first floor of Ottoman-era houses
Fli	A dish made by repeated layers of batter, interspersed with cream. See p. 24 for recipe
KLA	The Kosovo Liberation Army, established in 1998 as a guerrilla force to counter Serbian establishment repression of ethnic Albanians in Kosovo. The KLA was officially disbanded as part of the negotiations which ended the NATO bombing campaign against the Milošević regime in June 1999
Kulla	A Turkish word meaning 'tower' but used specifically to refer to the fortified three- or four-storey houses seen only in Kosovo and northern Albania
Mangall	A brazier which formed part of the furniture of the well-to-do home in Kosovo in the past
Minder	The integral cushioned seating running round the edge of the guest sitting room in traditional Kosovan homes
Oda	Turkish word meaning 'room', used in Kosovo specifically for the room where male members of the household and guests hung out
Pite	A pastry dish made of layers of filo pastry with filling which is usually savoury – cheese, spinach, nettles, pumpkin and others. See p. 109 for recipe
Raki	Spirits made, typically in a home still, from distilled juice (usually grape or plum though it can be as exotic as apricot or quince) – similar to Italian *grappa*
Tepsi	A round, deep baking tray which can be as small as 30cm diameter, or as large as 100cm diameter. It is used for baking many traditional Kosovan dishes including *fli*, *pite*, and baklava
UNMIK	The United Nations Mission in Kosovo, the mission which took over the administration of Kosovo in accordance with United Nations Resolution 1244 in 1999

A brief historical framework

1389   The Battle of Kosovo. Although the battle ended in a stalemate, it was the turning point in Ottoman efforts to conquer the Balkans. Shortly afterwards, Kosovo became part of the Ottoman Empire, and was to remain so until the twentieth century.

1987   Milošević's rise to power within Yugoslav politics, with an aggressive reassertion of Serbian rights and power, later to become ethnic cleansing. From this date on, and with increasing levels of severity, Albanians in Kosovo were discriminated against, threatened, and on occasion killed by the Serbian regime.

1999   Fuelled by fear of a repeat of Bosnian atrocities, Western frustration with Milošević and outrage at his policies of ethnic cleansing led NATO to launch its first ever humanitarian mission, a bombing campaign which lasted from March to June, and resulted in the withdrawal of Serbian troops from Kosovo, and the administration of Kosovo by the United Nations.

2004   Frustration at the slow progress of transfer of powers from the UN to local administration was brought to a head by what was in fact an unrelated incident in which three Kosovo Albanian children died, allegedly as the result of Serb actions, leading to widespread rioting by Albanian groups. Thirty-three major riots were reported and large ethnic Albanian crowds targeted Serb and other non-Albanian communities, burning at least 550 homes and 27 Serbian Orthodox churches and monasteries. Nineteen people were killed and over 1000 wounded.

2006-2008   The period when the action of this book takes place.

A note on pronunciation

Albanian is an almost entirely phonetically regular language. This means that once you have learned the sounds made by each of the Albanian letters (very similar to English in most cases) you would be able to read a newspaper out loud – even if with very little clue of what it means.

For the Albanian names in the book, the following alphabet equivalences will be helpful:

A	like *ar* in car
B	like *b* in blood
C	like *ts* in cats
Ç	like *ch* in church
D	like *d* in drone
Dh	like *th* in with
E	like *e* in egg
F	like *f* in freedom
G	like *g* in gold
Gj	like *j* in jug
H	like *h* in honey
I	like *ee* in bee
J	like *y* in yacht
K	like *k* in kite
L	like *lly* in fill your boots
Ll	like *l* in like
M	like *m* in microphone
N	like *n* in microphone
O	like *or* in for
P	like *p* in prince
Q	like *ch* in church
R	like *r* in rock
Rr	a rolled *r* that we don't have in English
S	like *s* in something
Sh	like *sh* in hush
T	like *t* in top
Th	like *th* in thing

U	like *oo* in cook
V	like *v* in violin
X	like *ds* in kids
Xh	like *j* in jug
Y	like the French *u* in 'tu'
Z	like *zz* in buzz
Zh	like *s* in pleasure

Index to recipes:

Bibliography

Assembly of Kosovo, Law no. 02-L-111 on apiculture, 2007: Pristina 'http://www.assembly-kosova.org/common/docs/ligjet/2007_02-L111_en.pdf. Accessed 6-6-08

Benjamin, A and McCallum, B, *A World without Bees*. Guardian Books, London, 2008

Defra, *Consultation on a Draft Strategy on Protecting and Improving the Health of Honey Bees in England and Wales.* Defra, London, 2008 http://www.defra.gov.uk/corporate/consult/bee-health/consultation.pdf Accessed 6-6-08

Di Lellio, A and Schwandner-Sievers, S, 'The Legendary Commander: the Construction of an Albanian Master-narrative in Post-war Kosovo', *Nations and Nationalism*, 12 (3), 2006, pp, 513-529

Elsie, R, *A Dictionary of Albanian Religion, Mythology and Folk Culture.* C Hurst and Co, London, 2001

European Stability Initiative, *A Future for Pristina's Past.* http://www.esiweb.org/pdf/esi_future_of_pristina%20booklet.pdf Accessed October 2009

European Stability Initiative, *Cutting the Lifeline.* http://www.esiweb.org/pdf/esi_document_id_80.pdf. Accessed March 2008

Flottum, K, *Beekeeping.* Apple Press, Hove, 2005

Gagica-Ukelli, F, *1000 receta për çdo familje* (*1000 recipes for every family*). Interpress R. Company, Pristina, 2007

Gjeçov, Sh (collected and arranged) and Fox, L (translated), *The Code of Lekë Dukagjini.* Gjonlekaj Publishing Co., New York, 1989

Gower, J, 'Bee Stings', *BBKA News* no. 177, June 2009

Hysa, K and R J, *The Best of Albanian Cooking.* Hippocrene Books, New York, 1998

Malcolm, N, *Kosovo: a Short History.* Macmillan, London, 1998

Muçolli, Z S, *Kalendari i Bletarisë* (*The Beekeeping Calendar*). Pristina, 2000

Ombudsperson Institution, Report Ex Officio No. 008/ 2007 Regarding the Incidents that Occurred during the 'Vetëvendosje' Protest on 10 February

2007, accessed online at:

http://www.ombudspersonkosovo.org/repository/docs/ex%20off%20008
-07%20Vetevendosje%20report-EnLG%20-%20final%2021-03-08.pdf
Accessed 6-6-08

Paçaku, K, *Lavustikorri* (*Dictionary*), Iniciativa 6, Prizren, 2004

Sejdiu (Kuqi), B, *Kuzhina Kosovare* (*The Kosovan Kitchen*). Tirana, 2006

Statistical Office of Kosovo, *Kosovo in Figures 2005*

http://www.ks-
gov.net/ESK/eng/index.php?option=com_docman&task=
cat_view&Itemid=8&gid=36 Accessed October 2009

Statistical Office of Kosovo, *Kosovo in Figures 2008*

http://www.ks-
gov.net/ESK/eng/index.php?option=com_docman&task=cat_view&Ite
mid=8&gid=36

Accessed October 2009

Stublla, Sh, *Mbijetesa* (Survival). Pristina, 2007

Sullivan, S, *Be Not Afraid For You Have Sons in America*. St Martin's Press, New
York, 2004

Thomo, K, *Për ju që keni bletë* (*For you who have bees*). 2002

Wilson, B, *The Hive*. John Murray, London, 2005